AGING:
The Process and the People

American College of Psychiatrists

OFFICERS
(at the time of 1978 Annual Meeting)

EDWARD O. HARPER, M.D., *President*

GENE USDIN, M.D.
President-Elect

WARREN, S. WILLIAMS, M.D.
First Vice-President

SHERVERT H. FRAZIER, M.D.
Second Vice-President

JOHN C. NEMIAH, M.D.
Secretary-General

CHARLES E. SMITH, M.D.
Treasurer

CURTIS G. SOUTHARD, M.D.
Archivist-Historian

Program Committee for 1978 Annual Meeting

ROBERT L. WILLIAMS, M.D., *Chairman*

H. KEITH H. BRODIE, M.D.
SHERVERT H. FRAZIER, M.D.
THOMAS H. HOLMES, M.D.
MORRIS A. LIPTON, M.D.

PETER F. REGAN, III, M.D.
JOSEPH J. SCHILDKRAUT, M.D.
JAMES N. SUSSEX, M.D.

Publications Committee

GENE USDIN, M.D., *Chairman*
CHARLES K. HOFLING, M.D., *Vice-Chairman*

D. EARL BROWN, JR., M.D.
HAROLD HIATT, M.D.
HENRY P. LAUGHLIN, M.D.
JERRY M. LEWIS, M.D.

MAURICE J. MARTIN, M.D.
JOHN C. NEMIAH, M.D.
HAROLD M. VISOTSKY, M.D.

AGING:

The Process and the People

Edited by

GENE USDIN, M.D.

Professor of Clinical Psychiatry
Louisiana State University School of Medicine

and

CHARLES K. HOFLING, M.D.

Professor of Psychiatry
St. Louis University Medical Center

BRUNNER/MAZEL, *Publishers* • New York

Library of Congress Cataloging in Publication Data

American College of Psychiatrists.
    Aging: the process and the people.
    Papers presented at the 1978 annual meeting of the American College of Psychiatrists.
    Includes bibliographical references and index.
    1. Aging—Psychological aspects—Congresses.   2. Aged—Psychology—Congresses.   3. Geriatric psychiatry—Congresses.   I. Usdin, Gene L.   II. Hofling, Charles K.   III. Title.   [DNLM: 1. Aging—Congresses.   WT150 A512a   1978]

BF724.55.A35A47   362.6'04'2   78-16777
ISBN 0-87630-178-2

Contributors

EWALD W. BUSSE, M.D.

Associate Provost and Dean, Medical and Allied Health Education, Duke University Medical Center

ROBERT N. BUTLER, M.D.

Director, National Institute on Aging, National Institute of Health, Bethesda, Maryland

MARJORIE H. CANTOR, M.A.

Director of Research and Faculty Development, Brookdale Center on Aging of Hunter College, School of Social Work, New York

CARL EISDORFER, Ph.D., M.D.

Professor and Chairman, Department of Psychiatry and Behavioral Sciences, University of Washington, School of Medicine, Seattle

CHARLES M. GAITZ, M.D.

Chief, Gerontology Research Section, Texan Research Institute of Mental Science and Clinical Professor of Psychiatry, Baylor College of Medicine, Houston

BENNETT S. GURIAN, M.Sc., M.D.

Director of Geriatrics, Massachusetts Mental Health Center and Assistant Professor of Psychiatry, Harvard Medical School

THOMAS H. HOLMES, M.D.

Professor of Psychiatry and Behavioral Sciences, University of Washington School of Medicine, Seattle

MORRIS A. LIPTON, Ph.D., M.D.

Biological Sciences Research Center, Department of Psychiatry, and Neurobiology Program, University of North Carolina School of Medicine

GEORGE L. MADDOX, Ph.D.

Professor of Sociology and of Medical Sociology in Psychiatry Director, Center for the Study of Aging and Human Development, Duke University

CHARLES B. NEMEROFF, Ph.D.

Biological Sciences Research Center, Department of Psychiatry, and Neurobiology Program, University of North Carolina School of Medicine

Contents

Contributors v

Introduction by Gene Usdin ix

1. OVERVIEW ON AGING 1
   by Robert N. Butler

2. THE SOCIAL AND CULTURAL CONTEXT OF AGING 20
   by George L. Maddox

3. THE BIOLOGY OF AGING AND ITS ROLE IN DEPRESSION 47
   by Morris A. Lipton and Charles B. Nemeroff

4. PSYCHOPHYSIOLOGIC AND COGNITIVE STUDIES IN THE AGED 96
   by Carl Eisdorfer

5. AGING RESEARCH: A REVIEW AND CRITIQUE 129
   by Ewald W. Busse

6. DEATH AND DYING 166
   by Thomas H. Holmes

7. MENTAL HEALTH AND COMMUNITY SUPPORT SYSTEMS
   FOR THE ELDERLY 184
   by Bennett S. Gurian and Marjorie H. Cantor

8. AGED PATIENTS, THEIR FAMILIES AND PHYSICIANS 206
   by Charles M. Gaitz

Index 241

Introduction

Who are the aged? Aside from constantly changing designated ages, they are more and more of us—increasingly more of us each year. As older persons constitute a significantly increasing proportion of our population, our way of life will be dramatically altered. Attitudes regarding aging are indeed not merely professional but personal issues for readers of this volume because what happens to the aged today presages what lies ahead for all of us. It behooves us to learn as much as we can about the issues of aging and how to cope with them. In learning to be of help to the aged, we help ourselves.

This volume addresses itself to this universal human development so long neglected by the medical profession. Better late than never. It is timely because it is being published in the year in which the American Psychiatric Association has made aging a major thrust of its annual scientific program. The book reflects the newer concepts of the aging process and significant breakthroughs—psychodynamically, physiologically and socioculturally—in the treatment of the aged. Not the least of its contributions is the exposure of many misconceptions that have persisted in Western society as well as in the medical profession. Readers cannot fail to be impressed by the contributors' concern not merely about the neglect of research in this area, but also about the often inhuman neglect of the aged themselves.

This volume is an outgrowth of the 1978 annual meeting of the American College of Psychiatrists, which brought together leading authorities in the field of gerontology who presented recent concepts in a thought-provoking manner. Appropriately, the overview is by Robert Butler, first and present Director of the recently established National Institute of Aging, one of the National Institutes of Health. Dr. Butler keynotes the challenges, is highly critical of the neglect of the field, and points out horizons which must be explored. The constant theme of neglect is balanced by presentation of exciting research findings which not only question many previously sacred and essentially nihilistic attitudes, but also offer new and hopeful vistas.

Generally speaking, we have accepted chronological age in a rigid fashion as a measure of the adequacy or inadequacy of people, and we have failed to appreciate the significant physiologic and psychologic differences between any two individuals, whether they are in their 20s or in their 70s. Personalities differentiate further and become more unique in proportion to the time they have lived and developed.

While the aged tend to have approximately 10 percent of the immune capacity of an adolescent, old age does not necessarily mean inevitable disease. It does mean that a longer life gives greater time for a disease to develop.

The assumption that chronic brain disease is inescapable leads to an unwarranted assumption that chronic brain disease is responsible for most of the problems of older persons. Many conditions develop extracerebrally and affect the brain by toxins or by constricting either nourishment or oxygenation. Of special interest to physicians is the fact that two of the leading causes of reversible brain syndrome are depression and drug misuse. Depression may be an early sign of chronic brain syndrome, but attention to early signs and symptoms may prevent significant functional impairment. There is increasing evidence that senile dementia may be an autoimmune process.

Throughout the volume there is recognition of the social issues impinging upon the care of the elderly—financial distress aggravated by inflation, lack of adequate public transportation, crime and other forms of victimization of the elderly, inadequate housing, problems regarding adequate utilization of Medicare and Medicaid, and the dumping of older persons into foster care and boarding homes. The latter often lack adequate trained personnel, facilities, and services; in nearly 80 percent of these homes, the primary motivation is profit. Nearly one million elderly persons live in nursing homes. Many are there by necessity, but many could live better elsewhere, even if the nursing homes were adequate. This indignity suffered by our elderly is not only a disservice to them, but also a disservice to each of us. What it comes to in the end is the value we place on human life and human dignity. This judgment will determine nothing less than the way we shall end our own lives. Perhaps the specter is too frightening, and physicians as well as patients tend to deny the unpleasant. How easy in our youth-oriented culture to think of youth as beautiful and age as ugly. In general, the lack of input regarding the problems of the aged and the declining general interest in community mental health centers, together with an unrealistically inadequate budget for the National Institute of Aging, substantiate the thesis of our society's neglect of the elderly.

The psychiatrist carries within himself or herself a personal value system not only about issues, but also about societal functioning in general. The medical profession, and psychiatry in particular, fancies itself as humanistic and has seldom refrained from being critical of neglect of health care. Yet, scant attention is currently paid in medical schools to the specialty of diagnosing, managing, and treating the elderly. Indeed, it is a rare medical school which provides its students even one visit to a nursing home; pediatrics and adolescent medicine are recognized as legitimate specific areas, while courses in gerontology are rarely taught.

The relatively recent development of gerontological societies, major research units in aging, and especially the recent founding of the National Institute of Aging are steps in the right direction. Yet they constitute a miniscule part of the needed effort, and the question is whether or not these efforts, including those of the National Institute of Aging, will be expanded enough to meet the need.

Of significance is the relatively small number of psychiatrists who offer dynamic psychotherapy to the older patient. Some attribute this to Freud's statements that psychodynamically-oriented therapy was of no value to the person over 40, but this is readily contradicted by the age of many patients whom he himself analyzed, as well as by his own productive later years. Actually, perhaps Jung was right when he said that a person can achieve his most significant growth in the latter half of his life. What may be appropriate is to recognize that Freud's analyses were often of extremely short duration and might be more correctly termed educationally-oriented self study. It would seem that a similar, brief, situation-oriented psychotherapy might be appropriate for the elderly. In fact, the elderly may be even more capable of effectively utilizing this type of therapy— especially in a society which is supportive and respectful.

Psychiatrists are not themselves immune to the emotional disturbances which they attempt to help their patients to understand. We share many of the apprehensions of our patients, including the fear of growing old. Like everyone else, we deny, we rationalize, we repress, and we do not like painful situations. It is notable that the life experiences of most physicians leave them ill-prepared for old age; when they do become patients, they are frequently difficult and uncooperative.

Dealing with the older patient can arouse memories about our relationships with our own parents; it can remind us of our own aging; we can play the "numbers game" when we realize that a feeble, depressed patient is but 10 or 15 years older than we are, and so find ourselves wondering how or where we will be at that age. Physicians have probably underestimated the resiliency of the older person, focusing primarily on the cliché that the older one is, the more rigid one gets. Physicians may believe that their time and energy should be spent treating younger people who have more years to live than with those who may soon die; their "omnipotence" as physicians may be threatened by the feelings of helplessness regarding what they cannot accomplish with some elderly patients. Especially frightening is the likelihood that aged patients may actually die while under their care.

In the gross anatomy laboratory, the young medical student often starts with the cadaver of an old person. Whether or not the resulting dehumanization of the aged is a protective device of the fledgling physician, medical students often come to attribute low social status to treating the aged.

Medicine needs a reevaluation of information and attitudes toward older persons. Physicians are in an almost unique position to lead the way toward a healthier society which recognizes the competency, experience, and adaptive capacities of most older individuals. In helping these older individuals, we need to see them in a broader sociocultural context. There is a need to improve their support networks, recognizing the specific difficulties with some of the tasks of daily living which the elderly often encounter.

We are learning that our society has been all too prone to rely on environmental manipulations in a stereotyped fashion, especially in the kinds of housing and the levels of income considered appropriate for older persons. We have paid insufficient attention to studying aging as an "individual experience." It is not surprising, considering the prevalent attitude of society and medicine, that older persons themselves become discouraged to the point of not feeling entitled to help. The older person may feel that it is too risky to reach out for help; rejection is all too likely. The classic expression, "I don't want to be a burden," is too often heard from the aged and serves as an indictment of all of us.

The prospect of retirement and the feelings of uselessness and loss of respect, real or imagined, may be devastating for some; but for others, retirement is a relief from difficult responsibilities or unrewarding activities. The diminishing autonomy of the very old is indeed a blow to the self-image of many. It is not surprising that depressions are more frequent, especially when self-respect is not encouraged or reinforced. The well-being of the retired person is affected by preretirement attitudes and expectations, social networks, modes of retirement, financial security, educational background, the type of work done before retirement, and especially the capacity to develop new and enjoyable interests and relationships. Two of the major psychodynamic themes of aging are loss and anger, each multiplying the other in a vicious cycle, often alienating the patient.

There have been dramatic breakthroughs in psychophysiologic and cognitive studies of the aged. We now know that progressive loss of cognitive functioning with aging is not inevitable. There is no precise definition of aging, any more than there is a precise definition of health. Laboratory and clinical studies should continue to bring major changes in our thinking regarding older persons. The finding of sex differences relative to the various processes of aging is exciting and provocative.

The idea that intellectual decline often forebodes death is pertinent. Certain components of cognitive functioning decline and others do not. The aged may perform more poorly on psychological tests because they fear the results as "proof" that they are "slipping." Actually, research has shown that older people can continue to grow in information, knowledge, and vocabulary, although at a somewhat slower rate than younger individuals. It is important to distinguish normal from pathological aging, but there is general agreement that senility is a poor term.

The more fully we understand the context of aging as a psychobio-sociologic process, the greater will be our capacity to deal with older persons and with our own aging.

We should take the contributions in this volume seriously, not simply out of guilt or even solely as a justifiable, social responsibility. The topic of *Aging* is interesting in itself, albeit uncomfortable at times. The idea that our later years may be stimulating and useful and not necessarily dreadful can be a source of strength in our personal life as well as providing an impetus to further research and clinical advances. We do not have to follow blindly the myths of yesteryear.

GENE USDIN, M.D.

AGING:
The Process and the People

1

Overview on Aging

Robert N. Butler, M.D.

Psychiatrists have an important role to play in working with the elderly and have already contributed to our understanding of aging, of the life cycle and the broad sweep of life. Still, psychiatrists have often failed to see the older person as a full and appropriate candidate for treatment and research. An important professional satisfaction exists in meeting the challenge of the elderly. We in the medical profession have extended life and now need to concern ourselves with the way those hard-won years are spent. It is an issue that concerns all of us, as what happens to the aged today predicts our own future lives. The facilities available, the level of standard treatments, and the attitudes toward the aged will affect us all regardless of personal education, status, income and achievement. It will touch us first, perhaps, with our parents and older relatives, but will eventually be a personal issue, for unlike other conditions or features of life, such as race and sex, old age may come to each of us.

Demographic studies show that aging is coming to an increasing number of Americans each year. Currently, some 23 million Americans are over 65 and, by the year 2030, 50 years ahead, we expect that 50 million Americans, or one in five, will be over 65 (see Figure

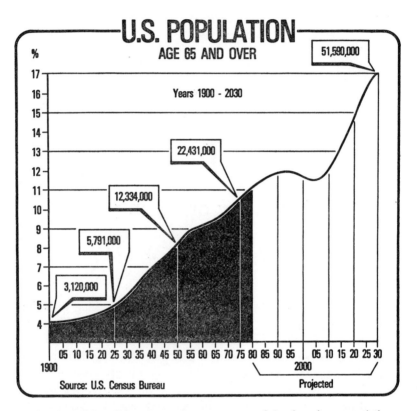

U.S. POPULATION
AGE 65 AND OVER

Years 1900 - 2030

51,590,000

22,431,000

12,334,000

5,791,000

3,120,000

05 10 15 20 25 30 35 40 45 50 55 60 65 70 75 80 85 90 95 | 05 10 15 20 25 30
1900   2000

Source: U.S. Census Bureau   Projected

AGE GAUGE — Chart shows the percentage of the American population 65 and older from 1900 to 1975, with predictions for 1980 to 2030.

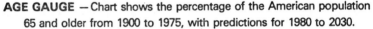

FIGURE 1

1). The same Americans who constituted the post World War II baby boom, those young people described as "greening" America, will "gray" America. The implications are stunning. It becomes clear that the welfare of one group is tied to the welfare of all, and that we must plan adequate social and medical care for the elderly which, in turn, will benefit the entire society.

The need for research is immediate. We do not know what aging really is. For far too long we have accepted the concept of total

years or chronological age as an adequate measure. This implies
that deterioration, illness and other problems advance consistently
with the years. This appears to be untrue. The saying, "You are
only as old as you feel" has more truth to it than the conventional
idea that old age arrives at 65.

When the National Institute on Aging was founded, the work in
progress at the Gerontology Research Center in Baltimore was included as an intramural program. There, under the direction of Dr.
Nathan Shock, a longitudinal study of about 1,000 men has gone on
since 1958. Dr. Shock has since retired, but work continues under
the direction of Dr. Richard C. Greulich. The Baltimore study includes the monitoring of cardiac, renal and pulmonary function;
body composition; exercise physiology; carbohydrate and lipid metabolism; drug pharmacokinetics; nutrition and endocrine factors; and
behavioral and social variables. The men who have been studied in
this longitudinal research are now from 20 to 96 years of age.
The combination of adequate baseline data with the ongoing study
of healthy men will allow us to study the aging process and begin
the vital task of sorting out aging from illness. Scrutiny of the condition and capacity of each man as he grows older allows for realistic
information about decline. This research team will soon add women
to the study, thus expanding the potential significance of its findings.

One early finding from this longitudinal study is that there are
wider differences, both physiological and psychological, between two
older persons of the same age than between two 20-year-olds. For
example, we need to know why one person lives an entire life in a
vigorous and healthy creative way, while another begins an early
decline. Study of healthy individuals is important, as then the problems caused by illness are not seen as the inevitable result of old
age. All too often studies of drug tolerance or assessment of emotional states occur when a person is evaluated for chronic brain
syndrome, given a competency test, or admitted to a hospital with
an acute illness, all inappropriate times to develop norms.

It is important to separate the changes intrinsic to aging—inevitable changes—from those caused by disease or social stress. Age-
standardized studies of metabolism are valuable. We know that in
the elderly, for instance, decreased glucose tolerance, decreased crea-

tinine clearance and higher blood pressure are often present, but not all elderly with these symptoms have kidney disease or are hypertensive. We know that older patients are more likely to have adverse drug reactions than younger patients, and also that drugs are very heavily prescribed for the elderly. Multiple drug prescriptions are common and often the elderly patient has to coordinate his or her own medical care, a precarious situation. Increasingly, gerontologists point out that old age does not necessarily mean inevitable disease, but that a long life may give a disease time to develop. We know, however, that the older person's ability to fight disease is limited; the aged tend to have only 10 percent of the immune capacity of an adolescent. This is a promising area of research, as we already know some ways to bolster immune capacity and undoubtedly can find more. Disease, of course, can be attacked. It was once common to hear that someone "died of old age." Now we more often hear the illness identified as cancer or stroke. This points out the breakdown of the long identification of aging with illness, a connection that must be broken down in order for appropriate and aggressive treatment to begin. Consider the 101-year-old man who went to the doctor complaining that his right leg hurt. The doctor told him he had to expect that at his age. The man replied that his left leg was the same age as his right, yet it did not hurt.

Research will help to give us a clear picture of what aging is and what it is not. Facts are needed about disability and the potential for continued health. Neither romanticism nor undue pessimism will help. All areas of life must be studied with regard to aging: the biological, psychological, and social.

EMOTIONAL AND MENTAL PROBLEMS

We know the elderly are disproportionately subject to emotional and mental problems. The incidence of psychopathology rises with age (1). Functional disorders, notably depression and paranoid states, increase steadily with each decade, as do organic brain diseases after age 60. One study by the National Institute of Mental Health (NIMH), reported by the World Health Organization in 1959, listed the following incidences of new cases of psychopathology of all types per 100,000:

Under age 15	2.3
Age 25-34	76.3
Age 35-54	93.0
Above 65	236.1

Schizophrenia is an exception, rarely occurring for the first time in the later years. Nevertheless, given the adverse circumstances that many of the elderly endure, it is impressive that many are able to manage as well as they do.

ORGANIC BRAIN SYNDROMES

We have a lot of myths concerning aging. One is that chronic (irreversible) brain syndrome—with its disturbing losses in intellect, memory, orientation, and judgment, as well as accompanying emotional problems—is an inevitable consequence of aging. We now know that only a third of those who die after age 80 have signs of senile brain disease. There is a peak onset at about age 80, and at that time, for some reason, more women than men develop this syndrome (2). Research has also revealed that senility—a word I use reluctantly as it is a wastebasket term—is not an inevitable consequence of aging, and that, in fact, the cerebral blood flow, which is an important factor, is not noticeably different in healthy, elderly men than in 20-year-olds (3).

On the other hand, those who do have chronic brain problems are a sizeable group for whom neglect has often been the therapy of choice. Estimates are that as many as 4.4 percent of our 23 million Americans over 65 have some degree of serious intellectual impairment. In absolute numbers this represents nearly one million U.S. citizens. It is estimated that about 65 percent, or some 600,000 of these, suffer from the Alzheimer's type dementia, an early form of senile brain disease, and in the absence of artificial survival methods, their life expectancy is reduced to about five years. Given these statistics, one might expect 100,000 deaths a year from senile dementia and Alzheimer's type dementia, making these diseases the fourth or fifth leading cause of death in the United States (4). Perhaps one reason these syndromes have not commanded proportionate research attention is that brain syndromes are rarely listed on death certificates and hence are not recognized as major killers.

The myth that chronic brain disease is inevitable leads to an assumption that it causes the problems seen in an older person. Not only do older people have the same range of medical and emotional problems as younger people, but they often have combinations of illnesses uncommon at early stages of life. Furthermore, many brain syndromes are reversible, commonly called "acute," although unfortunately if they go undiagnosed and untreated these reversible conditions may become chronic and irreversible. As astute diagnosticians have always found, researchers are also finding many causes for reversible brain syndromes. Some count nearly 100 possible contributing causes. Many conditions develop outside of the brain and affect the brain by constricting either nourishment or oxygenation. We know that cell functions in the brain are acutely dependent on blood supply, and that blood supply does not change markedly in healthy individuals as they age. We do not always know why it changes in illness. We do not know a great deal about microcirculation in the brain and how it changes with advancing years. Metabolism in the brain may change with age; drug sensitivity appears quite different in many cases. For example, it is well known that tardive dyskinesia can be produced in older persons, particularly women, through prolonged use of phenothiazines. Yet little work has gone on to standardize dosage according to age groups.

Among the causes that can lead to reversible brain syndromes are: depression; nonketotic hypersmolarity diabetic syndrome; normal pressure hydrocephalus; pernicious anemia; malnutrition, often caused by the "tea and toast" syndrome of the lonely, low-income older person; drug reactions; thyroid changes; noxious environmental toxins; heart attacks; viral infections; anxiety; steroids; injuries, particularly head injuries due to falls; alcoholism, which causes a brain syndrome at any age; brain surgery; and even fecal impactions. Tranquilizers given to allay anxiety before surgery may be continued too long and cause brain syndromes. Acute reversible brain disorders are often associated with illness, and psychiatric symptoms may be among the first clues to physical illness or dehydration. A behavioral change may reflect appendicitis, although there may be no pain at McBurney's point, no fever and no leukocytosis. Reversible brain syndromes are characterized by fluctuating levels of awareness which may vary from mild confusion to stupor or active delirium. Hallucinations may be present, usually of the visual rather than the auditory type. The patient is typically disoriented, mistaking one person for another, and other intellectual functions may be impaired. Restlessness, unusual aggressiveness or a dazed expression may be noted. The classic symptoms of brain disorders may be seen in varying degrees, at the same time or at separate intervals. Reversible syndromes may appear in a person already suffering a chronic condition, and any brain disorder may be complicated by psychotic, neurotic, or behavioral disorders, as well as by social crises.

Transient cerebral ischemic attacks may occur, marked by aphasia and paralysis. These are often mistaken for chronic brain disorders when they should instead be treated aggressively. There are many variants, such as little strokes, which are probably quite frequent. Transient dizziness, nausea, vomiting, confusion, and numbness of the extremities may be seen.

Many organic problems are first seen as psychiatric ones, and vice versa. Depression may be an early sign of chronic brain syndrome, signaling a latent awareness of the beginning of cognitive losses. Recognition of this dual problem may help the person make plans while still able to do so, and ensure that maximum functioning is retained as long as possible. Transient or reversible conditions can occur in a person already suffering from chronic brain syndrome, overlaying and confusing the diagnosis. If proper treatment is given, the previous level of functioning may be recovered; if not, immediate deterioration may ensue. Even with a patient whose chronic problems are well established, there is need for immediate—even emergency—diagnostic evaluation, prompt care and treatment.

Even in the presence of established chronic brain syndrome, we are learning that adequate medical care and a good environment—a prosthetic milieu—can help even the seriously injured patient. Simple measures can yield major results. Well marked spaces, with a continual effort at orientation, activities, and even social events can prevent the decline once thought inevitable. Psychotherapy, group therapy, drugs, and electroshock all have their place and, as with any age group, a combination of resources and genuinely motivated interest on the part of the professionals involved is essential.

It is clear that the personality of the individual plays a major role. Neuropathologic change alone will neither predict the amount of deterioration that will occur nor explain it.

DEPRESSION AND SUICIDE

Depressive reactions are very common in old age, and many of the conditions that foster depression, such as a loss of status or loss of a loved one, are pervasive in this stage of life. Signs of depression include feelings of helplessness, sadness, lack of vitality, frequent feelings of guilt, loneliness, boredom, sexual disinterest and impotence—these last two are as abnormal in the late years as earlier in life, despite folklore to the contrary. In severe depressions, insomnia, early morning fatigue, and marked loss of appetite may be seen. Hypochondriasis and somatic symptoms are common.

Depression frequently follows physical illnesses, including viral diseases, and is commonly seen in Parkinson's disease. Diseases that leave people incapacitated or in pain are often complicated by depression. Unfortunately, many doctors either view depression as an inevitable part of aging or hesitate to treat depression in the presence of a physical disease.

Although often thought of as a young person's solution, suicide rates increase with age, and the elderly, about 10 percent of the population, account for almost 25 percent of the reported suicides— from 5,000 to 8,000 a year (5). The highest suicide rates occur in white males in their eighties. We suspect the true rate is even higher as many families are unwilling to report suicides out of pain or guilt. Those who have been most disadvantaged throughout life, including blacks and minority group members, do not share this suicide pattern, leading some to the conclusion that the loss of status suffered by many in the later years is a factor in the high suicide rates. There may be many reasons for this phenomenon. In German, the word for suicide means self-murder, and Freud in 1925 (6) said that perhaps no one has the psychical energy to kill himself—unless he was thereby killing someone with whom he had identified himself. Menninger (7) noted that the suicide victim wishes to die, to kill, and be killed. Others postulate that suicide is a way of controlling the uncontrollable. Seneca said, "Against all the injuries of life, I have the refuge of death." There are other possible motivations. Some men envision with horror a deteriorating illness with disastrous economic costs, leaving their widows without a cent or even heavily burdened by debt. Suicide can also be subtle, occurring through many neglectful or smaller self-destructive acts, such as refusing to admit illness or follow treatment, or taking certain kinds of dangerous risks. Suicide threats or any other clues given by the elderly should be taken seriously. The warning signs are often subtle: perhaps an ironic lifting of depression as the decision is made. Psychotherapy is helpful; additional or emergency sessions may be needed. There should be frank discussion and the family should be involved if possible.

SOCIAL ISSUES—FINANCIAL

Another myth is that the elderly drain our country's financial resources. One hears that "Social Security will go down the drain by 1980" due to the retirees. A companion myth is that Medicare, Medicaid, and Social Security have already combined to provide a basic, limited but adequate, level of living for the elderly.

Unfortunately, approximately one-third to one-half of our oldest Americans live either below or at the poverty line (8). One-sixth, or about 3.3 million, are clearly below the official poverty threshold. Older persons have roughly half the income of their younger counterparts. In 1975, half of the families headed by an older person had incomes of less than $8,057, as compared with $14,698 for families with younger heads. The median income of older persons living alone or with nonrelatives was $3,311. Women and minority group members have the lowest incomes. And although poverty lines change, there is little doubt that many more elderly are living in deprived conditions. Many—over half—have no family or friends, are unable to buy new clothes and, even more seriously, cannot afford medication, food, telephones and other such necessities. It is estimated that over five million elderly cannot afford a telephone.

Most elderly have grown poor as they have grown old. Pension funds have shrunk due to inflation, or widows have suffered the dual

loss of a husband and a pension. Inflation has affected us all, but it
has dealt the elderly an especially fierce blow. Those on fixed incomes are at a particular disadvantage. And while there is no doubt
that the Social Security system has been crucial—about nine out
of 10 persons are eligible and may receive Social Security payments,
and one in 10 receives supplemental payments—it fails to solve the
problem of income for the vast majority. Even recipients receiving
both Social Security and supplemental payments would fall below
the poverty level if these were their only income. In 1975, after payments were doubled due to across-the-board increases, the average
payments were still minimal (8, p. 3):

> $217 ($2,604) for a retired worker alone
> $370 ($4,440) for a retired worker and wife
> $479 ($5,748) for a disabled worker with a wife and one or
>   more children
> $208 ($2,496) for an aged widow
> $243 ($2,916) for disabled workers

There are some improvements: The new extended mandatory retirement law will help many elderly have more income. In a sense, it
ratifies a known situation, as almost a third of the income the elderly
have to live on continues to come from current work, often in poorly
regulated, menial positions. Legislation was just defeated that would
have allowed the elderly unlimited earnings without reducing their
Social Security payment. Unfortunately, for the time being, they are
still penalized or feel forced to hide this income.

Other problems pile up: lack of good public transportation, high
prices, crime in our cities, the victimization of the elderly, and the
difficulty of maintaining old and deteriorating homes even if the
mortgage is paid. This country grosses almost a trillion dollars a
year, yet spends only 4.2 percent of the gross national product to aid
the old. Britain and France, with fewer resources, spend 6.7 and 7
percent of their respective gross national products on the elderly.

Medicare and Medicaid have been important, but far from perfect
solutions. Medicare was essentially designed as though for young
people. It has few provisions for the needs of the older person for
check-ups, foot care, dental care, glasses, or long-term outpatient

care, despite the fact that aged persons are more than four times as likely to have their activity limited by chronic health conditions than those under 65. Additionally, with the emphasis of Medicare and Medicaid on treatment rather than prevention and inpatient rather than ambulatory care, there has been a sharp rise in the number of old people entering nursing homes and a corresponding decline in the quality of long-term care.

There is another effect that concerns us deeply, and that involves those patients suffering from organic brain disease. Private profit and nonprofit care facilities can receive Medicaid funds, so long-term care in private facilities is far less expensive to the state, although the taxpayer pays one way or another to house patients in such facilities rather than in State institutions. Many states have, therefore, transferred—or, more accurately, "dumped"—patients into foster care and boarding homes which often lack adequate health care personnel, facilities or services. This trend was intensified by legal cases on behalf of patients urging "least restrictive" care and by the important concepts of the community mental health center movement. While it is true that a good community mental health network could probably help many people to stay out of hospitals, it is also true that few such networks exist, and that they are of little use to the patient who never reaches them in a poorly planned transfer from a hospital to the community. Many older patients have suffered lifelong, serious mental illness, have been institutionalized with all the loss of independence which that implies and, furthermore, have serious chronic brain syndromes. A more tragic situation is hard to imagine. The chronic mental patient is not the only one who suffers from this dumping; consider the situation of the frail, elderly, but mentally alert patient who is forced to enter a nursing home or long-term care facility and must then live with the mentally ill as well as perhaps with tubercular and other diseased patients. It is difficult to imagine a small institution that could adequately care for such a variety of ailments; in practice, very few do. Transferring older patients for any reason brings about a high risk of mortality—"transfer shock," as it is often called. This risk should be weighed against the value of a move to the patient before such a decision is made.

Nursing Homes

We now have over 1.2 million people in nursing homes, 950,000 elderly persons and about 250,000 who are younger (9). It can be said that many nursing homes are institutions with no nurses and hardly qualify under the fine term "home." Rarely do these community facilities offer psychiatric care or even good medical supervision. The December 1974 report of the U.S. Senate Special Committee on Aging describes the following:

> Of 815,000 registered nurses in the U.S. only 56,235 serve in nursing homes (usually in administrative positions) although there are more patients in nursing homes than hospitals. From 80 to 90 percent of care is provided by over 280,000 aides and orderlies, a few of them well-trained, but most literally hired off the streets. Most are gravely overworked and paid at, or near, the minimum wage. With such working conditions, it is understandable that their turnover rate is 75 percent a year (9, p. 8).

While no one would deny that a few institutions, such as the Philadelphia Geriatric Center, are fine and innovative, most nursing homes are outside of the medical tradition and offer only the minimum. Seventy-seven percent of the nursing homes in the United States are run for profit, and all nursing homes are eligible for a wide range of federal assistance programs (9, pp. 22-26). Many nursing homes are nevertheless unable to pass basic fire, safety, or sanitation inspections. Many referrals to nursing homes are made by physicians who have never visited the homes in question.

Many people could live independently or longer if minimal help were given. This might include help during a crisis or illness; help in shopping, meals-on-wheels, visits, phone calls, and development of a basic network of medical and mental health services. Community mental health services have, by and large, neglected the elderly, whether the elderly have sought to avoid hospitalization or have been "dumped" back into the community. For those newly discharged patients, particularly, there is little understanding. Their needs are immense; yet one major newspaper recently referred to such patients in a large State hospital by saying, "Their only illness is old age," (10).

Health care spending in the United States in 1976 reached $139.3 billion. Of that, about 29.4 percent went to the elderly. About half of our health care money goes for the treatment of chronic diseases in patients of all ages. In 1972, for the first time, Medicaid expenditures for nursing home care exceeded payments for surgical and general hospitals: $1.6 billion (34 percent) as compared to $1.5 billion (31 percent) (9). The elderly pay a considerable portion of their own medical expenses, and, indeed, in some cases have to deplete all savings to be eligible for federal programs.

Medicare and Medicaid are forming the basic building blocks for National Health Insurance and, therefore, assume even greater significance. Senator Frank Church's Senate Special Committee on Aging has been active in holding hearings and has concluded that Medicare and Medicaid are in need of revision. The members note with concern that increased costs result in decreased service to the patient. They report alarming abuse and fraud in the programs, manipulation by institutional administrators, and increasing resistance on the part of physicians to participate (11, pp. 4-5). A major need, they note, is rapidly improved community resources and home care. In 1975 there were twice as many elderly people bedfast and housebound in the community as there were elderly residents in institutions of all kinds (11, p. 33).

Not all increases are due to inflation; some are due to expensive new technology. Unfortunately, a question always arises as to the appropriateness of ordering extensive or expensive tests and treatments for the elderly patient. Most diagnostic problems of the elderly demand complex and multifaceted evaluation. For example, there is no simple laboratory test for senile dementia of the Alzheimer's type; such devices as the computerized axial tomogram (CAT), a revolutionary X-ray technique, have helped in diagnosis to the degree that they indicate brain atrophy and replace the risky and painful procedures of angiography and pneumonencephalography. However, such procedures are expensive. But missing a reversible condition is also costly. A bill for a $500 workup, including almost half for a CAT scan, is minimal in contrast to the $15,000 per year that one Medicaid nursing home bed costs in New York State.

PROFESSIONAL NEGLECT

An overemphasis on the organic problems of the elderly and personal, professional, and social issues have brought about a sad situation in which psychiatrists rarely offer psychotherapy or psychoanalysis to the older patient. This is unfortunate, as many could benefit from therapy—Freudian, Jungian, group psychotherapy, Rogerian, or almost any other sort. The reminiscence that goes on in psychotherapy is particularly appropriate for the older patient, as it coincides with a natural process of life review and allows important resolutions to be made. Psychotherapy is often helpful in a surprisingly brief time because of the sense of time being limited that the older person almost inevitably has. Group therapy is useful and also helps to overcome loneliness. Family therapy can be important in resolving old conflicts and healing rifts. Psychotherapy can be helpful even in the presence of chronic brain disorder.

All the various groups that work in mental health settings—psychologists, psychiatrists, social workers, occupational therapists, nurses, etc.—have neglected the older patient. A 1971 Group for the Advancement of Psychiatry Report, *The Aged and Community Mental Health,* listed some of the reasons: the old arouse therapists' apprehensiveness about their own old age; they arouse conflicts about the therapists' personal relationships with their own parents; therapists convince themselves that the old cannot change behavior; therapists believe it is a waste of time and energy to treat people who may soon die; therapists are threatened by feelings of helplessness at the thought that patients may actually die while in treatment; and, finally, therapists may be wary of the contempt of their colleagues if they show an interest in old age with its low social status (12).

Psychiatrists may have had their initial attitude towards the elderly set in medical school. The first older person that the average medical student meets in medical school, aside from some of his teachers, is the cadaver. Although "respect" is urged, little attention has been given to the distress this experience causes the student and the attitude that "death" and the "old person" are synonymous. One study of University of California medical students showed that their attitude towards old people deteriorated over their four years in medical school (13). There is little exposure to healthy older persons, nor is there the multidisciplinary development of a concept of geriatric medicine which might help students and young doctors more adequately treat the complex problems of the older person. Few medical schools, only 50 out of 120, have any instruction related to geriatric medicine and only Cornell has established a chair of geriatric medicine. Few psychiatric residents are assigned older patients; a survey of psychiatrists in a metropolitan area showed that 55 percent had no contact with the elderly, and the remaining group spent approximately 76 hours a year with those over 65—less than 2 percent of total psychiatric time (14).

A study by the American Psychoanalytic Association showed that 98 percent of psychoanalytic patients are white; 82 percent are under 45; and 78 percent are college-educated—figures which almost exclude the elderly (15).

Community mental health centers (CMHC) have failed the elderly. Although the system was enacted by Congress in 1963 to allow for widespread mental health care and to offer a variety of valuable services that would allow prompt and consistent treatment of the mentally or emotionally ill person in the community, it failed to develop as hoped. Chronic patients have not fared well, and some community mental health centers either refused or simply failed to treat the elderly. Fewer than 18 percent created geriatric programs of any sort. In many areas the centers did not develop at all. There has been virtually no interest on the part of CMHCs in the many former mental patients "placed in the community."

With regard to research, the same count-the-percentage-on-the-fingers-of-one-hand figures are found, with only 3 percent of the budget of the National Institute of Mental Health devoted to the study of the mental problems of old age. Similarly, the new National Institute on Aging commands only 1 percent of the National Institutes of Health budget.

The National Institute on Aging (NIA) is part of the National Institutes of Health (NIH) and is housed in Building 31 on the NIH campus in Bethesda. The NIA was authorized on May 31, 1974, and established on October 7, 1974. It has a total budget of

$37,000,000, of which $26,533,000 is allotted to extramural research and $7,945,000 to intramural research. The remaining $2,522,000 goes for administrative support of Institute programs.

NIA conducts research in its laboratories at the Gerontology Research Center in Baltimore, Maryland, and supports research through grants in universities, hospitals and research facilities in this country and abroad on a wide variety of biomedical, social, and behavioral aspects of the aging process and on the diseases, special problems, and needs of the aged. In addition, NIA supports the training of promising researchers.

CONCLUSIONS

Psychiatrists have a great deal to offer the elderly and will undoubtedly be increasingly involved in their care. More than other specialists, they are experienced in working with social agencies and other professionals, and this is particularly useful with the older patient. Also, psychiatrists understand the significance of social problems, of the background to illness, and of the wearing down of a person until he or she is unable to function. Psychiatrists are in a good position, too, to study younger patients for early warning signs. As in oncology, we need to learn prodromal signs. What are the physical indications that a person might be vulnerable to chronic brain disorders? We suspect that some preventive measures could be taken in the middle years. We know the cost of smoking and alcoholism and of some social patterns as well. One gerontologist, Wilma Donahue, noted that many of the young people involved in counterculture life-styles concern her, as they appear to have sacrificed the structure needed for a secure old age. Out of protest to the Vietnam War, they have become nomadic, broken off from family support, are disdainful of education, at times addicted to drugs, and isolated from the normal community. We do not yet know the validity of her concerns. On the other hand, Maggie Kuhn, director of the Gray Panthers, notes she has found one life-style variant useful—that of cross-generational communal style living which she sees as one creative answer to the isolation of the elderly.

Myths need to be challenged. Psychiatry has focused, perhaps due to Freud's emphasis, on the young, despite the fact that Freud himself did his most important work in his middle years and continued to work until his death, despite serious illness. Although others, such as Goldfarb (16) and Weinberg (17), have focused on later years, there needs to be a more even examination of the emotional life in the late years. Those who work with dying patients—and it really should be all of us—report gratification and personal growth from the experience. We live in a time of great change, with even greater change possible. Aristotle said, "What we have to learn to do, we learn by doing." We need to extend good medical care and good psychiatry to the elderly in every possible way and to proceed with research that will enlighten us about aging.

REFERENCES

1. "Mental health problems of aging and the aged." Sixth Report of the Expert Committee on Mental Health, WHO, Geneva, 1959, World Health Organization Technical Report Series, No. 171.
2. GRUENBERG, E.: "Senile brain diseases in people over 65." Unpublished paper. The Johns Hopkins University, School of Hygiene and Public Health. Baltimore, Md., October 1, 1976.
3. DASTUR, D. K., LANE, M. H., HANSE, D. B., KETY, S. S., BUTLER, R. N., PERLIN, S., and SOKOLFF, L.: Effects of aging on cerebral circulation and metabolism in man. In: J. E. Birren, et al. (Eds.), *Human Aging: A Biological and Behavioral Study*. Washington, D.C.: U.S. Government Printing Office, 1963.
4. BUTLER, R. N.: "Testimony before the President's Commission on Mental Health," September, 1977.
5. RESNICK, H. L. and CANTOR, J. M.: Suicide and aging. *Journal of the American Geriatrics Society*, 18:152-158, 1970.
6. FREUD, S.: Mourning and melancholia. In: *Standard Edition of the Psychological Works of Sigmund Freud*, Vol. 18. London: Hogarth Press, 1957, p. 163.
7. MENNINGER, K. A.: *Man Against Himself*. New York: Harcourt, Brace & World, 1938, p. 25.
8. "Developments in aging: 1976 (Part 1), A Report of the Special Committee on Aging." United States Senate, 95th Congress, Report No. 95-88. Washington, D.C.: U.S. Government Printing Office, 1977, pp. 4-5.
9. "Nursing Home Care in the United States: Failure in Public Policy." Introductory Report, Subcommittee on Long-Term Care of the Special Committee on Aging, United States Senate, 93rd Congress. Washington, D.C.: U.S. Government Printing Office, 1974.
10. "Maine Institute Official to Direct St. Elizabeth's." *The Washington Post*, September 14, 1977, p. A5.

11. "Health costs and problems in Medicaid and Medicare." *Developments in Aging*: *1976 (Part 1)*, *A Report of the Special Committee on Aging.* United States Senate, 96th Congress, Report No. 95-88. Washington, D.C.: U.S. Government Printing Office, 1977, pp. 4-5.
12. Group for the Advancement of Psychiatry. *The Aged and Community Mental Health*: *A Guide to Program Development.* Report Vol. 8, 1971.
13. SPENCE, D. L., FEIGENBAUM, E. M., et al.: "Medical student attitudes towards the geriatric patient." *Journal of the American Geriatrics Society*, 16:976-983, 1968.
14. BUTLER, R. N. and SULLIMAN, L. G.: "Psychiatric contact with the community resident, emotionally disturbed elderly." *Journal of Nervous and Mental Disease*, 137:180-186, 1963.
15. HAMBURG, D., et al.: "Report of Ad Hoc Committee on Central Fact Finding Data of the American Psychoanalytic Association." *Journal of the American Psychoanalytic Association*, 15:841-866, 1967.
16. GOLDFARB, A. I.: "The psychotherapy of elderly patients." In: H. T. Blumenthal (Ed.), *Medical and Clinical Aspects of Aging.* New York: Columbia University Press, 1962, pp. 106-114.
17. WEINBERG, J.: "1969 rehabilitation of geriatric patients." *Illinois Medical Journal*, 1963:63-66, 1970.

BIBLIOGRAPHY

The Aged and Community Mental Health: *A Guide to Program Development.* Report No. 81, New York, Nov. 1971.
BIRREN, J.: *The Handbooks of Aging: Three Volumes. Handbook of the Biology of Aging; Handbook of the Psychology of Aging; Handbook of Aging and Social Sciences.* New York: Van Nostrand Reinhold Co., 1977.
BIRREN, J. E., et al.: *Human Aging: A Biological and Behavioral Study.* Washington, D.C.: U.S. Government Printing Office, 1963.
BUTLER, R. N.: "The life review: An interpretation of reminiscence in the aged." *Psychiatry*, Vol. 26, 1963.
BUTLER, R. N.: *Why Survive? Being Old in America.* New York: Harper & Row, 1975.
BUTLER, R. N. and LEWIS, M. I.: *Aging and Mental Health, Positive Psychosocial Approaches.* St. Louis: C. V. Mosby Co., 1977.
BUTLER, R. N. and LEWIS, M. I.: *Sex After Sixty: A Guide for Men and Women in Their Later Years.* New York: Harper & Row, 1976.
DONAHUE, W. and CLARK, T. (Eds.): *Politics of Age.* Ann Arbor, Michigan: University Press, 1962.
ERIKSON, E. H.: *Identity and the Life Cycle. Psychological Issues.* Vol. 1, No. 1. New York: International Universities Press, 1959.

GOLDFARB, A. L.: "Patient-doctor relationship in the treatment of aged persons." *Geriatrics*, Vol. 12, 1964.

GOLDFARB, A. L.: "The psychotherapy of elderly patients." In: H. Blumenthal (Ed.), *Aging Around the World: Medical and Clinical Aspects of Aging.* New York: Columbia University Press, 1962.

HODGIN, E.: *Episode: Report on the Accident Inside My Skull.* New York: Atheneum, 1964.

HOLLINGSHEAD, A. B. and FREDERICK, S. R.: *Social Class and Mental Illness.* New York: John Wiley & Sons, 1958.

KAHN, R. L., GOLDFARB, A. I., POLLACK, M., and PECK, A.: "A brief objective measure for the determination of mental status of the aged." *American Journal of Psychiatry*, Vol. 117, 1966.

KRANT, M. J.: "The organized care of the dying patient." *Hospital Practice*, Vol. 7, 1972.

KUBLER-ROSS, E.: *On Dying and Death: What the Dying Have to Teach Doctors, Nurses, Clergy and Their Own Families.* London: Macmillan, 1969.

Our Future Selves: A Research Plan Toward Understanding Aging. National Institute on Aging, with the National Advisory Council on Aging. Washington, D.C.: U.S. Government Printing Office, 1977.

ROSSMAN, I. (Ed.): *Clinical Geriatrics in Medicine.* Philadelphia: J. B. Lippincott, 1971.

SAUNDERS, C.: *Care of the Dying.* London: Macmillan, 1959.

Special Committee on Aging. *Appendices, Developments in Aging: 1976.* United States Senate, April 1977.

2

The Social and Cultural
Context of Aging

George L. Maddox, Ph.D.

Popular as well as scientific interest in aging has increased markedly
in the past three decades. This interest has been stimulated by two
factors that have been difficult to ignore. One is a demographic explosion: The proportion of older persons* in modern societies has
doubled in this century; in the United States, for instance, the rate
of old persons exceeds that of any other category. In the United States
there are 23 million old persons, amounting to nearly 10 percent of
the population. Current estimates of Western European countries
places the figure at about 14 percent, and, depending on birth rates,
older persons may constitute as much as 16 percent of our population
early in the next century (1).

The demographic explosion has been accompanied by a marked increase in information about the biographical, behavioral, and social
aspects of aging. This knowledge has stimulated a need to know even

---

* In this paper the general sociological convention with respect to
terminology will be followed: unless otherwise stated, the terms "old,"
"older," and "aged," will refer to persons 65 and above.

more about the reciprocal influence of population aging and societal institutions.

The implications of the fact that biological and psychological aging occurs in a cultural and social context, as well as the specification of this context, will be the focus of this chapter. The shared construc- tions of reality that we call culture embody social preferences and ways of valuing people and things, as well as the roles and rules which structure interpersonal relationships, distinguish ordered from disor- dered behavior, and determine the allocation of status, honor, and opportunity. In simplest terms, culture comprises the institutionalized ways by which a society organizes everyday life. In regard to the life course, we would expect what we in fact observe: Societies have char- acteristic ways of thinking about and responding to aging and the aged. These ways of thinking and responding provide the context for aging and structure the experience of aging. A great deal of what we know about the sociocultural context of aging can be organized by addressing two questions: 1) How and to what extent are older per- sons integrated into various societies? 2) How and to what extent do older persons in various societies adapt in ways that are personally satisfying and socially adaptive? These questions lead to a third: 3) How and to what extent are the social integration and adaptation of older persons amenable to modification by guided social change? Be- fore any of these questions is addressed, however, it is important to stress the necessity and novelty of asking such questions at all. The questions have appeared to be relevant and urgent only in recent decades. The newness of societal aging explains in part the observed uncertainty about how to assess the related problems and the sense of urgency in identifying appropriate responses.

DEMOGRAPHIC CHANGE AND SOCIAL INSTITUTIONS

Recent Changes in Age Composition

Societies characterized by a large percentage of persons surviving well beyond adulthood are a distinctly modern achievement. Longev- ity *per se* is not unusual. All societies for which we have evidence have designations for *oldness* and have produced a few individuals who are chronologically very old. But longevity as a probable experience in a population has, until very recently, been quite unusual. The well-known figure adapted from Alex Comfort (2) by Leonard Hayflick (3) makes the point quite well (see Table 1). The current probability in the U.S. that approximately 75 percent of a birth cohort will survive to age 60 and 60 percent to age 70 is quite extraordinary when compared with the probabilities derivable from Table 1 and even more extraordinary when compared with historical evidence (4). There is some evidence from physical anthropology that most persons in the prehistoric era did not survive beyond age 30 and only rarely to age 50. By the late Roman Empire, however, about 20 percent of populations in Greece and Italy may have survived at least to age 70. Current data from life tables have been used to argue that the potential maximum life span of the species has continued to be about 94 years and might be extended under favorable conditions to a bit over 100 years. To date, improved sanitary conditions, nutrition and medical technology have increased the probability of achieving the estimated maximum longevity without increasing life span appreciably. In primitive and pre-modern societies, the proportion of older persons is about 3 percent. In contrast, in developed countries the result has been a notable rise in the proportion of older persons, with the proportion doubling in the first three-quarters of this century. (Model demographic profiles under varying assumptions are presented in Table 1.) In the United States this meant an increase of persons 65 years of age and older from 5 percent to 10 percent. In the countries of Western Europe the current percentage of older persons tends to range between 13 percent and 16 percent. About one-third of older populations are *very old*, that is, 75 years of age and older. The rapidly increasing numbers of older persons has contributed to their social visibility and has helped transform old age from a personal issue for a few persons into a societal issue. The transformation of aging into a social problem has been reinforced by the impact which an aging population has on social institutions.

Age Composition and Impairment

The key to understanding the societal impact of an aging population lies in the demonstrable association among adults between age and morbidity, a circumstance which increases the probability of phys-

TABLE 1

Model Demographic Profiles Under Varying Fertility and Mortality Levels

Population Characteristic	Primitive-stationary[a]	Pre-modern[b]	Transitional[c]	Modern[d]	Modern-stationary[e]
Birth rate	50.0	43.7	45.7	20.4	12.9
Death rate	50.0	33.7	15.7	10.4	12.9
Annual growth rate—percent	0.0	1.0	3.0	1.0	0.0
Age structure					
Percent under 15	36.2	37.8	45.4	27.2	19.2
Percent 15-64	60.9	58.8	52.0	62.4	62.3
Percent 65 and over	2.9	3.4	2.6	10.3	18.5
Average age	25.5	25.1	21.8	32.8	40.0
Dependency ratio	64	70	92	60	61
Youth dependency ratio	59	64	87	44	31
Aged dependency ratio	5	6	5	16	30
Percent surviving to age 15	41.0	55.9	78.8	95.6	98.9
Expectation of life at birth	20.0	30.0	50.0	70.0	77.5
Children ever-born to women age 50	6.2	5.5	6.1	2.9	2.1
Average number children surviving to age 20	2.3	2.9	4.7	2.7	2.0

a. Mortality level 1.
b. Mortality level 5.
c. Mortality level 13.
d. Mortality level 21.
e. Mortality level 24.
Source: Ansley J. Coale and Paul Demeny, *Regional Model Life Tables and Stable Populations*, Princeton, New Jersey: Princeton University Press, 1966. (Based on stable populations for "West" female.)

ical disabilities resulting in dependency. Standard life tables remind us that mortality is a function of age, and epidemiologic evidence confirms that morbidity and functional impairment are also related to age (5). A general implication of population aging is that increased dependency exacts social costs and forces new decisions about the allocation of health and welfare resources. About 5 percent of older persons in all Western societies are institutionalized. In the United States this translates into a million long-term care beds currently occupied primarily by older persons at a cost of some 10 billion dollars annually. And as a rule of thumb, older persons generate health bills roughly two-and-a-half-times greater than adults generally. Moreover, the financing of welfare has become a significant issue in allocation of social resources in all industrial societies.

AGING SOCIETIES AND SOCIAL CHANGE

Institutional arrangements that are adapted to the needs of a population with few older people may be mismatched with the needs of a population with a large proportion of older persons. Consider briefly, for example, the challenge which the aging of the U.S. population has posed for institutional arrangement involving income maintenance in retirement, health care delivery, transportation, and education.

Income Maintenance

Our current social security system emerged from rather modest beginnings as an Old Age and Survivors Insurance program in 1935. For all its limitations, the system has proven to be adaptable, politically viable and economically salvageable if not entirely sound at the moment. The system is an excellent illustration of a social contract between generations in which those currently in the work force share their wages with those outside the work force with the expectations that subsequent generations will continue to honor the contract when they are no longer at work. This understanding was not problematic when the economy was expanding, rates of inflation were modest, and the ratio of workers and retirees was favorable. The fact that none of these conditions holds currently underlies a growing concern not so much about the future of Social Security but about its cost, with estimates of increased Social Security taxation in the reasonably near future reaching as high as 300 percent above current rates (6,7). The unfunded debt obligation of the U.S. Social Security System is now larger than the Gross National Product. However, as costly as our social security system is perceived to be, it leaves about 11 percent of older persons below the poverty level and at least an equal proportion near poverty.

Health Care

Health care delivery in this country has tended to emphasize specialization of professionals and organizations and the dominance of medical centers. The result has tended to be fragmentation of care, the separation of health and welfare services, and relative neglect of primary care, preventive care, community based care, and long-term care. The areas of neglect have special significance for an aging population, whose perceived and actual needs are substantially mismatched with the types of care offered (8). And, interestingly, in spite of a general tendency toward specialization in health care, training of health care professionals has almost totally ignored formal training in geriatrics. Moreover, the legislative mandate to community mental health centers to develop special services for older persons has had relatively little effect on the services actually offered and/or utilized (9). Older individuals, who contribute a large proportion of first admissions to state mental hospitals, constitute a small fraction of the clients of community mental health centers.

Transportation

Geographic mobility is characteristic of all contemporary industrial societies. This mobility is reflected in frequent changes in residence, in the process of urbanization, and in the option for persons to live at considerable distance from work and from essential services. The private automobile has accentuated the perceived options in the arrangement of personal and social space. In an affluent society, physically unimpaired adults can accept or ignore both the very high cost of personal transportation and the threat of energy shortage. On the other hand, persons who are disabled or poor—conditions correlated

with advanced age—are particularly handicapped by the societal preference for private transportation. Almost half the population over age
65 does not own an automobile, and, as would be expected in a society
that favors private over public transportation, advancing age and low
income result in low rates of geographic mobility. Since problems of
transportation can be serious for rural and suburban elderly, it is not
surprising that surveys of perceived needs of older persons, many of
whom live in rural and suburban areas, typically list transportation
as an important unmet need (10).

Education

Formal education is distinctly associated with childhood and youth
for pedagogic, practical and economic reasons. Younger people need
to be trained; they are available to be trained, and the economic return from early training is higher than the return from later training.
These good reasons for associating education with youth have perverse
and unnecessary corollaries which are used to justify the failure to
provide learning opportunities for older persons. One hears, for example, that older people do not need or want more training, or that it is,
in any event, uneconomical. There is a pronounced tendency in this
country to think of adult learning as uninteresting as well as unnecessary. Although only a small fraction (less than 3 percent) of old adults
in the U.S. are active in continuing education programs, participation
rates among adults generally are increasing. At least three factors are
working to induce change. 1) There is a realization that continuing
education for professionals and other practitioners who depend on
up-to-date technical information is both prudent and necessary. (All
states now require some continuing education for some professionals.)
2) The educational attainment of the population is increasing, resulting in a large proportion of individuals who think of learning as a
good thing (28 percent of college graduates and 32 percent of post-
graduates participated in continuing education in 1975). 3) Institutions of higher learning are beginning to realize they may need older
students to reverse declining college enrollments. (Many states have
legislated free tuition to older learners on a space available basis.)

THE NATURE OF THE PROBLEM

A Question of Values

There are alternative explanations of the observed mismatch between demonstrable needs of an aging population and institutional arrangements for meeting those needs. The mismatch could be an expression of widespread hostility to older persons or to growing older, which is unconscious and therefore likely to continue. There is some basis for arguing that our national preference for youthfulness has as its counterpart a dislike of old age and older people. Perhaps our national heritage, which stresses newness, the breaking of traditional ties, and individual productivity, leads to such outcomes. And, psychodynamically, old persons do represent reminders of personal finitude and hence provide a basis for dislike, even hatred, and thus for rejection and isolation of the old. An equally plausible explanation of observed discomfort with old age is that the age composition of the population has simply outrun the rate of adaptive social change. We did not anticipate either the rapidity of aging in the population or the extent of institutional inadequacy. That is, we did not design a society in which it would be easy to grow old. We may be, and probably are, capable of institutional redesign that will accommodate current and projected changes in age composition. Sorting out facts about aging and the aged from preferences about aging and the aged has been a major task of the last three decades.

Aging and the Aged as Social Problems

Personal experience with aging is old, but scientific interest in aging and the aged is new. Concern about the aged as a social problem emerged about the same time that critics were worrying publicly about problems of modernization, industrialization and urbanization. Some observers wondered whether anyone would survive what was to be called later the future shock of rapid change, the dehumanization of the industrial workplace, and the alienating experience of urban living. Older persons were seen as especially vulnerable to disintegrative forces in a sociocultural context which threatened everyone. (See Arsenian and Arsenian on "tough cultures" (12).)

How a society identifies, defines, structures and responds to its social problems is a complex process. Personal troubles and individual misery, even if widespread, do not insure their perception as a social problem. Societies selectively dignify troubles and misery with the designation *social problem* when three conditions are met: 1) A basic societal value is challenged; 2) the problem appears to be avoidable; and 3) there is the possibility of social consensus about the procedures for correcting the perceived difficulty. Thus, the designation of aging as a social problem is implicitly optimistic, insofar as this implies that informed observers perceive trouble and misery associated with aging to be both undesirable and avoidable. But again, what needs fixing to ameliorate the perceived problems? Does the problem lie in the individual? In the organization of society? In the hierarchy of social values, alternative ways of structuring the problems of an aging society have each attracted proponents, and each way of structuring has consequences for how to proceed (13).

If the source of the problem lies in the aging of individuals, then we should find ways to modify the aging process. Alex Comfort, best known recently for his writings on the joys of sex, began his career as a biologist and gerontologist who wrote persuasively on the potential of transforming the aging process so as to delay, ameliorate, or obviate the biologically determined disabilities associated with late life. What we needed, according to Comfort, was more and better biochemistry and medical science. But the basic idea is straightforward. Transform individual capability, and you reduce the problems of late life. Comfort now stresses that the problem is more complex than this, and in his recent work (14) emphasizes prejudicial social attitudes and institutional barriers as important factors in creating problems associated with later life. This change in emphasis anticipates the second perspective.

Even healthy, functioning older persons face institutional barriers to meeting their needs. As noted above, the American way of living makes it difficult to maintain one's income at the end of life, makes primary, preventive and adequate long-term care inaccessible, and makes mobility and lifetime learning a challenge. Those who stress these factors believe that we need to transform institutional arrangements, whether or not we transform individuals. The remedies are, therefore, primarily political rather than biochemical or medical.

The third perspective on social problems emphasizes social preferences and power. Those who control society are in a position to define what is available and who ought to have access to resources. Hence the problems of aging lie substantially in our value system and the related distribution of power, prestige and material resources. Many of the problems associated with disability and with the low status and marginal welfare of older persons could be alleviated *if* the society committed its resources to achieve this objective. The problems of aging, from this point of view, derive as much from a value system that exaggerates the importance of independence, productivity, and economic consumption as from faulty biological organisms or faulty social institutions. The implication that a cultural revolution is required to deal with the real problem of aging is dramatically expressed in the final paragraph of Simone de Beauvoir's *The Coming of Age.*

> Society cares about the individual only in so far as he is profitable. The young know this. Their anxiety as they enter in upon social life matches the anguish of the old as they are excluded from it. Between these two ages, the problem is hidden by routine. The young man dreads this machine that is about to seize hold of him, and sometimes he tries to defend himself by throwing half-bricks; the old man, rejected by it, exhausted and naked, has nothing left but his eyes to weep with. Between youth and age there turns the machine, the crusher of men—of men who let themselves be crushed because it never even occurs to them that they can escape it. Once we have understood what the state of the aged really is, we cannot satisfy ourselves with calling for a more generous old-age policy, higher pensions, decent housing and organized leisure. It is the whole system that is at issue and our claim cannot be otherwise than radical—change life itself (15, p. 807).

Informed observers who agree that old age constitutes a social problem disagree honestly about which of these three perspectives provides the most accurate insights into the sources of the problem and into possible solutions. To some degree, all three perspectives provide useful insights which are complementary. In any case, we do not need to choose at this point and should not, until we review what we know about aging and the aged.

Aging as a problem for the biological, behavioral and social sciences came sharply into focus three decades ago. National and international societies and journals on aging appeared. Existing professional societies began to take note of aging. Centers and institutes on aging were created in universities. In the last two decades, three major sets of comprehensive handbooks on aging have been published to document what we know about human aging (16, 17, 18). In 1975 aging joined the pantheon of problems of relevance to health by becoming the focus of the newest institute in the National Institutes of Health. Since others in this conference have responsibility for discussing biological and psychological knowledge, this presentation will concentrate on social scientific knowledge and the themes and issues which have emerged in recent decades.

The Social Scientific Study of Human Aging

The identification of aging as a social problem was stimulated in part by the work of social scientists. Demographers documented the changing age structure of developed societies, and sociologists documented the evidence of social disorganization associated with industrialization and urbanization. The evidence led many informed observers in the early decades of this century to view with alarm the personal and social implications of aging and to worry about corrective action. The systematic social scientific study of aging, however, has its origins in the 1940s. A benchmark article appeared in the first issue of the *Journal of Gerontology,* the official journal of the Gerontological Society, which was founded in 1945. In the lead article of the first issue Lawrence K. Frank proposed a conceptualization of aging as a multidimensional biosocial phenomena to be understood in terms of "field theory," i.e., as person-environment interaction (19). At the same time, Leo Simmons published his pioneering study of old age in almost 100 preliterate societies, documented in the Yale Cross-cultural Area Files (20). Within a decade a number of major universities, including California (Berkeley and San Francisco), Michigan, Duke, and Chicago, began to assemble research scientists to study aging. The Social Science Research Council created a task force on aging. The American Psychological Association created a Division of Adult Development of Aging. By 1960 a large group of scientists, with federal support, produced the three previously noted substantial handbooks, which summarized a rapidly growing body of research evidence (16). In retrospect, the perceptiveness and foresight of the initial handbooks are impressive. These volumes document in considerable detail that aging is a social as well as a biological phenomenon, that chronological age is a deceptive and frequently unreliable indicator of functional capacity, and that environmental factors are important determinants of behavior in late life. These volumes also contain another message. They argue for a distinctly new discipline of gerontology, which is multidisciplinary and which weds scientific study to its application in social action. This latter point is noted in passing, because it sheds some light on the uneasy relationship which professionals who identify themselves as gerontologists have had with established academic disciplines. Established disciplines tend to prefer narrow theoretical paradigms and to avoid personal involvement in social movements. To many social scientists, social gerontology has appeared to be as much a social movement as a scientific undertaking, and they seem to be more interested in interdisciplinary than disciplinary research. By 1960, social scientists, whether or not they identified themselves as social gerontologists, had established their basic research agenda with regard to the study of aging. At the risk of considerable oversimplification, that agenda may be said to include examination of the three questions anticipated earlier:

1) Can the integration of older persons be satisfactorily achieved in modern, industrial urban societies?

2) Beyond social integration, can personal, satisfying adjustment be achieved by older persons?

3) Can sociocultural contexts be structured so as to maximize the achievement of social integration and personal satisfaction of older persons?

Social Integration

A deep and pervasive pessimism about the fate of modern men and women is a recurrent theme of humanists and scientists alike. There is a widespread suspicion that the world we have lost may have been

better than the world we have. In the language of sociology, there is
a generally distressing tendency for primary relationships to be replaced by secondary ones. Faceless factories and impersonal cities
tend to separate workers from their tools and rob them of their
pride in workmanship; community ties tend to weaken. Isolation,
alienation and future shock appear to be inevitable outcomes. Such is
the common fate of the modern individual; older persons are only a
special case insofar as they are more vulnerable than most. For evidence, all one had to do was to look at welfare departments, the slums
and state hospitals to see culture working against mankind (21).

With this perspective in mind, Leo Simmons looked longingly at the
preliterate world we had lost in our pursuit of modernity (20). In the
100 or so typically small, preliterate societies of his research, those
few individuals who survived into old age did appear to enjoy high
status and respect, and, on average, their welfare was as secure as, frequently more secure than, that of adults generally. Older persons—
usually older males, though Simmons did not dwell on the implications of this fact—presided over extended kinship groups, controlled
property, were the keepers of tradition, presided over ritual events,
and enjoyed positions of leadership. In preliterate societies, there was
no counterpart of retirement in the modern sense: Older persons maintained socially important roles and positions of power.

Contrasting preliterate and modern societies, Simmons induced a
persuasive hypothesis that has persisted: Modernization (i.e., industrialization, urbanization, rapid social change) is inversely related to
the status and welfare of older persons but, unfortunately, is directly
related to the probability of survival into old age. *Old* in modern society is associated with precarious welfare, low status, rolelessness,
social isolation, and alienation. Three decades later, Cowgill and
Holmes reported studies of 15 societies differing in their degree of
modernization and concluded that Simmons was more right than
wrong (22). The Cowgill and Holmes conclusions summarized in
Table 2 elaborate the original argument. Some qualifications of the
argument and the conclusions are required by the accumulating
evidence, however.

First, several societies rather clearly constitute negative evidence.
Consider Japan, one of the most urban and industrialized societies in

the world. In that country, extended kinship groups have been maintained, familism is incorporated in industrial firms that assume lifetime responsibilities for workers, and older persons are, as Erdman Palmore has documented, still "honorable elders" (23). Furthermore, societies with strong socialistic political traditions—Sweden, the Soviet Union, and the Kibbutz movement in Israel—manage to insure the welfare and status of older persons to an extent not predicted by the modernization hypothesis. Value systems apparently are countervailing forces which moderate the effects of modernization. Comparative studies of the United States, Britain, and Denmark also indicate that isolation of older persons from their kin is the exception rather than the rule (24).

Second, the more sociologists have studied the family relationship of older persons in modern societies, the more they are likely to propose revisions of the conventional wisdom about the isolation of older persons from their kin (25, 26). The preferred separate housing of generations and the related emotional detachment appear to be revocable. Intimacy between generations can be maintained at a distance, and substantial amounts of goods and services are exchanged between members of different generations. In a recent U.S. General Accounting Office study in Cleveland, Ohio, about 80 percent of the services provided to older persons were provided by kin and friends (27). In a recent unpublished report on research carried out in Cleveland, Ohio, for the U.S. Administration on Aging, Sussman (28) asked a large sample of adults whether they would accept an older person, presumably a kinsman, into their house to live. Sixty percent of respondents agreed that they would accept an older person without reluctance, and another 21 percent agreed that they would do so "under some circumstances." The remaining 20 percent maintained that they would never do so. Those who rejected the obligation of families to care for older members argued that this was an obligation of the state rather than of the family. Among the categories overrepresented in the 20 percent who said "never" were older adults, those reared on farms, Blacks, those without a religious preference, and those who had had minimal experience with older people. Also worth noting is the belief, held by 60 percent of the respondents, that care of older persons is primarily the responsibility of families and

TABLE 2

Summary of Propositions about the Status and Welfare of Older
Persons in Pre-modern and Modern Societies

UNIVERSALS

1. The aged always constitute a minority within the total population.
2. In an older population, females outnumber males.
3. Widows comprise a high proportion of an older population.
4. In all societies, some people are classified as old and are treated differently because they are so classified.
5. There is a widespread tendency for people defined as old to shift to more sedentary, advisory, or supervisory roles involving less physical exertion and more concerned with group maintenance than the economic production.
6. In all societies, some old persons continue to act as political, judicial, and civil leaders.
7. In all societies, the mores prescribe some mutual responsibility between old people and their adult chlidren.
8. All societies value life and seek to prolong it, even in old age.

VARIATIONS

1. The concept of old age is relative to the degree of modernization; a person is classified as old at an earlier chronological age in a primitive society than in a modern society.
2. Old age is identified in terms of chronological age chiefly in modern societies; in other societies onset of old age is more commonly linked with events such as succession to eldership or becoming a grandparent.
3. Longevity is directly and significantly related to the degree of modernization.
4. Modernized societies have older populations, i.e., high proportions of old people.
5. Modern societies have higher proportions of women and especially of widows.
6. Modern societies have higher proportions of people who live to be grandparents and even great grandparents.
7. The status of the aged is high in primitive societies and is lower and more ambiguous in modern societies.
8. In primitive societies, older people tend to hold positions of poli-

TABLE 2 (*continued*)

tical and economic power, but in modern societies such power is possessed by only a few.

9. The status of the aged is high in societies in which there is a high reverence for or worship of ancestors.

10. The status of the aged is highest when they constitute a low proportion of the population and tends to decline as their numbers and proportions increase.

11. The status of the aged is inversely proportional to the rate of social change.

12. Stability of residence favors high status of the aged; mobility tends to undermine it.

13. The status of the aged tends to be high in agricultural societies and lower in urbanized societies.

14. The status of the aged tends to be high in preliterate societies and to decline with increasing literacy of the populations.

15. The status of the aged is high in those societies in which they are able to continue to perform useful and valued functions; however, this is contingent upon the values of society as well as upon the specific activities of the aged.

16. Retirement is a modern invention; it is found chiefly in modern high-productivity societies.

17. The status of the aged is high in societies in which the extended form of the family is prevalent and tends to be lower in societies which favor the nuclear form of the family and neolocal marriage.

18. With modernization the responsibility for the provision of economic security for dependent aged tends to be shifted from the family to the state.

19. The proportion of the aged who are able to maintain leadership roles declines with modernization.

20. In primitive societies the roles of widows tend to be clearly ascribed, but such role ascription declines with modernization; the widow's role in modern societies tends to be flexible and ambiguous.

21. The individualistic value system of western society tends to reduce the security and status of older people.

22. Disengagement is not characteristic of the aged in primitive or agrarian societies, but an increasing tendency toward disengagement appears to accompany modernization.

Source: D. O. Cowgill and T. D. Holmes (Eds.), *Aging and Modernization.* New York: Meredith, 1972.

that institutions should be used only as a last resort. The image of families abandoning older members at the slightest provocation is not supported by Sussman's evidence or, in fact, by any systematic evidence. Functioning, modified kinship units characterized by separate households and residential mobility but also by intimacy at a distance and revocable detachment have been and are the rule.

Third, in the United States, at least, older persons have remained actively involved in the political process (29). Older persons are as interested and active in politics as adults generally and more active than young adults. The political alienation of older persons is not indicated by such evidence. The counterargument that the demographic projections plus the demonstrated political involvement of older persons insure the rise of a gerontocracy is also not supported by the current evidence (30). The response of older persons to political issues is better explained by their socioeconomic status than by their age. Moreover, older voters are emotionally identified with family groups, which are by definition multigenerational. Therefore, when faced with choices about the allocation of social resources, older persons—and adults generally—have an incentive to consider the interests of age categories other than their own. A politics based on age is conceivable but does not appear to be in prospect in any society that has been studied.

Fourth, the capacity and willingness of modern societies to secure the welfare of older persons seem to be greater than their willingness to provide unambiguously high status for the old. Yet, even this evidence is complex. Simone de Beauvoir (15) and, more recently, Fisher (1) have noted the varying perceptions of old age at different periods of European and American history. Irving Rosow (11) is so convinced that contemporary American society cannot tolerate functionless, roleless older persons that he recommends special colonies for older persons so that they can evolve their own status system. The late Yonina Talman (31) perceptively described the extent to which the socialization of older persons into a society characterized by a pervasive work ethic can exact its costs. She noted that, in an Israeli Kibbutz in which the founders had grown old working hard to realize the injunction "from each according to ability, to each according to need," the aging pioneers of the Kibbutz were uneasy in their retirement. In contrast, their relatives who came belatedly into the settlement from outside as guests enjoyed what they perceived to be a secure old age. The old pioneers of the Kibbutz had self-images which were more negative than their relatives who had not been reared in the Kibbutz. One suspects that Clark and Anderson (32) are right in arguing that a similar situation pertains in the contemporary United States, where an ideology of self-reliance generates a widespread terror of dependency. It is quite possible, therefore, that, even as public attitudes toward late life moderate in the face of growing evidence that old persons can be and are socially integrated for the most part, the most negative attitudes toward late life may be found among older persons themselves.

The balance sheet regarding the social integration of older persons, then, may be summarized as follows. While the full social integration of older persons in modern society is problematic, their essential integration into family groups and into political and social life commitments is not only possible, but also the rule. Palmore and Manton are probably on the right track in arguing that the relationship between modernization and the status and welfare of older persons may be curvilinear (33). The early phases of modernization probably do generate disruption of role relationships and stress institutional arrangements in ways which affect the status and welfare of older persons adversely. Advanced stages of modernization can and apparently do generate personal and social resources which make new and adequate forms of social integration of the generations both feasible and probable. We will return to this theme shortly.

Personal Adaptation

What do we know about the experience of growing old? This is a question worth asking quite independently of what we know about the social integration of older persons.

Although reserve capacity does decline with age, the fact is that most older individuals live out their lives in some community with dignity and with considerable competence and satisfaction. In all modern societies, no more than 5 percent of older persons are institutionalized at any point in time and these tend to be very old persons (average age about 80). Epidemiologic surveys indicate that an addi-

tional 5 to 10 percent living in the community are severely incapacitated (24). In the absence of incapacitating physical illness, intellectual functioning remains quite adequate into very late life (34). Moreover, surveys of life satisfaction consistently report, in the balance, a
fundamental sense of well-being (35, 36). Should we be surprised by
such evidence?

We would certainly be surprised by evidence of successful adaptation and widespread life satisfaction of older persons if we believed
that old age insures isolation and alienation; we would not be surprised if we knew the evidence reviewed above which indicates the
basic social integration of older persons. On balance, older persons
indicate that old age is not a particularly happy time in the sense of a
positive balance of affect but that, overall, late life can be and is
typically a satisfying time. This satisfaction appears to be explained
by three factors: 1) Age tends to be associated with substantial and
satisfying social and economic achievement; 2) these achievements
tend to approximate aspirations; and 3) alternative role relationships
and life-styles that were entertained in mid-life tend to lose their
salience over time.

Theories of human development have not helped very much in
understanding adaptation in late life. For the most part, developmental theory has ignored older adults. Erik Erikson provides a
notable exception (37), being one of the relatively few theorists who
has extended his theorizing beyond adolescence to include interest in
stages of development in adulthood: intimacy (adult sexual relations),
generativity (generational relationships), and integrity (managing the
prospect of death). Erikson has been popular with social scientists in
general and gerontologists in particular because his emphasis is consistently biosocial. Moreover, his conceptualization of ego identity
emphasizes not only a satisfying sense of sameness and of social competence but a satisfaction with self reinforced by the response of
significant others in the social environments. While Erikson is not on
record with estimates of the probability of maintaining a satisfying
sense of identity in late life, he provides no evidence which suggests
or demands a pessimistic conclusion.

Erikson was introduced into the gerontological literature in a very
provocative way by Cumming and Henry in their book *Growing Old*:

The Theory of Disengagement (38). Cumming and Henry used a hydraulic metaphor to describe an intrinsic and hence inevitable waning of physical and psychic energy in late life; decline in energy activates a mutual withdrawal of individual and society from one another. This inevitable disengagement, they argued, was the necessary condition of satisfaction in late life. It should be noted that this argument tended to make irrelevant the question of social integration. Cumming and Henry's intellectually provocative conclusions ran far ahead of their evidence, and current evidence has modified and qualified their thesis almost beyond recognition. On balance, Cumming and Henry were correct in observing that social involvement does tend to decrease with age. And a disengaged life-style is effective for some individuals. Yet, in general, socially involved and active individuals have been demonstrated to be more likely than others to report satisfaction with life, particularly if the individual's life-style has been characterized by social involvement in the middle years. This conclusion is supported by research in a variety of industrial societies (39).

Social survey research, which reflects an American preoccupation with knowing the reported happiness, satisfaction, well-being and concerns of the society, has provided some relevant insights into the experience of growing older. One of the most important insights is that the sense of well-being and of concern can be quite similar across the adult life course. In a recent report by Louis Harris and Associates (36) the similarity of responses by persons 18 to 64 and those 65 and older about their sense of well-being and their concerns is quite striking. Majorities of older as well as younger respondents agreed that "being younger is better." But only a minority of older persons, at the highest one in five, specified any "serious personal problems" (with money problems, loneliness, poor health, and fear of crime being the most common). Younger and older persons were essentially in agreement that such problems are, in general, widespread concerns in the society. Substantial majorities of both younger and older respondents felt that, compared with the past decade, Americans were better educated, in better health, and better off financially. On a scale of 0-12 assessing the public image of older people, both younger and older persons produced a very positive score (10.0 and 9.9 respectively). Did older persons in the Harris survey feel isolated from their families? Only 8 percent had not seen their children in the past three months. In contrast, 55 percent reported having seen a child "in the past day or so" and another 26 percent had seen a child within the past week. And what about the experience of retirement? Six out of ten retirees reported they had retired by choice, and a majority of retirees would not like to work even if they were offered a job. Only 11 percent of retirees indicated they would be definitely interested in considering a job offer.

Current research on adaptive capacity in late life leads to a similarly optimistic review of the resilience of older people. Colleagues at the Duke Center for the Study of Aging and Human Development have just completed a series of multidisciplinary studies on the management of the major challenges to personal integrity which are characteristic of the later years—retirement, widowhood, last child leaving home, and serious illness. The longitudinal evidence requires substantial modification of the hypothesis that such major events inevitably precipitate destructive stress of crisis proportion. The critical intervening variable in every instance has proved to be the availability of personal and social resources, particularly social support networks (on the importance of such networks see Lopata (40), Kaplan, et al. (41), and Lowenthal and Robinson (42)). In the case of retirement and the child-free state, the evidence has indicated that most individuals adapt surprisingly well, and rather quickly, as a matter of fact.

MAKING HISTORY

Modern men and women surely feel from time to time that they have to suffer history. But they certainly also entertain the notion that they can make history, and that reality is to a substantial degree a social construction amenable to reconstruction. By definition a social problem is an intolerable state of affairs that presumably is changeable and warrants changing. From this optimistic perspective, even the slender evidence that modernization tends to relate inversely to the status and welfare of older persons need not lead to passive acceptance of unwelcome outcome for the aged in modern society. The same impulse that led social scientists to identify this problematic relationship has generated research evidence about the modifiable factors which tend to explain the relationship. In the social sciences, not surprisingly then, interest has shifted from the documentation of societal change and its consequences to consideration of the potential for guided change (43, 44).

However, policy research relevant for guiding change in an aging society has been hampered by inadequate data sources. Part of the problem is the persistent preference of social scientists for survey research and of program analysts for routinely collected social system indicators. These preferences tend to insure that the policy analyst almost never has information simultaneously about the characteristics of individuals and environments in which and with which they interact. The results are the inability to implement even quasi-experimental research designs and unwarranted inferences about the effectiveness of alternative policies (45). Nevertheless, policy analysts have a considerable body of evidence about aging and the aged as a point of departure (16, 17, 18).

The available evidence has established some important substantive and methodological points. Substantively, a strong case has been made for what may be described as a *differential gerontology*. That is, while chronological age is a convenient administrative variable, persons of the same chronological age are enormously varied in functional capacity, in intelligence, in socioeconomic status, in coping styles, in social competence, and in life-styles. Stereotypes of the elderly are convenient fictions, which mask considerable variability and provide a dubious basis for the formulation of social policy. It is now clear that older persons between the ages of 65 and 75—the younger old, if you will—include a very high proportion of intellectually able and socially competent individuals who are considerably underused as a societal resource. In contrast, while most persons over the age of 75 are also able and competent, the probability of disability and related need for care is considerably increased with age. Older persons are also considerably different in terms of the social support networks which can be mobilized when significant role transitions are experienced. The impact of retirement, illness, widowhood, or the departure of children is demonstrably ameliorated by the mobilization and support of kin and friends. The availability of such support networks underlines the observation that most older people adapt quite adequately to major role transitions.

Methodological insights from gerontological research have also contributed an important dimension to the meaning of differential gerontology. The age category broadly defined as *older* is in fact a collection of successive age cohorts. These successive cohorts of individuals born at the same time are potentially very different in significant ways. A simple illustration of a consequential difference is cohort size. It is precisely the increased size of cohorts born following World War II that underlies the projected increase in the proportion of older persons shortly into the next century. Size of cohort, in turn, predicts both demand and competition for societal resources. Different cohorts, moreover, develop in environments that are variously supportive or threatening and thus arrive at old age with differing life-styles and resources (education, incomes, health, support networks). Thus references to *the elderly* perpetuate a misleading stereotype. The stereotype would be misleading to a program manager responsible for clients who are currently old and would be even more misleading to the policy analyst who must be concerned not only with issues affecting those who are currently old but, prospectively, also the future old. If these distinctions are not kept clearly in mind, we run the risk of attributing observed behavior of older people primarily to age, when the explanation is far more complex than that, and, worse, we would make the serious error of planning for older persons of the future on the basis of the characteristics of those who are currently old (46).

Looking Ahead

The study of aging by social scientists has made important contributions to our understanding of why old age is perceived as a social problem and to the factual base which will help in assessing policy options for dealing with various dimensions of the policies identified. The facts indicate that effective social integration of older persons in modern societies is feasible. The facts establish the considerable competence and adaptive capacity of older individuals. It is increasingly clear that the issue is not a matter of the feasibility of ameliorating the problems of older people in an aging society but the social will to do so and our creativity in restructuring the institutional arrangements for effecting the desired integration (47).

The aging of modern societies in general and of our society in particular confronts us with some interesting challenges. In regard to income maintenance, many older people in the United States subsist on incomes below the poverty level. We tend to define poverty in old age as a welfare issue rather than as an occasion to rethink our policy on income maintenance over the life course and on the distribution of work and leisure. In regard to health care, we appear to want to tamper with the structure of financing rather than confront the more basic issue, the fragmented disorganization of our health care system. In regard to transportation, we seem incapable of confronting the policy issues at all. In the face of a growing sense of urgency about the need for policies which provide for lifetime learning, many educational institutions want to do business as usual. The nation's limited capacity to move creatively in these various areas of our institutional life accentuates the problems of older persons in an aging society. Social arrangements lag behind demonstrated need. It should be quite clear, however, that the problems of an aging society are better understood as resulting from a crisis of national will, a failure of nerve, than as resulting merely from the fact that our population is aging.

REFERENCES

1. FISCHER, D. H.: *Growing Old in America.* New York: Oxford University Press, 1977.
2. COMFORT, A.: *The Biology of Senescence.* New York: Holt, Rinehart & Winston, 1964.
3. HAYFLICK, L.: Perspectives on human longevity. In: B. L. Neugarten and R. J. Havighurst (Eds.), *Extending the Lifespan: Social Policy and Social Ethics.* Washington, D.C.: U.S. Government Printing Office, 1977.
4. HAVIGHURST, R. J. and SACHAR, G. A.: Prospects of lengthening life and vigor. In: B. L. Neugarten and R. J. Havighurst (Eds.), *Op. Cit.*
5. SHANAS, E. and MADDOX, G. L.: Aging, health, and the organization of health resources. In: R. H. Binstock and E. Shanas, (Eds.), *Handbook of Aging and the Social Sciences.* New York: Van Nostrand Reinhold Company, 1976.
6. CAMPBELL, RITA R.: *Social Security: Promise and Reality.* Stanford, Calif.: Hoover Institution Press, 1977.

7. KREPS, J. M., SPENGLER, J., CLARK, R., and HERREN, S.: Economics of a stationary population—an executive summary. Durham, North Carolina: Center for the Study of Aging and Human Development, 1976.
8. MADDOX, G. L.: The unrealized potential of an old idea. In: A. N. Exton Smith and J. G. Evans (Eds.), *Care of the Elderly: Meeting the Challenge of Dependency*. New York: Grune & Stratton, 1977.
9. BROWN, BERTRAM, S., KORAN, L. M., and OCHBERG, F.: Community mental health centers—impact and analysis. In: L. Corey, M. Epstein, and S. Saltman (Eds.), *Medicine in a Changing Society*. St. Louis: Mosley, 1977.
10. REVIS, J. S.: *Transportation: Background and Issues*. Washington, D.C.: White House Conference on Aging, 1971.
11. ROSOW, I.: *Socialization to Old Age*. Berkeley, Calif.: University of California Press, 1974.
12. ARSENIAN, J. and ARSENIAN, J. M.: Tough and easy cultures. *Psychiatry*, 11:377, 1948.
13. MADDOX, G. L. and WILEY, J.: Scope, concepts and methods in the study of aging. In: R. H. Binstock and E. Shanas (Eds.), *Op. Cit.*
14. COMFORT, A.: *A Good Age*. New York: Crown, 1976.
15. DE BEAUVOIR, SIMONE: *The Coming of Age*. New York: Warner, 1970.
16. BIRREN, J. E. (Ed.): *Handbook of Aging and the Individual*. Chicago: University of Chicago Press, 1959.
    TIBBITS, C. (Ed.): *Handbook of Social Gerontology*. Chicago: University of Chicago Press, 1960.
    BURGESS, E. W. (Ed.): *Aging in Western Societies*. Chicago: University of Chicago Press, 1960.
17. RILEY, M. W. and FONER, A. (Eds.): *Aging and Society: An Inventory of Research Findings*. New York: Russell Sage Foundation, 1968.
    RILEY, M. W., RILEY, J., and JOHNSON, M. (Eds.): *Aging and the Professions*. New York: Russell Sage Foundation, 1969.
    RILEY, M. W., JOHNSON, M., and FONER, A. (Eds.): *A Sociology of Age Stratification*. New York: Russell Sage Foundation, 1972.
18. BINSTOCK, R. H. and SHANAS, E. (Eds.): *Handbook of Aging and the Social Sciences*. New York: Van Nostrand Reinhold, 1976.
    BIRREN, J. E. and SCHAIE, K. W. (Eds.): *Handbook of the Psychology of Aging*. New York: Van Nostrand Reinhold, 1977.
    FINCH, C. E. and HAYFLICK, L. (Eds.): *Handbook of the Biology of Aging*. New York: Van Nostrand Reinhold, 1977.
19. FRANK, L. K.: Gerontology. *J. of Gerontology*, 1:1-12, 1946.
20. SIMMONS, L. W.: *The Role of the Aged in Primitive Societies*. New Haven: Yale University Press, 1945.
21. HENRY, JULES: *Culture Against Man*. New York: Random House, 1963.

22. COWGILL, D. and HOLMES L. (Eds.): *Aging and Modernization.* New York: Appleton-Century-Crofts, 1972.
23. PALMORE, E. B.: *The Honorable Elders.* Durham, N.C.: Duke University Press, 1975.
24. SHANAS, E., TOWNSEND, P., WEDDERBURN, D., FRIIS, H., MILHOJ, P., and STEHOUWER, J.: *Old People in Three Industrial Societies.* New York: Atherton Press, 1968.
25. SHANAS, E. and STRIEB, G. F. (Eds.): *Social Structure and the Family: Generational Relations.* Englewood Cliffs, N.J.: Prentice-Hall, 1965.
26. LASLETT, P.: Societal development and aging. In: R. H. Binstock and E. Shanas (Eds.), *Op. Cit.*
27. Comptroller General of the United States: *Report to Congress on the Well-Being of Older People in Cleveland, Ohio.* Washington, D.C.: United States General Accounting Office, 1977.
28. SUSSMAN, MARVIN: Incentives and family environments for the elderly. A Report on Administration on Aging Grant 90-A-316, 1976 (unpublished).
29. HUDSON, R. B. and BINSTOCK, R. H.: Political systems and aging. In: R. H. Binstock and E. Shanas (Eds.), *Op. Cit.*
30. MADDOX, G. L.: Is senior power the wave of the future? In: L. F. Jarvik (Ed.), *Aging in the 21st Century: A Long Tomorrow.* New York: Gardner Press, 1977.
31. TALMON, YONINA: Aging in Israel—a planned society. In: B. L. Neugarten (Ed.), *Middle Age and Aging.* Chicago: University of Chicago Press, 1968.
32. CLARK, M. and ANDERSON, B.: *Culture and Aging.* Springfield, Illinois: C. C Thomas, 1967.
33. PALMORE, E. and MANTON, K.: Modernization and status of the aged: International correlations. *J. of Gerontology,* 29:205-210, 1974.
34. PALMORE, E. B. (Ed.): *Normal Aging, I: Report from the Duke Longitudinal Study, 1955-1969.* Durham, N.C.: Duke University Press, 1970.
    PALMORE, E. B. (Ed.): *Normal Aging II: Report from the Duke Longitudinal Studies, 1970-1973.* Durham, N.C.: Duke University Press, 1974.
35. CAMPBELL, A., CONVERSE P., and RODGERS, W.: *The Quality of American Life.* New York: Russell Sage Foundation, 1976.
36. HARRIS, LOUIS, and et al.: *The Myth and Reality of Aging in America.* Washington, D.C.: National Council on Aging, 1975.
37. ERIKSON, ERIC: Identity and the life cycle. *Psychological Issues,* Monograph I, 1959.
38. CUMMING, E. and HENRY, W.: *Growing Old: The Process of Disengagement.* New York: Basic Books, 1961.
39. HAVIGHURST, R. J., MUNNICHS, J., NEUGARTEN, B., and THOMAS, H. (Eds.): *Adjustment to Retirement: A Cross National Study.* Assen, Netherlands: Van Gorcum, 1969.

40. LOPATA, H.: *Widowhood in an American City.* New York: Schenkman, 1972.
41. KAPLAN, B., CASSEL, J., and GORE, S.: Social support and health. *Medical Care,* 15:47-58, 1977.
42. LOWENTHAL, M. F. and ROBINSON, B.: Social networks and isolation. In: R. H. Binstock and E. Shanas (Eds.), *Op. Cit.*
43. RIVLIN, A. N.: *Systematic Thinking for Social Action.* Washington, D.C.: The Brookings Institution, 1971.
44. CAMPBELL, D. T.: Reforms as experiments. In: E. Struening and M. Guttentag (Eds.), *Handbook of Evaluation, I.* Beverly Hills, Calif.: Sage, 1975.
45. MADDOX, G. L.: Aging, social change and social policy. In: M. Yinger, H. Mausch, and S. Cutler (Eds.), *Major Social Issues: A Multidisciplinary View.* New York: The Free Press, 1978.
46. ELDER, GLEN: *Children of the Great Depression.* Chicago: University of Chicago Press, 1974.
47. NEUGARTEN, B. L. and HAVIGHURST, R. J. (Eds.): *Social Policy, Social Ethics and the Aging Society.* Washington, D.C.: U.S. Government Printing Office, 1976.

3

The Biology of Aging and Its Role in Depression

Morris A. Lipton, Ph.D., M.D.
and
Charles B. Nemeroff, Ph.D.

> *Every man desires to live long;*
> *but no man would be old*
>
> JONATHAN SWIFT—"Thoughts on
> various subjects, moral and diverting."

INTRODUCTION

Although no age is immune to depression, it is well established that it is commonly frequent in the elderly. Separation from sustained meaningful human contact can produce depression in infants (1), and identity conflicts and existential despair are associated with depression and an alarming suicide rate among adolescents and teen-

Based on a presentation at the World Congress of Psychiatry, August 31-September 4, 1977, Honolulu, Hawaii and at the American College of Psychiatrists, February 9-12, 1978, New Orleans, La.

Preparation of this review was supported by NICHD HD-03110 and a NINCDS postdoctoral fellowship to CBN (NS-05722).

agers. The suicide rate is low in the twenties and thirties, but rises in the forties and fifties, peaking in the period from 55 to 70. There is some evidence that it drops after that age (2-5). Twenty-five percent of successful suicides is found among the elderly (6). Patients who have had previous depressions are likely to have them recur more frequently and with greater severity as they age (7). Men who have not had previous depressions are most likely to have their first hospitalization for this illness between age 45 and 60, while for women, in whom depression is more frequent, the peak age for hospitalization is about 50, with a slow decline till age 65 and a precipitous decline thereafter (7).

Emotional illness of many types increases with age, and 20-30 percent of patients over age 60 have significant psychiatric symptoms (8). The most common, it is generally agreed, is depression (9). Estimates of the population at large range from 2 percent (10), to 10 percent or higher (11). The variance in estimates may be due to the fact that depression in the elderly may mask as hypochondria or pseudodementia, which may be missed in routine examination (12). When the elderly have concomitant physical illness, the prevalence of depression is even higher. Thus, a study of acute medical and surgical admissions to a general hospital showed that 24 percent of patients over 65 had depression or alcoholic illness (12, 13).

There are many theories regarding the etiology of depression. They are the products of data obtained by differing types of investigations. An attempt has been made to diagram them in Figure 1. An elegant overview and attempt to integrate these has been made by Akiskal and McKinney (14). To the psychoanalytic school, depression is a consequence of object loss, loss of self-esteem, aggression turned inward and a negative cognitive set associated with hopelessness. To the sociologist, depression is associated with loss of role status and social support systems. The behaviorist views depression as learned helplessness in the face of uncontrolled aversive stimulation plus secondary rewards from the depressed role which substitute for the absent sources of reinforcement. To the existentialist, depression follows loss of meaning and purpose in life. The biological psychiatrist views depression to be a consequence of disordered neurotransmitter function with associated neuroendocrine malfunction.

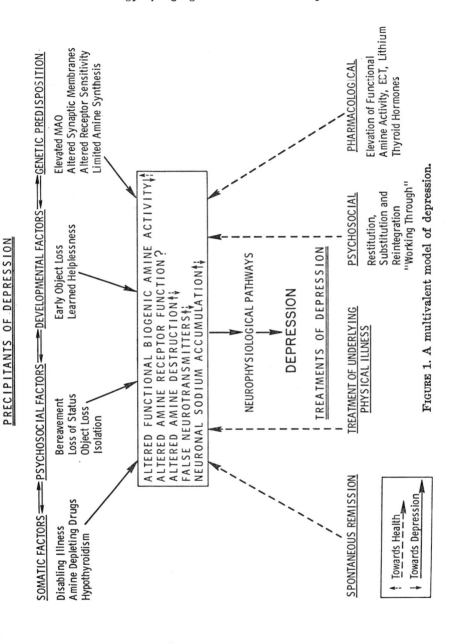

FIGURE 1. A multivalent model of depression.

All of these perspectives have some validity and are useful in attempts to comprehend and to manage the problem of depression, but clearly none is complete. We are reminded of the blind men and the elephant, each of whom feels and describes a part of the beast and attempts to describe the whole beast from his particular vantage. A possible integrating principle for these different perspectives is that all of the psychological, social and physical antecedents of depression are recognized by the organism as stress, which is responded to initially by coping and, when this fails, by depression with all of its physical and emotional features. But this principle is probably too simple and clearly a better integration of the results of different levels of investigation and conceptualization is badly needed.

This is especially true of depression in the elderly, who encounter all of the psychological, social and biological stresses noted as precipitants or determinants of depression by researchers from different specific disciplines. Thus, with aging there is greater bereavement and isolation than are characteristically associated with younger individuals. There is frequently loss of income with diminished responsibility and social status. There is increasing chronic physical illness and disability, and diminution of the capacity to see and hear. Some authors have indeed wondered whether the young might not be as vulnerable to depression as the elderly, if they had to endure the same physical and social vicissitudes (15, 16). Yet these commonsense explanations do not seem to fully account for the greater proneness of the elderly toward depressions severe enough to require treatment (3). Many, perhaps most, of the elderly encounter these vicissitudes without becoming depressed. Furthermore, bereavement and physical illness as precipitating causes are not found more frequently in late onset than in early onset depressions. The premorbid personalities of patients who develop their first depression late in life is generally considered to be exceptionally stable. Genetic studies have shown that early onset depressions have a stronger hereditary component than late onset depressions (3). Therefore, it appears likely that something about the aging process itself is involved in the apparent increase in susceptibility to depression among the elderly (3).

To examine this question properly it becomes necessary to discuss, first, the neurobiology of stress, then, the neurobiology of depression, and, finally, that of aging, seeking those common features which might help to suggest answers.

THE NEUROBIOLOGY OF STRESS

The action of at least three pituitary hormones (ACTH, growth hormone and prolactin) and at least two target organ hormones (testosterone and cortisol) are highly responsive to stress (17). The best studied and perhaps most relevant to depression is the pituitary-adrenal axis. Both physical and psychological stress stimulate the pituitary-adrenal axis in man and animals (18). This is shown by stress-induced elevations of 24-hour urinary adrenal steroids and their metabolites. A rough correlation between degree of stress and degree of adrenal activation has been found (19). Similar increases in adrenal steroids have been found in some depressed patients (21) and crises during a depressive illness cause even greater elevations (19). It seems safe to conclude that psychological stress is reflected by the adrenals as physiological stress, and by this criterion the state of depression is physiologically stressful.

Elevation of adrenal corticoids has many consequences. A recent report suggests that an age-related elevation of corticosterone may induce an age-related deterioration of hippocampal neurons (20). The loss of plasticity in these neurons may be associated with short-term memory loss (22, 23). Effects upon nuerotransmitters have been noted. Thus, these steroids induce tryptophan pyrrolase, perhaps making less tryptophan available for serotonin (5-HT) synthesis (24). They also increase norepinephrine (NE) inactivation by reuptake, making less transmitter available at the synapse (25). They increase the ratio of intraneuronal to extraneuronal sodium, perhaps by altering adenosine triphosphatase (ATPase) activity in the neuronal membrane (26). Changes in this transport system directly affect transport of amino acid precursors and amines and also affect synthesis of amines.

Growth hormone (GH) and prolactin (PRL) are both elevated in stress in humans. It has been suggested that GH elevation has a protective action, since it promotes healing and protects against other effects of stress (27). The function of the elevated PRL is unknown (28).

Stress also affects the neurotransmitters of the central nervous system (CNS) more directly. NE has been studied more extensively and seems to be more sensitive to stress than the other transmitters, but dopamine (DA) and 5-HT have also been studied. Immobilization stress lowers brain 5-HT in animals with adrenals but not after adrenalectomy. The effects on 5-HT may therefore be mediated through cortisol (24). With acute or moderately chronic stress, synthesis and breakdown (turnover) of NE increase with no change in brain levels (29). With more intense or prolonged stress, breakdown exceeds synthesis and levels fall (30, 31, 32, 33). The activity of tyrosine hydroxylase (TH), the first and rate-limiting enzyme in the synthesis of NE from tyrosine, increases in the brain with stress (34) and this may account for the increased turnover of NE in stress, but the capacity to increase may still not be sufficient and NE levels do fall with prolonged severe stress. The capacity to increase NE turnover in response to stress is related to the age of animals (35) and also seem genetically transmitted in mice (F. Goodwin, personal communication).

Regulation of NE synthesis and turnover is a complex matter (36). Feedback inhibition caused by NE in the post-synaptic neuron probably occurs. Inhibition of tyrosine hydroxylase by accumulated NE also has been demonstrated. These limit the production of NE. Changes in the configuration of the synthetic enzyme to make it more active have been proposed when NE levels fall. Stimulation of synthesis of new enzyme also occurs when NE levels fall (36). All of these tend to make more NE available when needed, but if stress is overwhelmingly prolonged, even these adjustments may not be sufficient and, therefore, NE levels may fall (30). Proponents of the NE hypothesis of depression would contend that this fall is a necessary precondition for depression. Contrariwise, if all of these adjustments were mobilized and central catecholamines were elevated while the need for them became diminished, mania or agitated depression might ensue.

THE NEUROBIOLOGY OF DEPRESSION

Neurotransmitters

The neurobiology of depression has been studied most intensively in primary or endogenous depressions which are prolonged and severe enough to require hospitalization (37). By definition, primary depressions occur in the absence of other psychiatric and serious physical illnesses. They are characterized by a severely dysphoric mood as well as five or more of the following: appetite disturbances, sleep disturbances, energy loss, slowed thinking, inappropriate guilt, recurrent suicidal thoughts and pyschomotor retardation (37, 38). The presence or absence of manifest precipitating causes does not differentiate primary depressions from others, nor are they good prognostic indicators of the severity of depression. What may initially appear to be a grief reaction takes on an autonomy and persists with symptom intensification. Primary depressions are usually recurrent and can frequently be subclassified as unipolar or bipolar.

It has been estimated that primary major depression represents about 20 percent of the depressions encountered in clinical practice (2, 38, 39). The remainder are secondary or mixed and are either associated with some other major mental or physical illness or are less severe, lacking one or more of the five characteristics noted above.

Depression in the elderly does not fit neatly into simple niches for classification. Environmental precipitants like physical illness, bereavement and social isolation are very common. Simultaneous organic brain disease is not infrequent, and its symptoms overlap sufficiently with severe depression to present diagnostic problems. Symptom intensity is also variable, but tends to be more severe in the elderly. Depression in the elderly is perhaps best visualized as a mood disorder with a wide spectrum of manifestations; it may be primary or secondary. Fortunately, secondary or mixed depressions usually respond to treatments similar to those used for primary endogenous depressions and there is no *a priori* reason to believe that the chemical changes in the neurotransmitters of the brain differ radically in different types of depression (40, 41, 42, 43). For the purposes of this review, we assume that they do not.

Several research strategies have been used to elucidate the chemical pathology of the brain in depression. The first and most important deals with determining the mode of action of those drugs which were empirically discovered either to be therapeutic or to cause depression. This strategy has led to emphasis upon neurotransmitter malfunction, because such drugs invariably have effects upon some aspects of one or more neurotransmitter malfunction, because such drugs invariably have effects upon some aspects of one or more neurotransmitter functions. With this established, a second strategy evolved, seeking chemical measures which would reflect changes in the metabolism of the neurotransmitters of the brain in the available tissues of patients before and after treatment. Ideally these should be sought in the brain directly, as is done with animals, but since this is clearly not feasible in human patients, studies have been limited to urine, blood and cerebrospinal fluid, except in those few instances where the brain becomes accessible through post-mortem examination. The interpretation of results from the study of peripheral tissues is fraught with difficulties, and definitive conclusions cannot be made. But strong inferences can be made, especially when the results of direct animal studies coincide with the results from indirect studies in man.

A third strategy for use in man has involved neuroendocrine studies (44, 45, 46). Thus, when particular CNS neurotransmitter systems were discovered to be involved in the activation or inhibition of hypothalamic-pituitary-end organ axes, the measurements in blood and urine of the concentrations of those hormones permitted some inferences about the activity of these neurotransmitter systems in the brain. These neuroendocrine studies have yielded additional valuable information in their own right about the pathology of depression.

A fourth strategy, particularly useful for studies of neurotransmitter enzymes, is based on the finding that some enzymes located in the brain are also found in peripheral tissues such as the blood platelets (47). Again, the inference is made that changes in the brain will be reflected in peripheral measurements. This approach may be particularly useful in evaluating the role of genetic factors in affective illness. Since all cells of the organism contain the same component of DNA, a deficiency of catecholamine biosynthesis would, if present, be measureable in all tissues in which the gene is expressed. This would include platelets, CNS, enterchromaffin tissue, etc. Another approach is to culture fibroblasts from tissue derived from psychiatric and control patients and then assay the activity of enzymes associated with neurotransmitter synthesis and degradation.

From such investigations in both animals and man, there have evolved hypotheses which implicate the neurotransmitters in the pathogenesis of affective disorders in man. The first neurotransmitter to be so implicated was NE, which is chemically a catecholamine. Somewhat later, 5-HT, an indoleamine, was shown to be involved. Very recently, DA and acetylcholine (ACh) have been implicated. Since all of these neurotransmitters are biogenic amines of endogenous origin, the hypotheses involving them may generically be called the biogenic amine hypothesis. In its briefest form, this hypothesis states that a functional deficiency of one or more of the biogenic amine neurotransmitters, usually NE or 5-HT, at significant receptor sites in the CNS is associated with depression. An excess is associated with mania. The evidence for this has been extensively and critically reviewed (48-55). The individual biogenic amine hypotheses have been constantly modified over the years. Originally, one or another of the various transmitters was considered to be the crucial determinant of depression; now there is evidence that the heterogeneity of depression is such that several transmitters may be involved (54, 55), and that depression may be a final common pathway of expression. A permissive hypothesis involving both NE and 5-HT simultaneously has been proposed (56). A cholinergic-catecholaminergic imbalance has also been proposed (55).

Early studies focused on neurotransmitter levels and the enzymes involved in their synthesis and degradation. More recently, it has been recognized that neurotransmitters act on receptors of the postsynaptic neurons. Attention is, therefore, increasingly being paid to the chemical nature of the receptor and to its alterations in affective illness (58, 66). Pre-synaptic receptors have also been discovered (58), but their relation to depression is still obscure.

It must be emphasized that the biogenic amine hypotheses have not been proven. Moreover, they leave many unanswered questions about depression. For example, why do depressions remit spontaneously when given enough time and why do they recur? Why do antidepressant medications which accelerate remission require weeks of treatment when their chemical effects are noted very quickly? Why can many of the effective drugs be discontinued after some months of treatment with permanent remission or only slow relapse? Why does reserpine, which effectively depletes neurons of both catecholamines and indoleamines, only cause depression in less than 15 percent of patients to whom it is administered for hypertension over long periods (59)? Why is lithium, which is effective in mania, also effective in preventing the recurrence of depression? These and many other questions remain unanswered. Despite the limitations of the neurotransmitter hypotheses, they are based on data which must be accounted for in any alternative hypotheses. The hypotheses are best considered incomplete rather than incorrect.

The evidence favoring a NE hypothesis has been reviewed many times (49-55). For example, it can hardly be accidental that totally different drugs like imipramine and the monoamine oxidase (MAO) inhibitors, which increase the concentration of NE in the synaptic cleft by different mechanisms, are both antidepressants. The two different classes of compounds achieve the same end by different mechanisms: the former by inhibiting NE inactivation by reuptake; the latter by inhibiting an enzyme involved in its degradation. Nor does it seem coincidental that reserpine causes depression in 15 percent of patients receiving this drug for hypertension. This drug lowers brain NE and 5-HT. Patients who become depressed on this drug frequently have a positive family history or have had previous episodes, so a predisposition to depression must also be involved (59, 60.)

Metabolic studies in man designed to measure CNS NE activity have depended upon the finding that in the CNS NE is metabolized into 3-methoxy-4-hydroxyphenylglycol (MHPG), whereas peripheral NE is metabolized to vanillyl mandelic acid (VMA) (61). MHPG measurements in urine or CSF, therefore, have been used as a marker for central NE metabolism. Some recent observations on monkeys whose central catecholamines have been depleted by 6-hydroxydopamine (6-HDA) suggest that this is not a reliable marker, but the point is controversial (62). It is noteworthy, then, that some depressed patients excrete lower than normal quantities of MHPG in their urine (49, 63), and such patients respond better to imipramine

(63) than to amitriptyline. Those with higher levels of MHPG respond better to amitriptyline (63). Manic-depressive patients excrete more MHPG when manic than when depressed or normothymic (64). Finally, the acceleration of the relief of depression by the addition of thyroid hormones to tricyclic antidepressants has led to the suggestion that the functional deficiency of NE systems may involve a receptor deficit (65, 66). This concatenation of results posits a role for the NE transmitter-receptor complex in depression which cannot be ignored. Yet other data do not fit. Depletion of NE by alpha-methyltyrosine does not cause depression. Augmentation by administration of l-DOPA does not relieve it except in a small minority of depressed patients (35, 70).

The serotonergic hypothesis of depression is supported by evidence similar to that which implicates NE. Reserpine lowers brain 5-HT levels in animals. MAO inhibitors block 5-HT destruction. Tricyclic antidepressants also block inactivation of 5-HT by reuptake. The autopsied brains from some depressed patients have low levels of 5-HT and its metabolite, 5-hydroxyindoleactic acid (5-HIAA) (67). The CSF from some depressed patients is low in 5-HIAA (68). But selective depletion of 5-HT by parachlorphenylalanine does not diminish mania (69). Tryptophan, the amino acid precursor of 5-HT, has been reported to be effective in the treatment of both depression and mania (56, 70).

The finding that tryptophan is effective in the treatment of both depression and mania, coupled with other evidence, led Prange et al. (56) to propose a permissive hypothesis of affective disorders. This view states that low functional 5-HT activity is a necessary but not a sufficient condition for both depression and mania. NE levels in the presence of low serotonergic function determine the specific nature of the affective disorder. When they are low, there is depression; when they are elevated, there is mania. The permissive hypothesis is attractive, because it attempts to integrate disparate findings. It, too, is probably incomplete. A cholinergic-adrenergic hypothesis of mania and depression (71, 72) has been proposed, based on the finding that an acetylcholinesterase (AChE) inhibitor has antimanic effects.

All of these results point to the probability that depressive disorders are pathogenetically heterogeneous and that there may be at least two depressive illnesses. One seems to have low NE, but normal 5-HT, and the other normal NE and low 5-HT (55). This hypothesis is currently being tested. As more neurotransmitters are shown to be implicated in depression, the probability rises that even more than two types will be shown to exist.

Neuroendocrine Studies

The functional activity of the hypothalamus is highly responsive to neural inputs from other areas of the brain. Various centers in the hypothalamus are innervated by NE neurons arising in the medulla and pons (73, 74). Serotonergic neurons have cell bodies in the raphe nuclei and form the ventral part of the medial forebrain bundle from which axons leave to innervate the hypothalamus. The hypothalamus possesses an intrinsic DA system, the tuberoinfundibular system, with cell bodies in the arcuate and periventricular nuclei that innervate the external layer of the median eminence (75). In addition, the median eminence also receives DA afferents from extrahypothalamic regions, most notably the midbrain (76). NE and 5-HT fibers terminate on hypothalamic neurons which innervate the median eminence and also may form axo-axonic synapses in the median eminence. Our laboratory has recently utilized biochemical and histochemical methods to discover a tuberoinfundibular cholinergic system with cell bodies in the arcuate nucleus that project to the median eminence (77). Extrahypothalamic cholinergic afferents also innervate the hypothalamus (77). There are, therefore, neuronal pathways and mechanisms by which monoaminergic neurotransmitters can affect the hypothalamus and, through it, the anterior pituitary.

Studies of ACTH secretion, for example, have shown that it is influenced positively by cholinergic, serotonergic and adrenergic pathways and decreased by dopaminergic pathways. A balance between serotonergic and cholinergic mechanisms may be involved in the circadian rhythm of ACTH secretion (78). Ettigi and Brown (44) suggest that adrenergic influences seem to be primarily inhibitory to hypothalamic corticotropin-releasing factor production while the central serotonergic influences are excitatory.

GH release seems to be positively controlled by DA, NE, and 5-HT (79, 80). Hypothalamic somatostatin (SRIF) inhibits GH secretion

(81). PRL, on the other hand, is negatively controlled by mono-aminergic activity. Thus, when DA activity is diminished, as, for example, as a consequence of chlorpromazine administration, there is increased pituitary PRL secretion. In fact, there is increasing evidence that DA is the physiological prolactin-inhibiting factor (78). There is some evidence that 5-HT may actively stimulate the release of PRL with an end effect similar to that achieved by reduction in catecholamine activity (78). Thyrotropin-releasing hormone (TRH), which releases TSH, also releases PRL, but the significance of this finding remains obscure (82). Thyrotropin (TSH) secretion seems to be positively stimulated by NE neurons, while 5-HT-containing neurons inhibit it. DA neurons may also be involved (78, 79, 83). The role of neurotransmitters in the control of gonadotropin (LH, FSH) secretion is not all together clear but cholinergic (84), dopaminergic (84, 85, 86, 87), noradrenergic (78) and serotonergic (84) circuits have all been implicated.

It is apparent that neurotransmitter control of the various hypo-thalamic releasing and release-inhibiting hormones which affect the pituitary is very complex. That neurotransmitters are involved in the dynamics of hypothalamic function seems beyond question. Altera-tions in neurotransmitter function doubtless have neuroendocrine con-sequences, but further work is required to define those precisely. The voluminous literature on neuroendocrine abnormalities in affective dis-orders has recently been reviewed (44, 87, 88). The hypothalamic-pituitary-adrenal (HPA) axis has been investigated in greater detail than have other neuroendocrine axes (89). Many depressed patients secrete abnormally large quantities of cortisol. The adrenal gland is normal, and its high secretion is a consequence of excessive stimulation by pituitary ACTH. The elevated cortisol in depression is freely dif-fusible, and target tissues, including the CNS (90, 91), are thus exposed to increased quantities of cortisol. Cortisol levels normally show a marked diurnal variation, but this is diminished in depression, suggesting a failure in tonic regulation of the HPA (89). HPA regula-tion involves the hippocampus, amygdala, septal region and midbrain, and these limbic areas are involved in regulation of mood and emo-tion (89). There is some evidence that central NE (17, 44) and 5-HT inhibit the elevation of cortisol response to stress. Thus, deficiencies of these transmitters may be responsible for the elevated cortisol in depression (17). Pituitary GH, normally very responsive to stress, sleep, fasting and many other environmental variables, is also under tonic control by the hypothalamus (92). GH regulation seems to be abnormal in some depressed post-menopausal women. This has been demonstrated by measuring changes in GH levels in response to provocative tests such as insulin hypoglycemia (17, 88). There is some evidence that the hypothalamic factors regulating GH are themselves under positive NE or DA control (80, 83, 86). This is consistent with the catecholamine hypothesis. GH response to thyrotropin-releasing hormone (TRH), rare in normal patients, is elevated in many depressed patients of both sexes (87).

Pituitary TSH secretion is under control of a hypothalamic hormone, TRH (82, 92). TSH levels seem to be within normal limits in depressed patients, but the elevation of TSH following TRH administration has been shown by many workers to be blunted in a significant number of depressed patients (87, 93). This characteristic seems to be a trait of depression-prone patients rather than a reflection of the state of depression (87, 93). The most common cause of a blunted TSH response to TRH is hyperthyroidism (92), but there is no evidence that depressed patients showing this blunted response are hyperthyroid. Excessive somatostatin production has been suggested as one possible cause (87), since this hypothalamic hormone inhibits TRH-induced TSH release, though most of the present data implicate the elevated cortisol levels alluded to earlier as an important etiological factor in this blunted response (94). Serum levels of luteinizing hormone (LH), regulated by luteinizing hormone-releasing hormone (LHRH) has been reported to be low in unipolar post-menopausal depressed women, when compared to normal women (88). Since NE is required for the rise in LH following gonadectomy or menopause, the finding of low LH in these patients also suggests diminished CNS noradrenergic function. Abnormal neuroendocrine function unquestionably exists in depression, and some of this dysfunction may be associated with the disorders of sleep, libido and eating so commonly found in primary depression. The fact that some neuroendocrine changes occur in only some depressed patients is in part due to poor methodology, but is probably more due to the heterogeneity of depression, which has not been adequately accounted for in many of the neuroendocrine studies.

THE NERVOUS SYSTEM AND AGING

Morphological Studies

There appears to be general agreement that a loss of neurons in the CNS occurs in animals and man with aging. Neuronal loss is not anatomically uniform: Brody (95) reported that it ranges from a high of approximately half the neurons in the superior frontal gyrus between 50 and 80 years to no loss in the inferior olivary nucleus. The loss of CNS neurons associated with advancing age probably accounts for the decline in brain weight between adulthood and senescence (96). By age 90 the human brain weighs the same as the brain of a three-year-old child (97). A marked loss of neuronal perikarya, but not of glia, in the substantia nigra of humans has recently been reported to occur with advancing age (98, Figure 2). Apart from neuronal loss, other neuroanatomical correlates of aging have been reported. Senile plaques (argyrophilic islets) have been observed in the neocortex and hippocampus of aged humans and animals. They are thought to be related to degradative changes in the neuronal and glial milieu. These have not, in general, been correlated with psychopathology in the aged; they have been observed in the brains of intellectually and emotionally intact individuals. One report (99) did correlate plaque concentrations and the subjects' ability to perform well on psychological tests.

Alzheimer (100) first described neurofibrillary tangles in the CNS in presenile dementia, and these are now known to be associated with the aging brain. Such structures are most easily seen in pyramidal cells of the cerebral cortex, various hypothalamic nuclei, the substantia nigra, the locus coeruleus, the reticular formation, and the hippocampus. They are invariably absent in Purkinje cells, primary sensory nuclei and Gasserian and spinal dorsal ganglia (96). Neurofibrillary tangles are abnormally large numbers of intracytoplasmic tubules running as compact parallel bundles which eventually push the cell nucleus to one side as they progressively fill the cytoplasmic en-

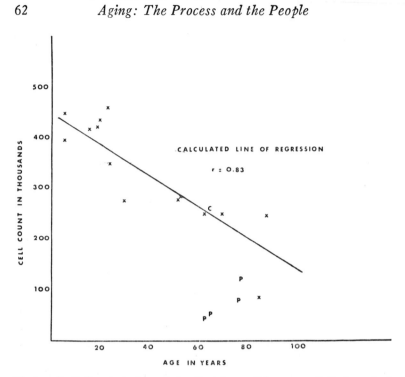

FIGURE 2. Cell counts in substantia nigra of humans plotted against age. X and line, those dying without neurological illness; P, Parkinsonian; C, choreic (from *Arch. Neurol.* 34, 1977, 33-35, copyright 1977, American Medical Association).

velope. They are believed to be the product of abnormal protein metabolism (101).

Lewy bodies and Hirano bodies are morphological structures which have been observed in nervous tissue of aged animals and man. The former consist of densely packed filaments; the later are eosinophilic rod-like structures (96).

Lipofuchsin and amyloid accumulate in the CNS with increasing age in animals and man (102, 103), and these events have been correlated with neuron loss. Lipofuchsin is observed in cell bodies of neurons and in glia whereas amyloid is found in extracellular locations. Of particular interest is the finding that a drug, centrophenoxine (meclofenoxate), with structural similarities to the plant growth hormone auxin, can remove lipofuchsin from tissue after *in vivo* administration to rats and monkeys (102). It is now being tested clinically in Europe for potential anti-aging properties.

There have been very few studies on age-related changes in the neuropil, i.e., dendrites, axons *en passage*, and axon terminals. Scheibel and Scheibel (101) have conducted Golgi investigations on aging tissue derived from laboratory animals. This procedure stains only 5 to 10 percent of neural elements but stains them completely. The earliest change they observed associated with aging was "loss of smooth, slightly concave contour of the cortical pyramidal cell body. The cell silhouette begins to bulge . . . and appears to become irregularly swollen." The dendritic shafts begin to swell and the basilar dendritic shafts decrease in length and number. Corresponding with these changes is a decrease in the number of horizontal and oblique branches of the apical shafts. The Scheibels believe that in many respects these progressive changes associated with senescence retrace the path followed in development. These changes may be due to the neurofibrillary tubules noted above; when present in large amounts, they may cut off transport of nutrients necessary for protein synthesis, membrane function, etc. They hypothesize that these changes in the complex horizontal dendritic systems in the cerebral cortex serve local programming and integrative functions and thus may be related to behavioral and psychomotor changes in senescence (101). Geinisman and Bondareff (104) recently reported a marked age-related decrease in the number of axo-dendritic synapses in the dentate gyrus molecular layer of the rat. They proposed that this age-related loss of synaptic contacts may result in a reduced capacity of the senescent brain for synaptic regeneration and remodeling.

Bondareff and Narotzky (105) reported a marked decrease (down 50 percent) in the size of the extracellular space of cerebral cortex of the rat derived from senescent animals (26 months old) when compared with young adults (three months old). It has been suggested that these changes induce alterations in the neuronal microenvironment during senescence. This same group (106) has also demonstrated a diminution in axonal transport of glycoproteins in the senescent rat brain.

Unfortunately, the morphological changes in the CNS that are associated with aging have provided no specific evidence for the assessment of the etiology of aging of the brain (107); nor do they contribute to an understanding of the predisposition to depression in the aged except that they may be related to a significant loss of plasticity, resulting in a reduced capacity to adapt to environmental alterations.

Biochemical Studies

Neurons undergo no further division after differentiation, whereas glial cells continue to proliferate throughout life. It is now almost universally accepted that when neurons are lost they are not replaced by division of the remaining cells. Thus, in chicks, DNA content of brain decreases by 20 months post-hatching (108, 109). In contrast, the DNA content of the mouse brain has been reported to remain unchanged with aging (111). These contradictory results between the two species remain unexplained. Since these studies did not differentiate between neuronal and glial DNA, and since there is clearly an increase in glia with aging, which is thought to represent a compensatory process of the CNS to overcome alterations in neuronal function (109), it is possible that the failure to find DNA changes in the aged mouse brain may be due at least in part to glial proliferation.

The majority of neurochemical studies concerned with the aging process have concentrated on alterations in functional activity of putative CNS neurotransmitters and related synthetic and degradative enzymes (Tables 1-5). These labile microconstituents are well known to be involved in interneuronal synaptic transmission. As noted earlier, their functional activity is altered by all of the psychotropic drugs employed in pharmacotherapy. Hence, they have been investigated in neurological diseases such as Parkinson's disease and Huntington's Chorea, in some forms of mental retardation, and in the so-called functional psychoses of schizophrenia and manic-depressive illness. Methods developed for the investigation of these disorders have been used to study the aging brain. Samorajski, et al. (112) studied behavioral and neurochemical correlates of aging in mice. Spontaneous locomotor activity and maze exploration decreased significantly with age. Whole brain levels of NE and 5-HT, as well as AChE activity,

TABLE 1

Age-Related Changes in Catecholomaines and Related Enzymes

Reference	Age-Related Changes	Species
1. Samorajski et al. (112).	↓ NE in whole brain	Mouse
2. Samorajski (113)	↓ DA in striatum ↓ NE in hypothalamus & brainstem ↓ NE in hypothalamus	Human Monkey Man
3. Finch (114)	No change in whole brain DA or NE ↓ Incorporation of ^{3}H-tyrosine & ^{3}H-DOPA into DA and NE in cerebellum, brainstem, striatum & hypothalamus	Mouse Mouse
4. Finch et al. (115)	↓ ^{3}H-tyrosine uptake into brain slices *in vitro*	Mouse
5. Jonec & Finch (116)	↓ DA uptake into synaptosomes derived from hypothalamus and striatum; NE uptake unchanged	Mouse
6. Vernadakis (109, 110)	NE levels of cerebral hemispheres and cerebellum unchanged ↓ ^{3}H-NE uptake into brain slices of cerebral hemispheres	Chick
7. McGeer et al. (119)	↓ tyrosine hydroxylase activity in caudate nucleus	Human
8. McGeer et al. (119)	↓ tyrosine hydroxylase activity in caudate nucleus, putamen and nucleus accumbens	Human
9. Ordy et al. (123)	↓ tyrosine hydroxylase activity in substantia nigra, caudate nucleus and putamen ↓ DOPA decarboxylase in hypothala- mus, substantia nigra, caudate nucleus and putamen	Human
10. Robinson et al. (126) Nies et al. (127)	↓ NE in hindbrain	Human
11. Gottfries et al. (131)	↑ HVA in CSF	Human
12. Carlsson (121)	↓ DA in putamen	Human

Abbreviations: NE = norepinephrine; DA = dopamine; HVA = homovanillic acid.

TABLE 2

Indoleamines

Reference	Age-Related Changes	Species
1. Samorajski et al. (112)	↓5HT in whole brain	Mouse
2. Samorajski (113)	↓5HT in hypothalamus	Man, Monkey
3. Finch (114)	5HT in whole brain unchanged	Mouse
4. Jonec & Finch (116)	5HT uptake into synaptosomes is unchanged	Mouse
5. Meek et al. (122)	↓5HT and tryptophan OHase in B_7, B_9, septum and hippocampus	Rat
6. Nies et al. (127) Robinson et al. (126)	5HT and 5HIAA unchanged in hindbrain	Human
7. Gottfries et al. (131)	↑5HIAA in CSF	Man
8. Vernadakis (109)	5HT in cerebral hemispheres and cerebellum unchanged	Chick

Abbreviations: 5HT = serotonin; tryptophan OHase = tryptophan hydroxylase; 5HIAA = 5-hydroxyindoleacetic acid; CSF = cerebrospinal fluid.

TABLE 3

Monoamine Oxidase

Reference	Age-Related Changes	Species
1. Prange et al. (125)	↑activity in heart; normal activity in brain	Rat
2. Robinson et al. (126) Nies et al. (127)	↑activity in hindbrain, platelets and plasma	Man
3. Robinson (128)	↑activity in globus pallidus, thalamus, hypothalamus, hippocampus, substantia nigra, reticular formation, cerebral cortex and caudate nucleus	Man
4. Shih (124)	↓activity when tyramine and benzylamine were used as substrates	Rat
	↑activity when 5HT was substrate	

TABLE 4

Cholinergic Systems

Reference	Age-Related Changes	Species
1. Samorajski et al. (112)	↓ AChE activity whole brain	Mouse
2. Vernadakis (108, 109)	↓ ChAc activity cerebral hemispheres	Chick
3. Timaras & Vernadakis (118)	↓ ChAc activity in spinal cord no change in cerebral hemispheres and cerebellum	Rat
4. McGeer et al. (119)	↓ ChAc activity in caudate AChE activity unchanged	Mouse
5. McGeer et al. (98)	↓ ChAc many brain regions	Man
6. Meek et al. (122)	↓ ChAc in caudate	Rat
7. Reichlmeier et al. (132)	↓ AChE in putamen, normal activity in cortex	Man

Abbreviations: AChE = acetylcholinesterase; ChAc = choline acetyltransferase.

TABLE 5

Amino Acid Transmitters

Reference	Age-Related Changes	Species
1. Vernadakis (108, 109)	↓ glutamate and taurine levels in spinal cord	Chick
2. Timaras & Vernadakis (118)	↓ aspartate in spinal cord, cerebral cortex & cerebellum	Rat
	↑ alanine, glycine and glutamine levels in many brain regions	
3. McGeer et al. (119)	↓ GAD in caudate nucleus	Rat
4. McGeer et al. (98)	↓ GAD in a variety of brain regions	Man
5. Ordy et al. (123)	↓ GAD in substantia nigra, caudate nucleus and putamen	Man

Abbreviations: GAD = glutamic acid decarboxylase.

decreased significantly with age. Further studies (113) revealed significant decreases in NE levels of the hypothalamus and brainstem of the rhesus monkey and the hypothalamus of man with increasing age. Hypothalamic 5-HT levels of rhesus monkey and man significantly decreased between the periods of development and senescence. DA levels in the striatum were also reduced in the human brain and this agrees with animal studies (114). This latter report also included findings of decreased synthesis of catecholamines (evaluated by studying conversion of ^{3}H-tyrosine and ^{3}H-DOPA into radiolabeled catecholamines) in a variety of brain regions (cerebellum, brainstem, striatum and hypothalamus) in senescent male mice. No change in the following parameters were noted with advancing age: whole brain weight, DNA content of cerebellum or brainstem, whole brain levels of DA, NE or 5-HT, hypothalamic and brainstem levels of NE, activity of DOPA decarboxylase. In a subsequent study (115), the effect of age on the *in vitro* active transport of catecholamine precursors into brain slices was examined. No age-related differences were observed in uptake of ^{3}H-DOPA or ^{3}H-tyrosine except when ^{3}H-tyrosine was present in low concentrations (< 0.01 ng/ml). In a later study, Jonec and Finch (116) demonstrated that DA uptake in synaptosomes derived from hypothalamus and striatum of senescent mice is diminished by 30 percent with compared with tissue from young adult controls. The affinity (K_m) of DA for the uptake system was altered in the aged animal brains. Uptake of NE, 5-HT and tyrosine was not affected. From these and other data, Finch (114, 117) postulated that CNS catecholamine systems may be pace-makers of aging. He visualizes a neuroendocrine cascade initiated by changes in monoamine neurotransmitter function that results in neuroendocrine changes, peripheral endocrine changes and thus changes in all body systems.

In the chick, the activity of AChE increases markedly in the cerebral hemispheres and cerebellum after hatching and from 20-36 months post-hatching. The activity of choline acetyltransferase (ChAc) increases in the cerebral hemispheres up to three months post-hatching and then decreases, reaching embryonic levels by three years (108, 109). Timaras et al. (118) found no change in ChAc in rat cerebellum and cerebral hemispheres from 2-20 months but a marked decrease in ChAc activity in the spinal cord was observed. These results suggested a decrease in the functional capacity of cholinergic neurons as evidenced by increased destructive (AChE) and decreased synthetic (ChAc) activity. Although Vernadakis (109, 110) observed no marked changes in levels of NE or 5-HT in the chick cerebral hemispheres or cerebellum, uptake of ^{3}H-NE in slices taken from the cerebral hemispheres increased during maturation but decreased with aging. This finding indicates a functional decline of brain NE systems associated with aging.

McGeer et al. (119) studied neurochemical sequelae of aging in rats (2-29 months old). They reported a decrease in tyrosine hydroxylase (TH), ChAc, and glutamic acid decarboxylase (GAD) activities in the caudate nucleus. No changes in these enzyme activities were noted in other brain areas, nor were any changes in AChE or succinic dehydrogenase activities or in levels of protein, NE or DA observed. These data indicate that TH activity of the caudate nucleus shows a sharp drop in aged rats, and that this change is both more pronounced and more clearly correlated with age than changes in ChAc, GAD or AChE. These data are in accord with a study of caudate enzymes in eight elderly human accident victims (120). The TH changes were interpreted as a specific change in the nigroneostriatal DA system and this can be correlated with the appearance of Parkinsonian symptoms (e.g., tremor) associated with senescence. These results have been confirmed in a more recent study (98) in which TH, GAD and ChAc were measured in 55 brain regions from 28 human brains. All three enzymes showed significant decrements with aging in many brain regions studied. The most dramatic effect was observed in TH activity in the caudate, putamen and nucleus accumbens, all areas receiving dense dopaminergic innervation. Cell counts in the substantia nigra (the site of origin of DA cell bodies of the nigroneostriatal system) indicate that the decrease in TH activity is partly due to cell loss (Figure 1), but probably also due to a decrease in functional activity of DA neurons. In agreement with these results, Carlsson (121) found a progressive decline with age in the DA concentration of the putamen in man. In a recent report utilizing sensitive microdissection methods to remove individual brain nuclei of the rat, Meek et al. (122) reported a marked loss of both 5-HT and tryptophan hydroxylase in areas containing 5-HT cell bodies and terminals (B_7, B_9, septum and hippocampus) in old (24-month) rats. These results suggest a loss of serotonergic cell bodies with age. Thus, 5-HT neural systems appear to degenerate with age. No changes in choline or ACh levels were observed in any brain regions studied, but a significant decrease in ChAc activity in the caudate nucleus was noted and this agrees with the studies of McGeer et al. (98). Ordy et al. (123) studied neurochemical changes in neurotransmitters and related enzymes associated with aging in humans (15-60 years). Essentially in agreement with McGeer et al. (98, 120), TH, DOPA decarboxylase and GAD decreased significantly in substantia nigra, caudate nucleus and putamen with senescence. In the hypothalamus, Ordy et al. (123) found that the activity of DOPA decarboxylase and GAD, but not TH, decreased significantly by 60 years of age.

Shih (124) has reviewed the literature concerning changes in monoamine oxidase (MAO) during aging (Table 3). Many studies, including one conducted in our laboratory (125), found various increases in MAO activity in heart and brain with advancing age. One group (126, 127) estimated MAO activity in brain derived from 55 humans and in platelets and plasma from 71 males and 91 females (21-84 years old). Hindbrain (rhombencephalon) 5-HT, NE and 5-HIAA were also assessed. MAO activity increased significantly with advancing age in human hindbrain and in platelets and plasma of normal subjects. NE levels in hindbrain decreased with age but neither 5-HT nor 5-HIAA levels exhibited any age-related alerations. In a more recent study, Robinson, et al. (126) measured MAO activity, utilizing benzylamine as the substrate, in eight brain regions of young ($<$ 45 years) and old ($>$ 45 years) humans ($n = 7$ per group); enzyme activity was greater in the older age group. Areas examined included the globus pallidus, thalamus, hypothalamus, hippocampus, substantia nigra, reticular system, cerebral cortex and caudate nucleus. The findings of increased MAO activity have been observed more frequently in rhesus monkeys and humans than in lower forms and may, therefore, represent a primate-only phenomenon (128). We now know that there are multiple forms of MAO. These are located in different tissues and are characterized by differences in activity with different subtrates. Shih (124) found a significant decrease in MAO activity of rat brain between three, four, and 24 months when tyramine and benzylamine were used as substrates. In contrast, MAO activity in the rat brain increased with age when serotonin was the substrate utilized. This finding may imply more rapid destruction of serotonin by the aged brain. This corresponds with the findings of decreased 5-HT in aged brains (113, 122). 5-HT has been implicated in depressive disorders (56) and elderly depressions may be serotonergic. We are unable to explain the conflicts in the literature concerning age-related changes in brain MAO activity, but these may depend upon the species examined or the substrate used in the MAO assay.

The cerebrospinal fluid (CSF) has also been used to examine the state of neurotransmitter function in man. With this technique, the levels of transmitter metabolites are measured. Since the spinal cord also contributes metabolites, the method does not have higher CNS specificity. Furthermore, since the metabolites are transported out of the CSF, the levels will be determined not only by rates of neurotransmitter synthesis and degradation in the brain and cord, but also by the rate of transport of the metabolites out of the CSF. The recent introduction of probenecid, which inhibits the transport of these acid metabolites out of the CSF, eliminates one of these variables (129). This method was not used in the older studies, and therefore it is difficult to assess central monoaminergic function in the aged from most of the reported studies, some of which give conflicting results. Thus Bowers and Gerbode (130) reported a U-shaped curve when CSF 5-HIAA, the major 5-HT metabolite, levels were plotted against age. Gottfries, et al. (131) reported that CSF concentrations of 5-HIAA and homovanillic acid (HVA), the major DA metabolite, were significantly elevated in the aged.

Gottfries, et al. (131) postulated that the results indicated an increased release and/or synthesis of monoamines in aged humans, though this is not consistent with the animal literature, which shows decreased activity of monoamine synthetic enzymes in aged rats (122). Reichlmeier et al. (132) measured the activity of a variety of enzymes in post-mortem human brain ($n = 36$, age 19-92 years). Cyclic adenosine 3'5'-monophosphate (cAMP) is known to be involved as a second messenger in neurotransmitter receptor function.

It is, therefore, interesting that cAMP-dependent protein kinase activity exhibited a gradual decline with increasing age, an effect more pronounced in cerebral cortex than in putamen. This may indicate diminished receptor function in the aged. AChE activity decreased in putamen but not in cortex, whereas carbonic anhydrase activity decreased in both areas. No changes in acid or alkaline phosphatase were observed. In a recent review, Meier-Ruge (107) summarizes several studies concerned with age-related changes in enzyme activity in the CNS. The following enzymes, in addition to those discussed above, have been reported to decrease in activity in old age: histone methylase, succinic dehydrogenase, lactic dehydrogenase, pyrophosphatase and Na^+/K^+-ATPase.

Levels of putative amino acid transmitters, as well as enzymes associated with them (e.g., GAD, see above), have been studied in relation to aging (Table 5). Levels of glutamate and taurine decrease markedly in the chick spinal cord with aging (108, 109). Aspartate levels decreased significantly in the cortex, cerebellum and spinal cord with aging (133). In contrast, alanine, glycine and glutamine levels rise in all brain structures studied. It is important to note that, in general, the brain levels of putative excitatory amino acid neurotransmitters exhibit age-related decreases, whereas levels of putative inhibitory transmitters increase.

In contrast to studying basal enzyme or neurotransmitter levels, McNamara (134) has suggested that "perhaps the study of aging is best approached by comparing biochemical and physiological responses to imposed stimuli . . ." She has examined the response of brain catecholamine systems in young and old rats subjected to electroconvulsive shocks (ECS). *In vivo* catecholamine synthesis was assessed by measuring conversion of tyrosine to l-DOPA after inhibition of DOPA decarboxylase with NSD 1015. Both young and old animals showed an increased synthesis of catecholamines after a single ECS, but the increase was much greater in the young rats (134,135). Assessment of serotonergic function, studied by measuring conversion of tryptophan to 5-HTP after decarboxylase inhibition, revealed no such effect. No change in brain levels of tyrosine or tryptophan was observed. These data indicate a reduced functional responsiveness of the brain catecholaminergic, but not of the serotonergic, systems in aged rats. This could generate an imbalance between these two transmitter systems under stress and this could be related to reduced adaptive capacity. In this regard it is of interest to cite the work of Gold and McGaugh (136), who have suggested that alterations in learning and memory processes which occur in old animals (e.g., reduced retention of new information) may be due to age-related alterations in central monoamine systems and/or alterations of endocrine homeostasis. These data also fit well with Smith's hypothesis (137) that central catecholamine systems subserve primarily an arousal function.

Endocrine Studies

Neuroendocrine regulation in response to a variable environment involves sensory input to higher centers and a downward path from these centers to the hypothalamus, pituitary and peripheral endocrine glands. There are also feedback loops from the endocrine end organs to the higher centers, hypothalamus and pituitary. Homeostasis is maintained by both neuronal and endocrine messages traversing back and forth throughout the CNS and the peripheral organs. Failure can occur at any one of several steps and it is important to examine where, in aging, they may occur. Several studies have reported a decline in one or another endocrine gland function with advancing age (Table 6). In addition, the increase in mortality with increasing age is frequently thought to be due to a failure of homeostatic mechanisms brought about by a gradual decline in neuroendocrine function (97), and this is important for the present discourse, since hormones may play a prominent role in depression (57).

The strategies employed to evaluate endocrine function in the elderly are: 1) measurement of basal serum and urinary levels of pituitary and end organ hormones, e.g., gonadal steroids, corticosteroids, TSH, etc.; 2) measurement of the response of endocrine organs to exogenous pituitary hormone administration, e.g., corticosteroid response to ACTH; 3) measurement of the pituitary response to exogenous hypothalamic releasing hormone administration, e.g., LH response to LHRH. The first evaluative method provides the least information. Only significant differences between basal levels in experimental and control groups can be interpreted as a dysfunction

TABLE 6

Age-Related Endocrine Alterations

I. PITUITARY-ADRENAL AXIS

Reference	*Age-Related Changes*	*Species*
1. Bowman & Wolf (138)	↓ 17-hydroxycorticosteroid response to ACTH	Monkey
2. Hess & Riegle (139)	Basal plasma corticosterone unchanged; ↓ corticosterone response to ACTH or ether stress	Rat
3. Riegle et al. (140)	Basal plasma corticosteroids unchanged; ↓ corticosteroid response to ACTH	Goat
4. Breznock & McQueen (141)	Basal plasma corticosteroid levels unchanged; corticosteroid response to ACTH-normal	Dog
5. Grad et al. (142)	Basal plasma corticosteroid levels unchanged; ↓ urinary corticosteroid levels	Man
6. Friedman et al. (143)	Cortisol response to ACTH normal or excessive	Man
7. Blichert-Toft (144)	Basal serum ACTH, cortisol and 24 hr urinary excretion of 17-ketogenic steroids unchanged secretory reserve of ACTH unchanged; normal glucocorticoid response to surgical trauma	Man

Abbreviations: ACTH = adrenocorticotropic hormone.

TABLE 6 (*continued*)

II. PITUITARY-THYROID AXIS

Reference	Age-Related Changes	Species
1. Snyder & Utiger (156)	↓ TSH response to TRH	Man
	↓ serum T₃ levels	
2. Finch (117)	Basal serum TSH levels unchanged	Mouse
3. Meites et al. (148)	↓ TSH response to TRH	Rat
4. Denckla (155)	↑ pituitary factor which blocks action of thyroid hormones	Rat

III. PITUITARY-GONADAL AXIS

Reference	Age-Related Changes	Species
1. Meites et al. (148)	Pituitary FSH content ↑, LH ↓; serum LH unchanged; Diminished post-castration rise in LH; Diminished pituitary responsiveness to estradiol benzoate;	Female Rat
	↓ LH response to LHRH	
2. Zumoff et al. (151)	↓ urinary androsterone/ etiocholanolone ratio	Man
3. Chan et al. (152)	↓ testosterone production ↓ testicular response to HCG	Male Rat
4. Clemens & Meites (147)	↑ LHRH content of hypothalamus	Female Rat
5. Tsai & Yen (164)	↑ LH and FSH in serum	Man
6. Kaplan & Hreschyshen (150)	↓ serum estrogen	Man

IV. MISCELLANEOUS HORMONE CHANGES

Reference	Age-Related Changes	Species
1. Meites et al. (148)	↑ serum prolactin	Female Rat
2. Kovacs et al. (149)	Prolactin cells of pituitary normal	Human
3. Blichert-Toft (144)	Normal basal serum GH levels; Normal secretory reserve of GH	

Abbreviations: TSH = thyrotropin; TRH = thyrotropin-releasing hormone; T₃ = triiodothyronine; FSH = follicle-stimulating hormone; LH = luteinizing hormone; LHRH = luteinizing hormone-releasing hormone; HCG = human chorioric gonadotropin; GH = growth hormone.

in the endocrine axis under study. The source of the disruption is not obvious from such measurements. Furthermore, the finding of a normal serum or urinary concentration of target gland hormones, e.g., estrogen, does not allow for an interpretation of "no change" between experimental and control subjects since changes in secretory reserve may exist. For this purpose, stimulation tests have been devised. Administration of exogenous pituitary hormones allows for the assessment of end organ responsiveness. Administration of hypothalamic-releasing hormones allows for the evaluation of pituitary responsiveness. These tests can, therefore, provide the data which may pinpoint where the endocrine deficits in the hypothalamic-pituitary-target gland axis reside. Unfortunately, not all of the data possibly obtainable by these methods has been investigated in the elderly. Furthermore, only two hypothalamic-releasing hormones (LHRH and TRH) are available for human pituitary stimulation tests. Of particular interest is the pituitary-adrenal axis, a major system in adaptation to stress, with significant abnormalities in depression. Since CRF, the corticotropin-releasing hormone, has not yet been chemically characterized, investigators have been able to study only basal corticosteroid levels in plasma and urine or adrenal responsiveness to stress or exogenous ACTH. Bowman and Wolf (138) reported that rhesus monkeys (15 years) showed a reduced (down 40 percent) 17-hydroxycorticosteroid response to ACTH when compared with sex-matched young controls (eight years). This suggests declining responsiveness of the adrenal cortex. In agreement with these results are those of Hess and Riegle (139), who reported that, although no age-related differences existed in basal plasma corticosterone levels in rats, exposure to ether as a stressor or to exogenous ACTH resulted in significantly smaller increments in plasma corticosterone in old animals when compared to young. Riegle, et al. (140) found no change in basal plasma corticosteroids in old versus young goats, but older animals showed a significantly smaller corticosteroid response to ACTH than young ones. In contrast, Breznock and McQueen (141) found no differences between old and young dogs as regards either basal corticosteroid levels or corticosteroid response to ACTH. Conflicting results have been obtained in humans. Grad, et al. (142) measured plasma and urinary corticoids in young and old persons. No significant differences in plasma corticosteroids due to age or sex were observed but the old had significantly less urinary corticoids than the young. Friedman et al. (143) reported that in geriatric patients (average age — 80 years), the adrenocortical response to porcine ACTH is excessive when compared to normal adults. Cortisol response to insulin-induced hypoglycemia, exogenous synthetic ACTH gel and $ACTH_{1-24}$ was normal. Thus, this study provides no evidence for a deficit in the functional capability of the HPA axis in the aged human. In a more recent study, Blichert-Toft (144) studied the secretion of ACTH and growth hormone (GH) in 447 subjects aged 14-95. No age-related differences were observed in resting serum levels of ACTH, cortisol or in 24-hour urinary excretion of 17-ketogenic steroids (17-KGS). GH levels in serum showed no change in males with advancing age, but females exhibited increased basal levels. In addition, secretory reserve of ACTH and GH, determined by metyrapone and arginine stimulation tests respectively, showed no age-related differences. No evidence of a reduced reserve of the glucocorticoid system or GH secretion was observed in connection with surgical trauma in elderly subjects. From this study there is little evidence that ACTH and GH secretion are impaired in response to acute stress in old age. These findings were obtained in experiments with acute stress, but studies on the effects of chronic stress on pituitary-adrenal function in the elderly have not yet been reported. Such data could have important clinical implications since Friedman et al. (145) reported that treatment of old rats with cortisol or posterior pituitary extracts significantly prolonged their life span when compared with untreated controls. There is also considerable interest in the use of ACTH and ACTH fragments as psychopharmacological agents for disorders of learning and memory in the aged. DeWied and his collaborators have elegantly demonstrated that fragments of the ACTH molecules which lack steroidogenic properties (e.g., $ACTH_{4-10}$) are capable, in low doses, of improving the acquisition and inhibiting the extinction of active and passive conditioned avoidance behavior in rats (see 146 for review). In view of these studies, Cole and his associates (165) have recently demonstrated an amelioration of neuropsychological symptomatology associated with senile organic brain syndrome with $ACTH_{4-10}$. Subcutaneous injection of 30 mg $ACTH_{4-10}$ resulted in a reduction in depression and confusion and an increase in vigor. Memory retrieval was also enhanced.

Hypothalamic-pituitary-gonadal function in aging has been studied at the three levels. Clemens and Meites (147) reported an increase in LHRH content of the hypothalamus of old female rats. This may be due to decreased release of the decapeptide with advancing age. Meites et al. (148) have studied the functional capacity of the pituitary-gonadal axis in old (20-24 months) female rats. Pituitary content of FSH and LH was increased and decreased, respectively. Serum LH was normal in old rats, but serum PRL was elevated six-fold. This latter finding may well be due to a functional deficit in hypothalamic DA systems known to tonically inhibit PRL secretion. Such a deficit has been noted in the aged mouse (116), but not in man (149). Further work revealed that young female rats exhibit a 26-fold post-castration rise in serum LH whereas old female rats showed only a three-fold increase. In addition, estradiol benzoate treatment markedly reduced the LH rise (after castration), but had a much smaller effect in the castrated aged animals. Serum LH elevations produced by intravenous LHRH were much higher in young rats than in old ones. Taken together, these results suggest a decreased responsiveness of senescent adenohypophyseal receptors to both feedback (i.e., estrogen) and feed-forward (i.e., LHRH) control mechanisms. Kaplan and Hreschyshen (150) reported a large fall in serum estrogen in post-menopausal women. Zumoff et al. (151) reported that in man there is a progressive decrease in the mean urinary androsterone/etiocholanolone ratio, a measure of testosterone metabolism. Chan et al. (152) reported a decreased testicular production of testosterone and 5-α androstene-3-α, 17-β-diol in aged rats. The testicular response to human chorionic gonadotropin was also impaired. Thus, both pituitary and end-organ failures apparently occur in the pituitary-gonadal axis as a consequence of aging.

A decreased metabolic rate associated with aging is well known. For several years Denckla (153-155) has suggested the presence of a polypeptide pituitary factor, which appears during puberty and progressively (with age) blocks the effects of thyroid hormones on peripheral tissues. Since hypothyroidism in young persons produces symptoms resembling old age, and since thyroidectomy, but no other endocrine ablations (except hypophysectomy), produces decreases in O_2 consumption similar to those observed in aging, Denckla has hypothesized that this pituitary factor, acting in concert with other unknown endocrine factors, results in deterioration of two systems: the circulatory and the immune system. The outcome is death. Denckla's pituitary factor has not yet been chemically characterized.

Meites et al. (148) reported a significant decrease in the magnitude of the TRH-induced TSH response in old rats when compared to young controls. This finding has been reported in elderly human subjects as well (154,157). These data suggest an impairment in the pituitary-thyroid axis analogous to that observed in the pituitary-gonadal axis, i.e., alteration in pituitary receptor sensitivity. This is of considerable importance, since a blunted TSH response to TRH has been observed in depressed patients and in alcoholics (87, 93, 94), but not in normal controls or schizophrenics.

Physiological Studies

Cerebral blood flow decreases with increasing age, and it was found to be even lower in arteriosclerotic and senile psychotic patients (158, 159). There is also a gradual decline in cerebral oxygen uptake with increasing age, with lower values in senile psychotic patients. These changes can have profound effects on electrophysiological correlates of CNS function. Peng et al. (160) have recently reported that *in vitro* oxygen consumption of brain slices derived from hippocampus, hypothalamus and amygdala is significantly reduced in aged rats.

Neurophysiological correlates of aging have been reviewed (118). In an early study on peripheral nerves Norris et al. (161) reported a decrease in average conduction velocity of motor fibers of human ulnar nerves with advancing age. The effect is not due to nerve fiber degeneration. Declining sensory function associated with aging is well documented, and it includes impaired vision and audition. EEG changes associated with aging have been reported, including shifts in the frequency spectrum, resembling the pattern observed in children. The temporal lobe, more than any other brain area, is prone to develop such slow activity. In old age, the frequency and duration of spontaneous awakening from sleep increase markedly. Furthermore,

Stage 4 EEG is virtually absent, sleep spindles are greatly reduced and the proportion of REM sleeps begins to decline. With increasing age, sympathetic and parasympathetic nervous effects on organs and tissues decline (118). In order to reproduce various effects mediated by the autonomic nervous system in old animals, it is necessary to stimulate cholinergic and adrenergic fibers with strong electric currents (162).

Frolkis et al. (162) have conducted extensive physiological studies concerning alterations in hypothalamic function in aging. These include assessment of neurosecretory activity, electrophysiological function, sensitivity to humoral factors, and an analysis of hypothalamic influences on cardiovascular and respiratory systems. Using Gomori staining techniques, they concluded that the marked increase of neurosecretory substances observed in the hypothalamo-neurohypophysial system of 24-month-old rats was due to retarded secretion (rather than increased production). They have also applied painful electrical stimulation to the skin of young and old rats to assess hypothalamic function by activating neurosecretory processes and have observed a sluggish response in the aged animals. Direct electrical stimulation of the amygdaloid complex activated neurosecretory processes in young adults, but not in old animals. In contrast to neural stimulation, intraperitoneal injection of epinephrine induced "a more evident stimulation of neurosecretion in old rats" than in young controls. In concert with these findings, they also demonstrated that noxious stimulation of the skin leads to larger physiological changes in young adults than in old animals, i.e., a large drop of blood eosinophils, a larger increase in urinary 17-ketosteroids, etc., whereas humoral stimulation (adrenalin injection) led to larger changes in old animals than in young adults. Furthermore, in old animals, "disruption and exhaustion of the adaptive mechanisms due to prolonged stress stimulation occur much quicker than in adults." Microinjection of ACh and NE revealed an age-related increase in sensitivity of the hypothalamus to humoral factors, as measured by electrical changes, cardiovascular and respiratory responses. They hypothesized that the mechanism of the increase in the sensitivity of the hypothalamus to humoral factors is due to changes in cell membrane receptor function.

CONCLUSIONS

We have reviewed the literature on the neurobiology of depression and on the neurobiology of aging in an effort to find correlations which might offer hints as to what changes in aging might predispose to depression. A myriad of findings emerges, which may do more to confuse than to enlighten. Several factors account for this confusion. Hypotheses regarding the biological substrates of depression are incomplete and sometimes contradictory. The research strategies used to obtain the data base for these hypotheses have involved the study of depressed patients without drug treatment and after drug accelerated remission, as well as the direct study of drug effects upon the brains of animals. A systematic investigation of the neurobiology of elderly depressed patients has not been conducted. Such studies would require sex-matched aged normal controls that are apparently hard to come by. Hence we are limited to information, often cursory, which is obtained during the conduct of research which is oriented towards different goals.

Studies of the neurobiology of aging are numerous and are conducted on both aging animals and man with the reasonable expectation that the animal results are relevant to man. Unfortunately, most of the studies in humans do not focus on depression, and the use of animal models for the study of the human condition is open to question. On the other hand, physical and psychological stress can be created in animals and the neurobiological results from such investigations are probably relevant to man. Unfortunately, very few systematic studies of aged animals and of their capacity to tolerate such stress or of the consequences of such stress have been done.

Despite these limitations, some tentative conclusions may be drawn. Severe depressions are associated with diminished function of one or more neurotransmitters or of an imbalance among them. In the elderly, several changes occur which might explain the increased vulnerability to this illness. Though results are not always consistent, there seems to be diminution of tyrosine uptake into brain and a decrease of tyrosine hydroxylase activity associated with aging. Since this is the rate limiting enzyme in synthesis of DA and NE, this finding may account for the diminution of the content of these two neurotransmitters in the brain which has been reported by many workers. Interestingly, the most extensive and consistent data relate aging to DA diminution in the substantia nigra, caudate nucleus and putamen. Since the nigroneostriatal tract is involved in the control of movement, this may account for tremor and other motor disturbances in the elderly. Diminution of tryptophan hydroxylase and of 5-HT content has also been reported in aging, particularly in the septum and hippocampus and these limbic system changes may also predispose to serotonergic depression.

In the face of diminished synthetic capacity for both catecholamines and indoleamines, there is increased activity of MAO—a major degrading enzyme for both types of biogenic amines—in the aging organism. There is also diminished NE receptor function. This concatenation of events offers a persuasive argument that diminished biogenic amine function may be involved in the increased risk for depression in the aged.

In aging, changes in other transmitters may also occur. Both the synthetic and degrading enzymes for ACh diminish with aging, though the consequences of this and the role of ACh in the pathogenesis of depression are uncertain. Levels of excitatory amino acid neurotransmitters decrease, while those of inhibitory ones increase. The significance of this is unclear, because no role for these amino acids in depression has been established.

Neuroendocrine changes also occur with depression and aging. In depression, there is evidence for heightened and uncontrolled HPA activity similar to that found in stress. There is also evidence for disturbed regulation of the thyroid axis, for low levels of LH, and for alterations in GH regulation (148, 156, 157). In aging, the results are inconsistent. In the monkey, rat and goat there is diminished adrenal response to ACTH, but in dogs and man the adrenal response is intact.

In depression, some alteration of the hypothalamic-pituitary-thyroid axis occurs because some patients show a blunted TSH response to TRH and because thyroid hormones accelerate antidepressive medication. In aging, there is diminution in thyroid activity, perhaps due to a thyroid-inhibiting factor produced in the pituitary, as proposed by Denckla, because the basal metabolic rate falls despite normal levels of circulating thyroid hormone. It is not difficult to infer that diminished thyroid function associated with aging predisposes to depression, but this is not proven.

GH regulation in depression is aberrant, since the GH response to insulin hypoglycemia is diminished in some depressed post-menopausal women. GH levels and the pituitary GH reserve in aging are normal in the one study we have noted.

In depression, there have been a few studies of LH. One study reported low LH levels in post-menopausal depressed women compared with normal post-menopausal women. In aging, there is a report of LHRH elevation in the aged hypothalamus and varying results in the study of the pituitary response to this releasing factor. Diminished gonadal activity with aging seems to be associated with both diminished pituitary activity and diminished gonadal responsiveness.

Although the similarity of many of the neuroendocrine changes in depression and in aging is striking, the role of these changes in the affective changes of depression is far from clear. On the other hand, a role in the vegetative changes associated with depression may readily be presumed.

In the many studies of aging, very few things have been reported to prolong life. Partial starvation early in life has long been known to do so, perhaps by delaying the genomic time table for maturation, senescence and death. Cortisol or adrenal steroids and meclophenoxate, a drug which removes lipofuchsin, are also reported to do so. It is, therefore, of exceptional interest that the late Dr. George Cotzias, who discovered the utility of l-DOPA in the treatment of Parkinson's disease, recently reported (163) that the addition of l-DOPA (40 mg/g) to the diet of rats extended the life span of rats by 50 percent. No mechanism has been proposed, but the ready conversion of this amino acid precursor to DA and NE and the known relations of these transmitters to CNS function and to neuroendocrine regulation suggest that these mechanisms may be involved.

REFERENCES

1. SPITZ, R.: Anaclitic Depression. *Psychoanalytic Study of the Child*, 2:313-342, 1946.

2. SILVERMAN, C.: *The Epidemiology of Depression.* Baltimore: Johns Hopkins Press, 1968, pp. 55-71.
3. POST, F.: Diagnosis of depression in geriatric patients and treatment modalities appropriate for the population. In: D. Gallant and G. Simpson (Eds.), *Depression: Behavioral, Biochemical, Diagnostic and Treatment Concepts.* New York: Spectrum Publications, Inc., 1976, pp. 205-231.
4. WATTS, C.: *Depressive Disorders in the Community.* Bristol: John Wright & Sons Ltd., 1966.
5. RIPLEY, H.: Depression and the life span-epidemiology. In: G. Usdin (Ed.), *Depression: Clinical, Biological and Psychological Perspectives.* New York: Brunner/Mazel, 1977, pp. 1-27.
6. VERVOERDT, A.: *Clinical Geropsychiatry.* Baltimore: Williams & Wilkins, 1976, pp. 213-222.
7. POST, F.: The factor of aging in affective illness. In: A. Coppen, A. Welk (Eds.), *Recent Developments in Affective Disorders.* Brit. J. Psychiatry Special Publication, 1968, 2:105-116.
8. BUSSE, E.: Aging and psychiatric diseases in later life. In: S. Arieti (Ed.), *American Handbook of Psychiatry*, Vol. 4. New York: Basic Books, 1975, pp. 67-90.
9. GOLDFARB, A.: Depression in the old and aged. In: F. Flach and S. Graghi (Eds.), *The Nature and Treatment of Depression.* New York: John Wiley & Sons, 1975, pp. 119-144.
10. POST, F.: Psychological aspects of geriatrics. *Postgrad. Med. J.*, 44:307-318, 1968.
11. BUSSE, E. and PFEIFFER, V.: *Mental Illness in Later Life.* Washington: Am. Psychiatric Association, 1973.
12. SCHUKIT, M., MILLER, P., and HAHLBOHM, D.: Unrecognized psychiatric illness in elderly medical-surgical patients. *J. Gerontology*, 30:655-660, 1975.
13. VERWOERDT, A.: Emotional responses to physical illnesses. In: C. Eisdorfer and W. Fan (Eds.), *Psychopharmacology and Aging.* New York: Plenum Press, 1973, pp. 169-181.
14. AKISKAL, H. and MCKINNEY, W., JR.: Overview of recent research in depression. *Arch. Gen. Psychiat.*, 32:285-305, 1975.
15. LIPSHITZ, K. and KLINE, N.: Psychopharmacology of the aged. In: J. Freeman (Ed.), *Clinical Principals and Drugs in the Aging.* Springfield, Ill.: Charles C Thomas Publishers, 1963, pp. 421-547.
16. LIPTON, M.: Age differentiation in depression: Biochemical aspects. *J. Gerontology*, 31:293-299, 1976.
17. SACHAR, E.: Hormonal changes in stress and mental illness. *Hospital Practice*, 10:46-64, 1975.
18. MASON, J.: Specificity in the organization of neuroendocrine response profiles. In: P. Seeman and G. Brown (Eds.), *Frontiers in Neurology and Neuroscience Research.* Toronto: University of Toronto Press, 1974, pp. 68-80.

19. FAWCETT, J. and BUNNEY, W., JR.: Pituitary-adrenal function and depression. *Arch. Gen. Psychiat.*, 16:517-535, 1967.
20. LANDFIELD, P. and LYNCH, G.: Brain aging and plasma steroid levels: Quantitative correlations. *Neuroscience Abstracts*, 3: 111, 1977.
21. SACHAR, E., HELLMAN, L., ROFFWARG, H., et al.: Disrupted 24 hour patterns of cortisol secretion in psychotic depression. *Arch. Gen. Psych.*, 28:19-24, 1973.
22. ORDY, J. and BRIZEE, K.: Age declines in learning, short-term memory, arousal and aggression in relation to cell loss from the cortex and hippocampus of the rat. *Neuroscience Abstracts*, 3:115, 1977.
23. LANFIELD, P. and LYNCH, G.: Impaired monosynaptic potentiation in *in vitro* hippocampal slices from aged, memory-deficient rats. *J. Gerontol.*, 32:523-533, 1977.
24. CURZON, G.: Tryptophan pyrrolase: A biochemical factor in depressive illness? *Brit. J. Psychiatry*, 115:1367-1374, 1969.
25. MAAS, J. and MEDNICKS, M.: Hydrocortisone effected increase of norepinephrine uptake by brain slices. *Science*, 171:178-179, 1971.
26. MAAS, J.: Interactions between adrenocortical steroid hormones, electrolytes and the catecholamines. In: B. Ho and W. McIsaac (Eds.), *Brain Chemistry and Mental Disease*. New York: Plenum Press, 1971, pp. 177-195.
27. BROWN, G. and REICHLIN, S.: Psychologic and neural regulation of growth hormone secretion. *Psychosomatic Med.*, 34:45-61, 1972.
28. HORROBIN, D.: *Prolactin: Physiology and Clinical Significance.* London: MTP Medical and Technical Publishing Co., Ltd., 1973, p. 23.
29. THIERRY, A., FRANCE, J., GLOWINSKI, J., et al.: Effects of stress on the metabolism of norepinephrine, dopamine and serotonin in the central nervous system of the rat. Modifications of norepinephrine. *J. Pharmacol. Exper. Ther.*, 163:163-171, 1968.
30. BLISS, E., AILION, J., and ZWANZIGER, J.: Metabolism of norepinephrine, serotonin and dopamine in rat brain with stress. *J. Pharmacol. Exper. Ther.*, 164:122-134, 1968.
31. BLISS, E. and ZWANZIEGER, J.: Brain amines and emotional stress. *J. Psychiat. Res.*, 4:189-198, 1966.
32. WELCH, B. and WELCH, A.: Differential activation by restraint stress of mechanism to conserve brain catecholamines and serotonin in mice differing in excitability. *Nature*, 218:575-577, 1968.
33. WELCH, A. and WELCH, B.: Failure of natural stimuli to accelerate brain catecholamine depletion after biosynthetic inhibition with alpha-methyl-paratyrosine. *Brain Res.*, 9:402-405, 1968.
34. MUSACCHIO, J., JULOU, L., KETY, S., GLOWINSKI, J., et al.: Increase in rat—rat brain tyrosine hydroxylase activity pro-

duced by electroconvulsive shock. *Proc. Nat. Acad. Sci. (USA)*,
63:1117-1119, 1969.

35. GOODWIN, F. and BUNNEY, W., JR.: Psychobiological aspects of
stress and affective illness. In: *Separation and Depression*.
Washington: AAAS, 1973, pp. 91-112.

36. WEINER, N.: Factors regulating catecholamine biosynthesis in
peripheral and central catecholaminergic neurons. In: D.
Tower (Ed.), *The Nervous System Vol. I: The Basic Neurosciences*. New York: Raven Press, 1975, pp. 341-354.

37. SPITZER, R., ENDICOTT, J., and ROBINS, E.: Clinical criteria for
psychiatric diagnosis and DSMII. *Amer. J. Psychiat.*, 32:1187-
1192, 1975.

38. GOODWIN, F.: Diagnosis of affective disorders. In: E. Jarvik
(Ed.), *Psychopharmacology in the Practice of Medicine*. New
York: Appleton-Century-Crofts, 1977, pp. 219-228.

39. DOVENMUEHLE, R. and VERVOERDT, A.: Physical illness and depressive symptomatology. *J. Amer. Geriatrics*, 10:932-947,
1962.

40. GOODWIN, F. and EBERT, M.: Recent advances in drug treatment of affective disorders. In: E. Jarvik (Ed.), *Psychopharmacology in the Practice of Medicine*. New York: Appleton-
Century-Crofts, 1977, pp. 277-287.

41. LEHMANN, H.: Depression: Somatic treatment methods. In:
G. Usdin (Ed.), *Depression: Clinical, Biological and Psychological Perspectives*. New York: Brunner/Mazel, 1977, pp.
235-270.

42. PRANGE, A.: The use of antidepressant drugs in the elderly patient. In: C. Eisdorfer and W. Fann (Eds.), *Psychopharmacology and Aging*. New York: Plenum Press, 1973, pp.
225-237.

43. GOODWIN, F. and EBERT, M.: Specific antimanic and antidepressant drugs. In: E. Jarvik (Ed.), *Psychopharmacology in the
Practice of Medicine*. New York: Appleton-Century-Crofts,
1977, pp. 257-273.

44. ETTIGI, P. and BROWN, G.: Psychoneuroendocrinology of affective disorder: An overview. *Amer. J. Psychiat.*, 134:493-501,
1977.

45. RUBIN, R. and KENDLER, K.: Psychoneuroendocrinology: Funda-
mental concepts and correlates in depression. In: G. Usdin
(Ed.), *Depression: Clinical, Biological and Psychological
Perspectives*. New York: Brunner/Mazel, 1977, pp. 122-138.

46. FAWCETT, J. and BUNNEY, W., JR.: Pituitary-adrenal function
and depression: An outline for research. *Arch. Gen. Psychiat.*,
16:448-460, 1967.

47. MURPHY, D. and WEISS, R.: Reduced monoamine oxidase activity
in blood platelets from bipolar depressed patients. *Amer. J.
Psychiat.*, 128:1351-1357, 1972.

48. LIPTON, M.: Theories of the etiology of schizophrenia. In: I.

Forest and E. Usdin (Eds.), *Psychotherapeutic Drugs*. New York: Marcel Dekker, 1976, pp. 225-274.

49. SCHILDKRAUT, J.: Biogenic amines and affective disorders. *Ann. Rev. Med.*, 25:333-348, 1974.

50. MENDELS, J., STERN, S., and FRAZER, A.: Biological concepts of depression. In: D. Gallant and G. Simpson (Eds.), *Depression: Behavioral, Biochemical, Diagnostic and Treatment Concepts*. New York: Spectrum Publishers, 1976, pp. 19-74.

51. BALDESSERINI, R.: Biogenic amines and behavior. *Ann. Rev. Med.*, 23:694-701, 1976.

52. BARCHAS, J., PATRICK, R., RAESE, J., and BERGER, P.: Biochemical research in affective disorders. In: G. Usdin (Ed.), *Depression: Clinical, Biological and Psychological Perspectives*. New York: Brunner/Mazel, 1977, pp. 166-197.

53. GOODWIN, F. and SACK, R.: Affective disorders: The catecholamine hypothesis revisited. In: E. Usdin and S. Snyder (Eds.), *Frontier in Catecholamine Research*. London: Pergamon Press, 1973, pp. 1157-1164.

54. SCHILDKRAUT, J.: Biochemical research in affective disorders. In: G. Usdin (Ed.), *Depression: Clinical, Biological and Psychological Perspectives*. New York: Brunner/Mazel, 1977, pp. 166-197.

55. DAVIS, J.: Central biogenic amines and theories of depression and mania. In: W. Fann, I. Karacan, A. Pokorny, and R. Williams (Eds.), *Phenomenology and Treatment of Depression*. New York: Spectrum Publications, 1977, pp. 11-32.

56. PRANGE, A., JR., WILSON, I., LYNN, C., et al.: L-tryptophan in mania: Contribution to a permissive hypothesis of affective disorders. *Arch. Gen. Psychiat.*, 30:56-62, 1974.

57. PRANGE, A., JR., LIPTON, M., NEMEROFF, C., et al.: The role of hormones in depression. *Life Sci.*, 20:1305-1318, 1977.

58. BUNNEY, W., JR. and MURPHY, D.: Strategies for the systematic study of neurotransmitter receptor function in man. In: E. Usdin and W. Bunney, Jr. (Eds.), *Pre and Postsynaptic Receptors*. New York: Marcel Dekker, 1975, pp. 283-311.

59. GOODWIN, F. and BUNNEY, W., JR.: Depressions following reserpine: A reevaluation. *Seminars in Psychiatry*, 3:435-448, 1971.

60. GERSHON, E., DUNNER, D., and GOODWIN, F.: Toward a biology of affective disorders: Genetic contributions. *Arch. Gen. Psychiat.*, 25:1-15, 1971.

61. MAAS, J., DEKIRMENJIAN, H., and FAWCETT, J.: MHPG excretion by patients with affective disease. *International Pharmacopsychiat.*, 9:14-26, 1974.

62. KRAEMER, G., McKINNEY, W., BRESSE, G., and PRANGE, A., JR.: Behavioral and biochemical effects of microinjections of 6-hydroxydopamine into the substantia nigra of the rhesus monkey. *Neuroscience Abstracts*, 2:494, 1976.

63. BECKMAN, H. and GOODWIN, F.: Antidepressant response to tricyclics and urinary MHPG in unipolar patients: Clinical re-

sponse to imipramine or amitriptyline. *Arch. Gen. Psychiat.,* 32:17-21, 1975.

64. SHOPSIN, B., WILK, S., SUTHANANTHAN, G., GERSHON, S., DAVIS, K.: Catecholamines and affective disorders revisited: A critical assessment. *J. Nerv. Ment. Dis.,* 158:369-383, 1974.

65. PRANGE, A., WILSON, I., RABON, A., et al.: Enhancement of imipramine anti-depressant activity by thyroid hormone. *Amer. J. Psychiat.,* 126:457-468, 1969.

66. PRANGE, A., WILSON, I., KNOX, A., et al.: Thyroid-imipramine clinical and chemical interaction: Evidence for a receptor deficient in depression. *J. Psychiat. Res.,* 9:187-205, 1972.

67. BOURNE, H., BUNNEY, W., COLBURN, R., et al.: Noradrenaline, 5-hydroxytryptamine, and 5-hydroxyindoleacetic acid in hindbrains of suicidal patients. *Lancet,* 2:805-808, 1968.

68. VAN PRAAG, H. and KORF, J.: Endogenous depressions with and without disturbances in the 5-hydroxytryptamine, metabolism: A biochemical classification? *Psychopharmacologia,* 19:148-152, 1971.

69. GOODWIN, F. and MURPHY, D.: Biological factors in affective disorders and schizophrenia. In: M. Gordon (Ed.), *Psychopharmacological Agents.* New York: Academic Press, 1975, pp. 9-35.

70. BURNS, D. and MENDELS, J.: Biogenic amine precursors and affective illnesses. In: W. Fann, I. Karacan, A. Pokorny, and R. Williams (Eds.), *Phenomenology and Treatment of Depression.* New York: Spectrum Publications, 1973, pp. 33-68.

71. JANOWSKY, D., EL-YOUSEF, M., DAVIS, J., et al.: A cholinergic-adrenergic hypothesis of mania and depression. *Lancet,* 2:632-635, 1972.

72. JANOWSKY, D., EL-YOUSEF, M., and DAVIS, J.: Parasympathetic suppression of manic symptoms by physostigmine. *Arch. Gen. Psych.,* 28:542-547, 1973.

73. HOKFELT, T. and FUXE, K.: On the morphology and the neuro-endocrine role of the hypothalamic catecholamine neurons. In: K. Knigge, D. Scott, A. Weindl, and S. Basel (Eds.), *Brain-Endocrine Interaction: Median Eminence Structure and Function.* Karger, 1972, pp. 228-265.

74. HOKFELT, T., FUXE, K., GOLDSTEIN, M., et al.: Immunofluorescence mapping of central monoamine and releasing hormone (LHRH) systems. In: W. Stumpf, L. Grant, and S. Basel (Eds.), *Anatomical Neuroendocrinology.* Karger, 1975, pp. 381-392.

75. FUXE, K. and HOKFELT, T.: Central monoaminergic systems and hypothalamic function. In: L. Martini, M. Motta, and F. Franchini (Eds.), *The Hypothalamus.* New York: Academic Press, 1970, pp. 123-138.

76. KIZER, J., PALKOVITS, M., and BROWNSTEIN, M.: The projections of A8, A9 and A10 dopaminergic cell bodies: Evidence for a

nigral-hypothalamic-median eminence dopaminergic pathway. *Brain Research*, 108:363-370, 1976.

77. CARSON, K., NEMEROFF, C., RONE, M.: Biochemical and histochemical evidence for the existence of a tubero-infundibular cholinergic pathway in the rat. *Brain Res.*, 129:169-173, 1977.

78. McCANN, S. and OJEDA, S.: Synaptic transmitters involved in the release of hypothalamic releasing and inhibiting hormones. In: S. Ehrenpreis and I. Kopin (Eds.), *Reviews and Neuroscience*, Vol. 2. New York: Raven Press, 1976, pp. 91-110.

79. FROHMAN, L.: Neurotransmitters as resulators of endocrine function. *Hosp. Prac.*, 10:54-67, 1975.

80. MARTIN, J.: Brain regulation of growth hormone secretion. In: L. Martini and W. Ganong (Eds.), *Frontiers in Neuroendocrinology*, Vol. 4. New York: Raven Press, 1976, p. 129.

81. BRAZEAU, P., VALE, W., BURGUS, R., et al.: Hypothalamic polypeptide that inhibits the secretion of immunoreactive pituitary growth hormone. *Science*, 179:77-79, 1973.

82. VALE, W. and RIVIER, C.: Hypothalamic hypophysiotropic hormones. In: L. Iversen, S. Iversen and S. Snyder (Eds.), *Handbook of Psychopharmacology*. New York: Plenum Press, 1975, pp. 195-238.

83. NEMEROFF, C., GRANT, L., BISSETTE, G., et al.: Growth, endocrinological and behavioral deficits after monosodium-L-glutamate in the neonatal rat: Possible involvement of arcuate dopamine neurone damage. *Psychoneuroendocrinol.*, 2:176-196, 1977.

84. KORDON, C., HENRY, M., and ENJALBERT, A.: Neurotransmitters and control of pituitary function. In: F. Labrie, J. Meites and G. Pelletier (Eds.), *Hypothalamus and Endocrine Functions*. New York: Plenum Press, 1976, pp. 51-61.

85. NEMEROFF, C. B., KONKOL, R. J., BISSETTE, G., et al.: Analysis of the disruption in hypothalamic pituitary regulation in rats treated neonatally with monosodium-glutamate (MSG): Evidence for the involvement of tuberoinfundibular cholinergic and dopaminergic systems in neuroendocrine regulation. *Endocrinology*, 101:613-622, 1977.

86. KIZER, J. S. and YOUNGBLOOD, W. W.: Neurotransmitter systems and central neuroendocrine regulation. In: M. A. Lipton, K. F. Killam, and A. DiMascio (Eds.), *Psychopharmacology: A Generation of Progress*. New York: Raven Press, 1977.

87. PRANGE, A. J., JR.: Patterns of pituitary response. In: W. E. Fann, I. Karaca, A. D. Pokorny, and R. L. Williams (Eds.), *Phenomenology and Treatment of Depression*. New York: Spectrum Publications, Inc., 1977, pp. 1-15.

88. SACHAR, E. J., GRUEN, P. H., ALTMAN, N., HALPERN, R. S. and FRANTZ, A. G.: Use of neuroendocrine techniques in psychopharmacological research. In: E. J. Sachar (Ed.), *Hormones,*

Behavior and Psychopathology. New York: Raven Press, 1976, pp. 161-176.

89. CARROLL, B. J. and MENDELS, I.: Neuroendocrine regulation in affective disorders. In: E. J. Sachar (Ed.), *Hormones, Behavior and Psychopathology.* New York: Raven Press, 1976, pp. 193-224.

90. McEWEN, B. S.: Endocrine effects of the brain and their relationships to behavior. In: G. J. Siegel, R. W. Albers, R. Katzman and B. W. Agranoff (Eds.), *Basic Neurochemistry.* Boston: Little, Brown and Co., 1976, pp. 737-765.

91. REES, H. D., STUMPF,W. E., and SAR, M.: Autoradiographic studies with ³H-dexamethasone in the rat brain and pituitary. In: W. E. Stumpf and L. D. Grant (Eds.), *Anatomical Neuroendocrinology.* Basel: S. Karger, 1975, pp. 262-269.

92. MARTIN, J. B., REICHLIN, S., and BROWN, G. M.: *Clinical Neuroendocrinology.* Philadelphia: F. A. Davis Company, 1977.

93. LOOSEN, P. T., PRANGE, A. J., WILSON, I. C., et al.: Thyroid stimulating hormone response after thyrotropin releasing hormone in depressed, schizophrenic and normal women. *Psychoneuroendocrinology,* 2:137-148, 1977.

94. NEMEROFF, C. B., LOOSEN, P. T., BISSETTE, G., et al.: Pharmacobehavioral effects of hypothalamic peptides in animals and man: Focus on the thyrotropin-releasing hormone (TRH) and neurotensin. *Psychoneuroendocrinology,* in press.

95. BRODY, H.: Aging of the vertebrate brain. In: M. Rothstein (Ed.), *Development and Aging of the Nervous System.* New York: Academic Press, 1973, pp. 121-133.

96. WISNIEWSKI, H. M. and TERRY, R. D.: Morphology of the aging brain, human and animal. In: D. H. Ford (Ed.), *Neurobiological Aspects of Maturation and Aging.* Amsterdam: Elsevier; *Prog. Brain Research,* 40:167-187, 1973.

97. KAACK, B., ORDY, J. M., and TRAPP, B.: Changes in limbic, neuroendocrine and autonomic systems, adaptation, homeostasis during aging. In: J. M. Ordy and K. R. Brizzce (Eds.), *Neurobiology of Aging.* New York: Plenum Press; *Adv. Behav. Biol.,* 16:209-231, 1975.

98. McGEER, P. L., McGEER, E. G., and SUZUKI, J. S.: Aging and extra pyramidal function. *Arch. Neurol.,* 34:33-35, 1977.

99. ROTH, M., TOMLINSON, B. E., and BLESSED, G.: Correlation between score for dementia and counts of senile plaques in cerebral gray matter of elderly subjects. *Nature,* 209:106, 1966.

100. ALZHEIMER, A.: *Allg. Z. Psychiat.,* 64:146, 1907.

101. SCHEIBEL, M. E. and SCHEIBEL, A. B.: Structural changes in the aging brain. In: H. Brody, E. Harman and J. M. Ordy (Eds.), *Aging,* Vol. I. New York: Raven Press, 1975, pp. 11-37.

102. BOURNE, G. H.: Lipofuchsin. In: D. H. Ford (Ed.), *Neurobio-*

logical Aspects of Maturation and Aging. Amsterdam: Elsevier; *Prog. Brain Res.*, 40:187-201, 1973.
103. BRIZZEE, K. R., HARKIN, J. C., ORDY, J. M., et al.: Accumulation and distribution of lipofuchsin, amyloid and senile plaques in the aging nervous system. In: H. Brody, D. Harman and J. M. Ordy (Eds.), *Aging*, Vol. I. New York: Raven Press, 1975, pp. 39-78.
104. GEINISMAN, Y. and BONDAREFF, W.: Decrease in the number of synapses in the senescent brain: A quantitative electronmicroscopic analysis of the dentate gyrus molecular layer in the rat. *Mech. Aging Devel.*, 5:11-23, 1976.
105. BONDAREFF, W. and NAROTZKY, R.: Age changes in the neuronal microenvironment. *Science*, 176:1135-1136, 1972.
106. GENINSMAN, Y., BONDAREFF, W., and TELSER, A.: Diminished axonal transport of glycoproteins in the senescent rat brain. *Mech. Aging Devel.*, 6:363-378, 1977.
107. MEIER-RUGE, W.: Experimental pathology and pharmacology in brain research and aging. *Life Sciences*, 17:1627-1636, 1975.
108. VERNADAKIS, A.: Comparative studies of neurotransmitter substances in the maturing and aging of central nervous system of the chicken. In: D. H. Ford (Ed.), *Neurobiological Aspects of Maturation and Aging*. Amsterdam, Elsevier: *Prog. Brain Res.*, 40:231-243, 1973.
109. VERNADAKIS, A.: Neuronal-glial interactions during developing and aging. *Fed. Proc.*, 34:89-95, 1975.
110. VERNADAKIS, A.: Uptake of ^{3}H-norepinephrine in the cerebral hemispheres and cerebellum of the chicken throughout the lifespan. *Mech. Aging Devel.*, 2:371-379, 1973.
111. HOWARD, E.: DNA content of rodent brains during maturation and aging, and autoradiography of postnatal DNA synthesis in monkey brain. In: D. H. Ford (Ed.), *Neurobiological Aspects of Maturation and Aging*. Amsterdam: Elsevier; *Prog. Brain Res.*, 40:91-114, 1973.
112. SAMORAJSKI, T., ROLSTEN, C., and ORDY, J. M.: Changes in behavior, brain and neuroendocrine chemistry with age and stress in C57BL/6J male mice. *J. Gerontol.*, 26:168-175, 1971.
113. SAMORAJSKI, R.: Age-related changes in brain biogenic amines. In: H. Brody, D. Harman and J. M. Ordy (Eds.), *Aging*, Vol. I. New York: Raven Press, 1975, pp. 199-214.
114. FINCH, C. E.: Catecholamine metabolism in the brains of aging male mice. *Brain Res.*, 52:271-276, 1973.
115. FINCH, C. E., JONEC, V., HODY, G., et al.: Aging and the passage of l-tyrosine l-dopa, and insulin into mouse brain slices in vitro. *J. Gerontol.*, 30:33-40, 1975.
116. JONEC, V. and FINCH, C. E.: Aging and dopamine uptake by subcellular fractions in the C57BL/6J male mouse brain. *Brain Res.*, 91:197-215, 1975.
117. FINCH, C. E.: The regulation of physiological changes during mammalian aging. *Quart. Rev. Biol.*, 51:49-83, 1976.

118. TIMARAS, P. S. and VERNADAKIS, A.: Structural, biochemical and functional aging of the nervous system. In: P. S. Timaras (Ed.), *Developmental Physiology and Aging*. New York: Macmillan Co., 1972, pp. 502-526.

119. McGEER, E. G., McGEER, P. L., and WADA, J. A.: Distribution of tyrosine hydroxylase in human and animal brain. *J. Neurochem.*, 18:1647-1658, 1971.

120. McGEER, D. G., FIBIGER, H. C., McGEER, P. L., et al.: Aging and brain enzymes. *Exp. Gerontol.*, 5:391-396, 1971.

121. CARLSSON, A.: Comments on dopamine and substance P. In: E. Usdin, D. Hamburg and J. D. Barchas (Eds.), *Neuroregulators and Psychiatric Disorders*. New York: Oxford Univ. Press, 1976, pp. 14-18.

122. MEEK, J. L., BERTILSSON, L., CHENEY, D. L., et al.: Aging induced changes in acetylcholine and serotonin content of discrete brain nuclei. *J. Gerontol.*, 32:129-131, 1977.

123. ORDY, J. M., KAACH, B., and BRIZZEE, K. R.: Life-span neurochemical changes in the human and non-human primate brain. In: H. Brody, D. Harman and J. M. Ordy (Eds.), *Aging*, Vol. I. New York: Raven Press, 1975, pp. 133-168.

124. SHIH, J. C.: Multiple forms of monoamine oxidase and aging. In: H. Brody, D. Harman and J. M. Ordy (Eds.), *Aging*, Vol. I. New York: Raven Press, 1975, pp. 191-198.

125. PRANGE, A. J., JR,. WHITE, J. E., LIPTON, M. A., et al.: Influence of age on monoamine oxidase and cathechol-o-methyltransferase in rat tissues. *Life Sci.*, 6:581-586, 1967.

126. ROBINSON, D. S., NIES, A., DAVIS, J. M., et al.: Aging, monoamines and monoamine oxidase. *Lancet*, 1:290-291, 1972.

127. NIES, A., ROBINSON, D. S., DAVIS, J. M., et al.: Changes in monoamine oxidase with aging. In: C. Eisdorfer and W. E. Fann (Eds.), *Psychopharmacology and Aging*. New York: Plenum Press, 1973, pp. 41-54.

128. ROBINSON, D. S.: Changes in monoamine oxidase and monoamines with human development and aging. *Fed. Proc.*, 34:103-107, 1975.

129. VAN PRAAG, H. M., KORF, J., LAKKE, L. P. W. F., et al.: The significance of dopamine in the diagnosis of depression, psychotic disorders and Parkinson's disease. In: J. R. Boissier, H. Hippius and P. Pichot (Eds.), *Neuropsychopharmacology*. Amsterdam: Excerpta Medica, 1975, pp. 186-194.

130. BOWERS, M. B. and GERBODE, R. A.: Relationship of monoamine metabolites in human cerebrospinal fluid to age. *Nature*, 219:1256-1257, 1968.

131. GOTTFRIES, C. G., GOTTFRIES, I., JOHANSSON, B., et al.: Acid monoamine metabolites in human cerebrospinal fluid and their relations to age and sex. *Neuropharmacol.*, 10:665-677, 1971.

132. REICHLMEIER, K., SCHLECHT, H., and IWANGOFF, P.: Enzyme activity changes in the aging human brain. *Experientia*, 33:798, 1977.

133. TIMARAS, P. S., HUDSON, D. B., and OKLUND, S.: Changes in central nervous system free amino acids with development and aging. In: D. H. Ford (Ed.), *Neurobiological Aspects of Maturation and Aging.* Amsterdam; *Prog. Brain Res.,* 40: 267-275, 1973.

134. McNAMARA, M. C.: Aging and the brain: The effect of electrically induced seizure on brain tyrosine and tryptophan hydroxylation *in vivo* in young and old rats. Ph.D. dissertation, University of North Carolina, Chapel Hill, North Carolina, 1975.

135. McNAMARA, M. C., MILLER, A. T., JR., BENIGNUS, V. A., et al.: Age-related changes in the effect of electroconvulsive shock (ECS) on the *in vivo* hydroxylation of tyrosine and tryptophan in rat brain. *Brain Res.,* 131:313-320, 1977.

136. GOLD, P. E. and McGAUGH, J. L.: Changes in learning and memory during aging. In: J. M. Ordy and K. R. Brizzee (Eds.), *The Neurobiology of Aging.* New York: Plenum Press; *Adv. Behav. Biol.,* 16:145-158, 1975.

137. SMITH, G. P.: The arousal function of central catecholamine neurons. *Ann. N.Y. Acad. Sci.,* 270:45-56, 1976.

138. BOWMAN, R. E. and WOLF, R. C.: Plasma 17-hydroxycorticosteroid response to ACTH. In M. Mulatta: Dose, age weight, and sex. *Proc. Soc. Exp. Biol. Med.,* 130:61-64, 1969.

139. HESS, G. O. and RIEGLE, G. D.: Adrenocortical responsiveness to stress and ACTH in aging rats. *J. Gerontol.,* 25:344-348, 1970.

140. RIEGLE, G. D., PRZEKOP, R., and NELLOR, J. E.: Changes in adrenocortical responsiveness to ACTH in fusion in aging goats. *J. Gerontal.,* 23:187-190, 1968.

141. BREZNOCK, E. M. and McQUEEN, R. D.: Adrenocortical function during aging in the dog. *Amer. J. Vet. Res.,* 31:1269-1273, 1970.

142. GRAD, B., KRAL, A., PAYNE, R. C., et al.: Plasma and urinary corticoids in young and old persons. *J. Gerontol.,* 22:66-71, 1967.

143. FRIEDMAN, M., GREEN, M. F., and SHARLAND, D. E.: Assessment of hypothalamic pituitary adrenal function in the geriatric age group. *J. Gerontol.,* 24:292-297, 1969.

144. BLICHERT-TOFT, M.: Secretion of corticotrophin and somatotrophin by the senescent adenohypophysis in the old rat by adrenal and neurohypophyseal hormones. *Gerontologia,* 11:129-140, 1965.

145. FRIEDMAN, S. M., NAKASHIMA, M., and FRIEDMAN, D. L.: Prolongation of life span in the old rat by adrenal and neurohypophyseal hormones. *Gerontologia,* 11:129-140, 1965.

146. DeWIED, D.: Pituitary-adrenal hormones and behavior, In: F. O. Schmitt and F. G. Worden (Eds.), *Neurosciences:*

Third Study Program. Cambridge: Cambridge Univ. Press, pp. 653-666.

147. CLEMENS, J. A. and MEITES, J.: Neuroendocrine status of old constant-estrous rats. *Neuroendocrinology,* 7:256-279, 1971.

148. MEITES, J., HUANG, H., and REIGLE, G. D.: Relation of the hypo-thalamo-pituitary-gonadal system to decline of reproductive functions in aging female rats. In: F. Labrie, J. Meites, and G. Pelletier (Eds.), *Hypothalamus and Endocrine Functions.* New York: Plenum Press, 1976, pp. 3-20.

149. KOVACS, K., RYAN, N., HORVATH, E., et al.: Prolactin cells of the human pituitary gland in old age. *J. Gerontol.,* 32:534-540, 1977.

150. KAPLAN, H. G. and HRESCHYSHEN, M. M.: Gas-liquid chroma-tographic quantitation of urinary estrogens in non-pregnant women, post-menopausal women and men. *Amer. J. Obstet. Gynecol.,* 111:286-390, 1971.

151. ZUMOFF, B. , BRADLOW, H. L., FINKELSTEIN, J., et al.: The influ-fluence of age and sex on the metabolism of testosterone. *J. Clin. Endocrinol. Metab.,* 42:703-706, 1976.

152. CHAN, S. W. C., LEATHEN, J. H., and ESAS, H. I. T.: Testicular metabolism and serum testosterone in aging male rats. *Endo-crinology,* 101:128-133, 1977.

153. DENCKLA, W. D.: A pituitary factor inhibiting the effects of the thyroid: Its possible role in aging. In: C. Eisdorfer and W. E. Fann (Eds.), *Psychopharmacology and Aging.* New York: Plenum Press, 1972, pp. 77-80.

154. DENCKLA, W. D.: A time to die. *Life Sci.,* 16:31-44, 1975.

155. DENCKLA, W. D.: Pituitary inhibitor of thyroxine. *Fed. Proc.,* 34:96, 1975.

156. SNYDER, P. J. and UTIGER, R. D.: Response to thyrotropin-re-leasing hormone (TRH) in normal man. *J. Clin. Endocrinol. Metab.,* 34:380-385, 1972.

157. DAVIS, P. J.: Endocrines and aging. *Hospital Practice,* 12:118-128, 1977.

158. KETY, S. S.: Human cerebral blood flow and oxygen consump-tion as related to aging. *J. Chron. Dis.,* 3:478-486, 1956.

159. SOKOLOFF, L.: Circulation and energy metabolism of the brain. In: G. J. Siegel, R. W. Albers, R. Katzman, and B. W. Agra-noff (Eds.), *Basic Neurochemistry.* Boston: Little, Brown & Co., 1976, pp. 388-413.

160. PENG, M. T., PENG, Y. I., and CHEN, R. M.: Age-dependent changes in the oxygen consumption of the cerebral cortex, hypothalamus, hippocampus, and amygdaloid in rats. *J. Geron-tol.,* 32:517-522, 1977.

161. NORRIS, A. H., SHOCK, N. W., and WAGMAN, I. H.: Age changes in the maximum conduction velocity of motor fibers of human ulnar nerves. *J. Appl. Physiol.,* 5:589-593, 1953.

162. FROLKIS, V. V., BEZRUKOV, V. V., DUPLENKO, Y. K., et al.: The hypothalamus in aging. *Exp. Gerontol.*, 7:169-184, 1972.
163. COTZIAS, G. C., MILLER, S. T., LANG, T. C., et al.: Levodopa, fertility and longevity. *Science*, 196:549-551, 1977.
164. TSAI, C. C. and YEN, S. S. C.: Acute effect of intravenous infusion of 17-estradiol on gonadotrophin release in pre- and post-menopausal women. *J. Clin. Endocrinol. Metab.*, 32:766, 1971.
165. BRANCONNIER, R. J., COLE, J. O., GANDOS, G.: ACTH$_{4-10}$ in the amelioration of neuropsychological symptomatology associated with senile organic brain syndrome (submitted).

4

Psychophysiologic and Cognitive Studies in the Aged

Carl Eisdorfer, Ph.D., M.D.

Central to much of the clinical and investigative interest in aging and geriatric psychiatry lies a concern with the issues of cognitive change. Studies of the central nervous system (CNS) and autonomic nervous system (ANS), using an array of psychophysiologic, biochemical and behavioral techniques, are often oriented to an understanding of differences in persons across and within age groups and address the question: What, if any, changes result from the aging process?

Though loss of ability with aging is often recognized, the results of numerous longitudinal studies do not support the hypothesis of a universal, progressive loss of cognitive functioning with advancing age (1). It remains to be determined whether cognitive change relates to primary or secondary aging (2), i.e., to aging as a process or to changes secondary to the disorders and traumata associated with longevity. Research methodology has itself brought the issue of change into sharp focus, since very different findings have resulted from the application of cross-sectional, longitudinal and cross-sequential strategies, as well as from differences in the populations studied using these designs.

This chapter reports on a number of fundamental issues related to the investigation of aging as a process and reviews attempts to identify and understand age-related change. The initial section describes psychophysiologic studies of the aged. Those studies selected for review are focused upon determining what CNS and ANS events are associated with aging, as well as upon the ways these events may be associated with the assessment of cognitive functioning. In addition, age-related differences between men and women are briefly discussed. The analysis of psychophysiological and performance differences in older men and women highlights a central issue in the comparative study of aging populations: individual differences in longevity and morbidity. Women live longer than men by rather substantial and growing amounts (3, 4). A later section selectively reviews the controversial literature on cognitive change and aging with an emphasis upon the difficulties in the study of change. This includes a particular emphasis and critique of the clinical measures applied in the assessment of cognition and change in cognition among the unimpaired aged. Furthermore, an analysis of assessment among the aged with cognitive impairment emphasizes the need to develop an improved behavioral technology to monitor change during aging. The final section focuses upon the need for future studies to bear upon the development of biobehavioral theories of change and aging.

PSYCHOPHYSIOLOGIC STUDIES

The field of study which addresses the interaction of physiologic and mental phenomena is eclectic and is subsumed under a variety of titles including biobehavior, behavioral physiology, behavioral biology, brain and behavior, neuropsychology and psychophysiology. Among these descriptors the use of the term psychophysiology has come to signify investigations which involve a simultaneous focus upon behavior and central or autonomic nervous system activity, reflected in a number of bioelectric measures and/or detectable physiologic assays of such tissue as blood or urine. In a review of a decade of psychophysiologic research in aging, Storrie and Eisdorfer

(5) reported that a number of shifts in research strategy had taken place in the period from the mid-1960s to 1976. These involved trends toward the use of multiple measures of somatic activity, more studies of "faster" bioelectric phenomena, and the simultaneous measurement of cognitive, affective and/or psychomotor performance in samples of subjects of different ages. Occasionally, these studies have involved longitudinal rather than simple cross-sectional observations of single age samples. More careful screening of older subjects has included health as well as cognitive controls, so that the "aged" are no longer represented from among those primarily in long-term care institutions or mental hospitals. Increasing the focus upon ANS-CNS activity and interaction has become fashionable, reflecting a trend toward the testing of hypotheses concerning state of arousal, the effects of feedback, anxiety and performance alteration rather than a collection of empirical data used primarily to document age differences.

However, difficulties still present themselves in our effort to improve psychophysiological research among the aged. Among these problems are the issues of age and cohort effect as they relate to sampling in cross-sectional and longitudinal studies, the necessity for more precise definitions of "health," as well as the difficulties in relating health to age (2). Furthermore, the measurement of cognitive performance relies upon the relatively poor instruments currently available, a matter which is particularly critical in the assessment of those elderly with cognitive impairment. There are other artifacts of measurement in old and young subjects relating to a number of somatic changes among the aged which could confuse the data between age groups, e.g. changes in skin texture and heart rate. Vascular responsivity and other somatic parameters also affect basal measurement, and therefore create statistical and interpretive problems in the definition of change from the different base rates of activity.

Age itself, as a variable, has often not been adequately sampled. Most studies aggregate all adults 65 years and older and then compare them with younger adults whose ages cover four or five decades of life span. The aged are a heterogeneous population: An emerging data base has described important differences observed between the "young-old," i.e., 60-75, and the "old-old," i.e., those 75 years and older. Despite these and other problems, a substantial information base has evolved as a foundation for understanding the psycho- physiology of aging and this, in turn, has become an important tool in understanding cognitive change in later life.

The next section of this paper will focus upon a few of the major areas of psychophysiologic study: changes in the electroencephal- ogram, the galvanic skin response (GSR) and electrodermal re- sponse (EDR), cardiovascular response (CVR) and other indices reflecting ANS activity relatable to cognition and learning.

Electroencephalographic Studies

Changes in the electroencephalogram (EEG) with age have been reported by numerous investigators, and Berger (6), Obrist (7, 8), Marsh and Thompson (9). Storrie and Eisdorfer (5) have con- tributed reviews of much of the work in the field. Busse and his col- leagues (10) were perhaps the first to report a diffuse, slow wave EEG activity among the elderly. Controversy has existed regarding the precise significance of this finding, but Obrist and others (11) ob- served that among the institutionalized aged there was a striking cor- relation bewteen slowing and motor performance on psychological tests. This pattern was not found in the community sample. Obrist (7) also reported that focal slowing on the left anterior temporal area did not correlate with WAIS performance on 48-hour memory reten- tion. Wang and others (12) similarly found no verbal-performance discrepancy on the WAIS in the community sample with left temporal foci, although they noted a decline in verbal scores for those subjects who manifested left temporal slowing across a three-and-one-half- year period.

Among patients with low blood pressure and vascular disease, a significant majority also show diffuse EEG slowing, according to Obrist (8) and Busse and Wang (13). In his analytic review Obrist (7) contends that EEG slowing in the aged reflects impaired cerebral circulation with resultant neuronal loss and cognitive defi- cit. Among those with known vascular disease or severe EEG shift, a relationship between cognition, cerebrovascular state and EEG has been established (7). Recent reports (14, 15) may support Obrist's thesis, at least with regard to cognitive impairment of the type associated with the senile dementias. However, while this model is justified by data among patients with demonstrable vascular problems and clear CNS disturbance, the studies of EEG and cognition among those free from known vascular disease are somewhat less clear. Wang and his associates (12) and Marsh and Thompson (9) present no data strongly supportive of Obrist's hypothesis as it relates to normal aging.

Marsh and Thompson (9) emphasize that, in contrast to the relatively slow alpha activity, beta activity on the EEG, i.e., 14-40 HZ low voltage "fast" waves, has received relatively little attention in studies of the aging. While it has been reported that the extent of beta activity increases in some portions of the aged population (16), additional supporting information is still needed, and the significance of that finding needs to be pursued.

The relationship between alpha rhythm and performance as a focus of investigation was restimulated, in part, by Liberson's (17) report that cerebral dysfunction could be examined by quantification of the blocking of alpha waves with the resultant appearance of low voltage fast activity. This blocking is accomplished through sensory stimulation. An analysis of the phenomenon has led to an activation theory, which predicts that the emerging increased EEG activity is correlationally associated with behavioral arousal reflected by change in a variety of parameters, e.g., faster reaction time (RT). In pursuit of this hypothesis, Wilson (18) demonstrated that elderly subjects do show less alpha blocking. Older subjects also habituated faster in Wilson's experiment, in contrast to findings of Thompson and Wilson (19). They observed differences in reactivity but no differences in resting EEG in two groups of older men who differed in learning ability, response to photic stimulation and alpha frequency.

Surwillo (20) summarized a series of EEG and reaction time studies and concluded 1) that the alpha rhythm reflects a timing or pacing mechanism and 2) that slowing of alpha is directly correlated with slowing in simple reaction time as well as complex decision-making time. While he has performed a series of elegant investigations, the data are only moderately supportive of his overall hypothesis. Woodruff's (21) attempt to test Surwillo's theory, using EEG biofeedback to first influence the alpha frequency and then measure RT, has yielded interesting, albeit somewhat confusing, results. She did, in fact, observe a significant shift in RT in the expected direction; subjects' attempts to increase their alpha rate resulted in decreased, i.e., faster, RT. Although RT shifted, however, there was no change in alpha. Therefore alpha frequency did not correlate with RT change. The inability of subjects to shift their mean alpha frequency is contrary to Woodruff's finding in a different portion of the study, demonstrating that older subjects not engaged in a performance task do indeed have the ability to alter alpha frequency through biofeedback.

When evoked responses in the brain are averaged (AER), responses to visual auditory or somatosensory stimulation do appear to change with age. Early components of AER show increases in latency and amplitude with increasing age through the middle years, while later components stabilize in youth and increase somewhat in later life. These late components seem more related to cognitive processing than information loading (9). The late positive component, referred to as P-3 or P-300, does not show specific age changes in relation to auditory stimulation (22), but does increase with visual stimulation (9).

Marsh did not observe age-related differential asymmetry between cerebral hemispheres in his attempt to study verbal and visual motor discrepancy in IQ tests. However, recent evidence suggests that patients with significant cognitive disorders, e.g., senile dementia, may show hemispheric differences in evoked potentials (23). Visser and colleagues (24) also studied evoked potentials in older persons with Alzheimer's disease of early and late onset, the commonest form of cognitive disorder in the elderly. Compared with normals, the Alzheimer's patients had longer latencies for all but the earliest components. John and his colleagues (25) also reported that "neurometric" profiles derived from a computer-assisted analysis of the EEG yield differences between cognitively impaired and non-impaired aged patients. Many aspects of the EEG and evoked potential are mathematically treated in the automated computer-based technology which is part of John's strategy to develop a numerical taxonomy based upon EEG findings and performance as well as diagnostic criteria.

An interesting phenomenon of the EEG, termed the contingent

negative variation (CNV), results when two stimuli appear sequentially with the subject being alerted by the first to react behaviorally to the second. The resultant negative shift in average potential is presumed to be an index, or at least a correlate, of attention or arousal. Marsh and Thompson (26) and McCallum and Walter (27) have shown that CNV's have smaller amplitude in older persons. Harkins and others (28), in a study of 12 healthy men (aged 64-77), reported that CNV was predictive of the speed of RT. In addition, McCallum and Walter showed that younger subjects who are anxious have patterns during acquisition of the CNV similar to older subjects. Further investigations with the CNV are now in progress and may yield interesting insights as to older persons' ability to attend and as a measure against which to compare other changes.

Sleep EEG studies have demonstrated that older persons spend less time in rapid eye movement (REM) activity (29) and that Stage IV or slow wave sleep is also diminished (30, 31, 32). This change is particularly impressive in pathologic states. These findings have led to the postulation of a relationship between REM and/or slow wave deficits in sleep and cognition (32). In a report of a longitudinal study (33), it was indicated that diminished WAIS performance was correlated with a reduction in REM and slow wave activity. Although Eleftheriou and others (34) reported similar findings in mice, they observed important differences across strains. It is of interest that in those mice in which REM activity was observed to be totally absent, the authors reported an accelerated aging process reflected in a number of biologic changes.

In their excellent review of the use of the EEG in the assessment of life span changes, Michalewski and Thompson (35) report that, while the EEG provides information about the brain and insight into brain-behavior relationships in the aged, tests have not yet been developed which can put much of this information into practice. They particularly feel that data from studies of the evoked potential of special slow wave recordings may be of value in the future. Storrie and Eisdorfer (5) comment that further dynamic testing, better understanding of sleep EEG records, as well as the development and evaluation of complex, computer-assisted interpretive technologies such as those of John and his associates (25), are promising avenues to understanding how brain electrical activity reflects subtle changes in brain-behavior relationships. These strategies can be implemented through technological advances that facilitate the collection and analysis of massive amounts of data. The result may be the development of better correlates of the discrete components of the EEG patterns in conjunction with blood flow and delineated behavioral measurements. There has been a long-standing criticism of the EEG as an envelope of electrical activity that is difficult to decipher without being opened and its parts better defined. While this criticism is still valid, recent major strides have been made in measurement and understanding of the complex elements of brain electrical activity with evoked as well as resting and sleep records.

Galvanic Skin Response

The galvanic skin response (GSR) has been a frequently employed technique in psychophysiology and one of the earliest used in gerontologic research to reflect autonomic arousal. In general, the findings argue that older subjects show a reduction in electrodermal functioning (9) and present "underaroused" patterns in comparison with young adults. This is not entirely the case, however; Shmavonian and Busse (36) demonstrated that, although aged subjects generally had a less responsive GSR than younger subjects, the GSR response of older subjects was greater than that of the young in reaction to words which were emotionally charged for the aged. Their data suggest that highly meaningful material minimized age differences in GSR, and a recent study (37) supports these findings. While young subjects had higher tonic skin conductance levels than old subjects, the age difference did not reach significance, and both groups showed the same magnitude of specific response during learning (37).

The experimental design involved the simultaneous presence of an indwelling venous catcher and other psychophysiologic sensors, which could have influenced basal autonomic levels such that even the baseline measures may have indicated some heightened autonomic activity. Interestingly enough, Wilkie and Eisdorfer (37) reported that the EDR was associated with fewer omission errors in learning among the aged, and this is reminiscent of the Shmavonian and Busse (36) finding of better memory for words associated with heightened GSR in older subjects.

Eisdorfer, Doerr and Follette (38) have recently reported a study of age and sex differences on the GSR, using a relatively nonthreatening strategy. Resting electrodermal (EDR) levels were obtained for 98 men and women who were in one of three age groups: young (21-26); middle-aged (36-59); and old (61-79). Subsequent to the obtaining of a basal level of electrodermal activity, each subject was asked to perform a valsalva maneuver. As expected, there was a significant age effect in basal conductance level with older persons, showing a reduction in basal activity compared with the young. When the specific EDR in response to the valsalva maneuver was expressed relative to the basal level, however, there was no difference in response magnitude and, indeed, the aged approached higher levels of specific relative response.

Of particular interest, too, is the finding that in comparison with men, women at every age level showed lower resting EDR and also significantly greater elevation in specific EDR relative to their basal levels. The results of this study, in demonstrating a different pattern between the sexes, raise the question of whether this reflects a greater efficiency in specific autonomic response to stimulation among women, while men routinely manifest a higher degree of autonomic activity, even at rest. The interpretations regarding age-related changes are interesting in their own right, but several questions are raised by this cross-sectional design. It remains to be determined whether there is a relative survivorship of persons with lower basal electrodermal responsivity, e.g., women and the aged, or whether a change in electrodermal level occurs with aging which reflects autonomic nervous system change through the years.

Clearly, the cumulative data on electrodermal responses are interesting, but at the same time they highlight the complex issues of investigating individual differences, including sex differences, in age-related change. In recent years there has been a tendency to couple EDR performance with measures of heart rate, and the relationship has not been a simple one to establish.

Heart Rate

Studies of heart rate, per se, have been confusing, but the Laceys' (39) description of heart rate deceleration preceding reaction time has been valuable in stimulating interest in this phenomenon as a mechanism for the facilitation of externally demanded performance such as reaction time. While older persons show less deceleration than do the young (40, 41) their reaction time is unimpaired. This would suggest that the precise significance of the relationship between cardiac deceleration and performance could be reinterpreted. Data collected from elderly subjects since the report of Nowlin and his colleagues (41) indicates that the aged are not greatly different from the young in responsivity, despite a change in psychophysiologic pattern. Indeed, the latter may be a reflection of the ability of older persons to show a shift in total configuration of autonomic activity which is unrelated to behavior. However, as indicated earlier, this result requires further confirmation.

Other ANS Measures

The hypothesis that internal activity uniformly drops with age is disputed by the findings of Powell and others (42) and Wilkie and Eisdorfer (37, 43), who demonstrated heightened ANS activity among the aged in a serial learning task. Circulating levels of serum free fatty acid (FFA) were measured throughout the duration of learning, and aged males (65-79) showed significant elevations in FFA levels compared to the younger (25-45-year-old) men (43). The FFA levels remained elevated for a longer period among the aged.

Wilkie and Eisdorfer (37) recently reported the results of concurrent measurements of FFA, GSR and heart rate in relation to learning in men aged 19-25 years (mean age 22 years), and 60-79 (mean age, 68). They replicated the now often repeated finding that old men appear to have poorer learning scores compared to the young, primarily because of heightened omission errors. Of salient interest here are the psychophysiologic data indicating no basal difference in heart rate or tonic electrodermal response (EDR) but a lower heart rate in the young. While the young had a significantly greater percent increase in heart rate (HR) during learning, they began the drop to their resting HR level during the task, while the older subjects' HR's remained elevated. The EDR reactivity pattern was not significantly different for young and old men, corroborating the observations of Eisdorfer, Doerr and Follette (38).

In the instance of FFA, the aged show significant elevation in absolute levels of circulating plasma levels during the resting, late learning, and recovery phases of the study. Furthermore, the earlier observation (44) that FFA levels peak among the aged 15 minutes after the end of learning was replicated in the Wilkie and Eisdorfer study (43). In that study there was also the finding of greater relative FFA increase in younger men during one of the three blood samples drawn during learning. It is notable, however, that aged subjects seem more aroused than young ones during the resting phase of the Wilkie and Eisdorfer (37) study in two of the three psychophysiological measures taken (HR and FFA). While on all of the indices young men peaked and began to return to resting level during the learning phase itself, older persons did not show their peak ANS response until late in learning or until the post-learning measurement during the resting phase.

In his recent overview of a series of studies, Frolkis (45) reports heightened electrical thresholds for a variety of ANS end organ receptors. At the same time, he reports marked increases in end organ receptivity to the neurochemical environment, including neurotransmitters such as serotonin, acetylcholine and hormones such as thyroxin and insulin. It is Frolkis' contention that with aging there is a significantly increased sensitivity of receptor sites to neurotransmitters, and that hypersensitivity may characterize certain ANS and CNS end organ receptor sites. The resultant dyssynchrony in ANS-CNS activity could be the etiology of a host of age-related problems, including sensitivity to drugs, CNS-ANS dissociation and disruption in homeostasis among older persons.

Eisdorfer and his colleagues (31, 42, 46, 47) have performed a series of studies and postulated that heightened arousal in older men might account for the greater tendency toward omission errors and resultant poorer performance in learning. Indeed, they indicated that impairment in test performance, rather than learning per se, may be a major factor in creating the observed pattern of age-related learning deficit. They employed a beta adrenergic blocking agent (propranolol) in a study of learning among older men and did improve responsivity in learning performance above that of a control group who received a saline placebo (47). Although improvement in performance was associated with diminished FFA and EDR levels of arousal in persons given propranolol, the group receiving the saline placebo and showing no such physiological effect also demonstrated a significant improvement in learning, albeit the improvement was significantly less among the placebo group than among the subjects who received propranolol and manifested beta blockade. Froehling (48) administered a lower dose of propranolol to a group of brighter subjects instructed to perform a paired associate rather than a serial rote learning task, and did not observe improved learning performance. However, the data collected in the two studies are somewhat difficult to compare, since the subjects in the Froehling study had higher levels of performance on the initial task and did not show the GSR blockade, perhaps because of the drug dosage employed. They did, however, show partial FFA blocking.

More work needs to be done to explicate this area, since Herr and Birren (49), using an animal model, supported the Eisdorfer, Nowlin and Wilkie (47) finding. Of particular importance is the relationship between FFA and arousal. These biochemical data have, in general, supported the thesis that autonomic arousal is observed during advancing age, whereas other measures, e.g., GSR, have tended not to support it. While Eisdorfer's thesis and pattern of results are in general agreement with the Frolkis hypothesis, the data regarding underlying events at the synaptic end organ level are still too ambiguous to make such an ambitious speculation.

The general hypothesis that hyperarousal is associated with diminished responsivity, as well as the inference that older persons are caught up in a failure to reinforce their responses with lessened ability and then greater tendency to inhibit responses, is still compelling. However, the counterhypothesis that lower levels of activity lead to a lower base rate of responsivity is equally if not more difficult to reject in view of the available evidence. Proponents of the overarousal hypothesis have speculated that the need to achieve as a motivating force among the young may be complicated by a fear of failure emerging in later life, which results in a tendency in the aged to become more conservative in their response patterns. This could impact upon personal style and problem-solving abilities.

The possibility that different physiologic measures may reflect aging in differential ways has also been raised by the findings of Wilkie and Eisdorfer (37, 43) that the correlation between concurrent psychophysiologic measures is not significant, even though individual measures correlate with performance. This supports the Laceys' (39) contention that marked individual differences in psychophysiologic patterns exist among individuals and suggests that aging change may be best studied by examining multiple concurrent psychophysiologic measures in a longitudinal or cross-sequential rather than cross-sectional paradigm.

In summary, it seems clear that any simplistic notion that there are unidirectional psychophysiologic changes among the aged, or that the aged are not as autonomically responsive as the young, must be discarded in the light of the current data, however confusing these data may appear to the scientists currently involved in their collection.

Sex Differences

In view of the increased life expectancy of women over men, as well as in relation to other social changes, it is interesting to note the emergence of limited data contrasting behavioral and psychophysiologic functioning in older men and women. Both longitudinal and cross-sectional studies have supported the general conclusion that older women seem to perform better on verbal tasks, while men do better on spatial tests (50). Wang and Busse (16) found faster EEG frequency and greater amplitude among older females, and Wilkie and Eisdorfer (51) found that, while highly intelligent older men and women performed similarly in a paced serial learning task, average older women (age 60-79) performed significantly better than age- and intelligence-matched males at the fast (4 sec.) but not at the slow (10 sec.) pace. The tendency of women to respond was the crucial variable and may reflect one of the several reported differences in reported cognitive style between the sexes (52, 53). These data raise speculation about cerebral dominance patterns at various life stages.

It may be that earlier lateralization of the left cerebral hemisphere in females (52) results in better patterns of verbal abilities, while males may maintain bilateral functioning for both verbal and spatial abilities, thus perhaps developing better spatial abilities or at least better performance in spatial tasks. Although these hypotheses still require much data, research in this area seems to be developing apace. Apart from yielding valuable information of possible differential abilities of the sexes, it could yield valuable insights into an understanding of cerebral hemisphere dominance in performance. In addition, the genetic and environmental influences upon sex hormonal configuration on these variables throughout the developmental life cycle is an important area for investigation. Study of differential patterns of cognitive functioning between the sexes only highlights the need for a strategy directed toward elucidating the pattern of individual differences versus cognitive changes throughout life.

Intellectual and Cognitive Functioning and Adult Life Change

It is particularly noteworthy that the investigation of intellectual changes with advancing age in adults has generated a heated controversy in the behavioral sciences literature. A number of authors have contended that the cross-sectional studies of intellectual functioning have yielded spurious results, implying a progressive loss of intelligence with advancing age post-maturity (54, 55). After a series of papers best characterized by the title of one of them, "Aging and IQ: The Myth of the Twilight Years," Baltes and Schaie (54) review their cross-sequential studies of intellectual functioning from mid-life into the sixth decade. Jarvik (56) emphasized "from our own research at the New York State Psychiatric Institute, if illness does *not* intervene, cognitive stability is the rule and can be maintained into the ninth decade. . . ." Wilkie and Eisdorfer (57) are among the few investigators who have specifically examined health status and cognition and reported that elevated diastolic blood pressure rather than age per se was a factor in the intellectual decline of a group of subjects seen initially at ages 60-69 and followed over a ten-year period using the WAIS. Subjects were drawn from the Duke Longitudinal Study and showed no decline until at least the eighth decade of life if they had normal or slightly elevated blood pressure. Those hypertensive subjects initially seen between ages 70 and 79 did not survive the ten-year followup.

On the other side of this controversy are a number of authors, including Botwinick (1) and Horn (58), who indicate that age clearly is associated with deficits in performance affecting a variety of cognitive measures. The resolution of this issue appears to reside in the comparison of data from differing research strategies and is in part a semantic problem. In interpreting the data, it is important to define more precisely the age of the target population in the various studies, the measures which are used, and the research methodology employed.

The controversy may stem in part from Wechsler's (59) initial conclusion that most human abilities decline progressively after the mid-20s. There are now data from a number of studies which question these conclusions (54, 60, 61) and which have produced evidence that there is no clear peaking of intelligence with age during the third decade of life. Even Botwinick (1), Horn (58), and others who have been major proponents of the hypothesis supporting the decline of intelligence in adulthood agree that there is no simple unidimensional drop in intelligence past the third decade of life. The question, then, becomes not so much decline versus no decline, but a matter of what, if any, components decline, and when and under what conditions, if at all, decline is observed.

Eichorn (62), assessing data from the Berkeley Growth Study, states, "That increments in mental ability occur during adulthood no longer seems debatable. The questions become: in what, for whom, and when? In the Berkeley Growth Study the overall trend from 16 to 36 years is an increase, although at a decelerating rate for males, while females show a very slight decline after 26 years. No subtest, however, conforms exactly to this pattern."

Owens (63, 64) reported that those inductees who scored high on their intelligence tests on induction into the military in World War I sustained their ability into their late adult years. His results seem to indicate that subjects scoring higher on intelligence tests stay brighter longer. In their report of a ten-year study of subjects in the Duke Longitudinal Study I, Eisdorfer and Wilkie (66) indicated that their data reflected in part the effects of a differential dropout of lower scoring nonsurvivors. The surviving subjects seem to have had higher initial scores on the WAIS testing with more stable levels on repeated examinations. In their conclusions Eisdorfer and Wilkie (65) indicated that there was far more intellectual decline over a ten-year period in a group of subjects who were seen initially at age 70 or above than among those who were in their 60s at the time of the original testing. In a study of younger subjects, Honzik and Macfarlane (66) reported that "intellectual functioning was relatively stable over the age period 6-40 years for a representative urban sample." Bayley (67) developed a theoretical curve of the growth of intelligence to the mid-30s. Horn (58) indicates that while some functions "are markedly decreasing throughout adulthood, there are indications of intelligence which either are not decreasing or are decreasing at only a slow rate. Indeed, [sic] these results suggest that major components of crystallized intelligence (Gc) are increasing during the same period that fluid intelligence (Gf) increases." In the statement of Horn we also see the emergence of another major variable, namely that in part the determination as to whether the decline does or does not exist may reside in the particular component of intelligence being measured.

Thus, using standardized psychometric tests of intelligence, the data would indicate that there may not be a profound drop in overall intellectual ability at least during the middle years of life and that initial level and a variety of other factors play a role in performance. It seems clear from an impressive array of evidence that decline in intelligence reported to begin from the mid-20s (59) is based on a purely cross-sectional strategy and is perhaps not a valid position in the light of consistent current findings that some intellectual factors are stable or increase perhaps to ages in the early 30s and even on to the 50s (54, 63, 64).

On the other side of the argument is Horn's (58, 68) position that intelligence is a complex structure and, depending upon what is being measured, we may see decline at various ages. Definitions of intelligence have, of course, been an elusive challenge in psychology. Intelligence in its broad dimensions has been identified as an adaptive capacity, but in developing tests of intelligence it has never been clear precisely what is being adapted to. Since educational needs have dominated psychometric test development, school performance, occupational achievement or the lack of ability to achieve in school, i.e., children with mental retardation, are the most likely criteria for the tests developed. Operationally, however, intelligence becomes that which is measured by the test.

Horn (58, 69, 70, 71) perhaps has made the most systematic effort to develop a psychometric strategy for the measurement of intelligence or human ability systems in middle-aged and older populations. He and his colleagues (59, 68, 70, 71) have adopted and adapted a series of measures to define intellectual and cognitive ability. Briefly their view is that results now indicate the presence of a fairly substantial number of primary cognitive abilities which emerge from factor analytic studies of intelligence. Horn (58) estimates that there are now in the neighborhood of 25 distinct components of intelligence, and he posits broad abilities, which include creativity, verbal-productive thinking, expressional fluency, associational fluency, general reasoning and visualization, as well as spatial-perceptual-practical intelligence. Auditory abilities, such as rhythm, nonsymbolic recognition memory, masked speech comprehension and auditory reasoning, represent others.

In an effort to simplify this very complex array of factors, Horn has grouped these abilities into two second-order factor dimensions, crystallized intelligence (Gc) and fluid intelligence (Gf), a theoretical structure postulated by Horn and Cattell (70). Crystallized intelligence involves awareness of concepts and terms pertaining to a large array of subjects, including information, vocabulary and a variety of verbal areas associated with accumulated knowledge. Its counterpart, fluid intelligence (Gf), relates to facility in problem solving and reasoning involving the learning and manipulation of new information. Fluid abilities relate particularly to manipulation of nonverbal symbolic and semantic materials, including certain verbal abilities, letter series and word groupings. From much of Horn's work it becomes clear that the patterns of change, of crystallized and fluid intelligence through age, are quite different. Crystallized intelligence would appear to increase throughout adult life into the 50s, while Gf appears to grow and then level and begin to drop off, perhaps as early as age 20. In accord with the argument of Horn and his colleagues, it is important to recognize that there is no simple answer to the issue of decline in age. In assessing change, individual components of intelligence, or at the very least Gc and Gf, must be identified and treated almost independently. It has already been demonstrated that, by varying the subtests of Gc and Gf, a pattern of decline or nondecline can be fitted to an aged population (58). This was accomplished by development of an omnibus intelligence test, which showed no decline by simply varying the ratio of Gc and Gf power within the aggregated test.

It is clear that intellectual growth and change during the life span are complex multidetermined phenomena. Jarvik and her associates (55, 72) have shown the importance of genetics in predicting intellectual change throughout the life span, and Cohen and Wilkie (50) have described differences between the sexes in the pattern of cognitive performance in later years. Wilkie and Eisdorfer (57) have demonstrated that blood pressure is an important factor in intellectual performance as well as longevity, and Eisdorfer and Wilkie (73) have summarized a considerable number of studies involving physical and stress-related variables which affect cognitive performance.

Among the various factors associated with change in intellectual functioning, one phenomenon has generated particular interest (65, 74), that of the so-called terminal drop. Kleemeier (74) reported that intellectual decline, particularly among performance-type measures, preceded death by only a few years. Jarvik and Falek (55) also reported a decline in intellectual performance preceding death (over a longer period), while Berkowitz and Green (75), who studied a younger population, did not. Eisdorfer and Wilkie (65) reported higher initial test scores among the group of survivors in a longitudinal study, and Botwinick's (1) review suggests that "certain test performance levels or changes in these levels over time relate to closeness to death." Siegler's (76) analysis of eight longitudinal investigations indicates that the phenomenon of "terminal drop" is more complex than suspected. While the extent of any such drop is still subject to some question, the data indicate that poorer health or health-shortening variables, e.g., blood pressure, cholesterol, are associated with poorer performance and that higher test performance usually occurs with greater distance from death.

Memory

The data on age differences in memory are difficult to assess. Craik's (77) recent review reflects the emergence of much information which is as yet relatively unsystematized, and much of which does not apply specifically to the aged. A three-stage process was envisioned for memory, including perception, short-term and long-term storage. This view is now being redefined, since short-term memory and long-term memory appear to be overlapping constructs, and there is no discrete short-term to long-term memory shift. Primary memory (PM) and secondary memory (SM) are constructs which are currently being considered as the processes by which events are incorporated and stored. Primary memory follows adequate sensory stimulation and refers to material which is still in the mind and being processed, while SM is stored. Material from SM must be retrieved to be identified; thus "immediate recall" will involve reports from some PM and retrieval from SM. PM is served by different processes than SM and these processes are currently under investigation.

Age differences in PM are negligible according to Craik's (77) analysis of a variety of studies. Secondary memory (SM) is impaired among older, normal subjects in comparison with the young under a variety of conditions, but recognition is minimally, if at all impaired, in contrast to recall of material. Older subjects may learn material initially less well than do the young and therefore show more difficulty in subsequent recall (77), and they may be more subject to interference from other material (78). The widespread belief that very long-term memory remains intact in the aged is not supportable (77).

The primary need in studies of memory is for more longitudinal parametric data, as well as controlled experimental data. Since memory and memory testing are so potentially valuable (79) for our consideration of clinical states, the paucity of information directly applicable to older, normal and pathologically impaired subjects is particularly disturbing.

Neuropsychology

The difficulty in defining normal patterns of intellectual change with aging has created serious problems in our attempt to assess abnormal or clinically deviant cognitive performance. Since clinical assessment of cognition among the aged is of such practical concern, it is no surprise that several strategies have been employed to distinguish normal from pathologic aging. The two primary approaches to clinical assessment have been through the use of the traditional psychometric approaches and through the use of neuropsychological techniques. The two strategies share much in common but have evolved from somewhat different heritages. The psychometric approach has had its roots in the assessment of intelligence and performance related to such predictors as school or military achievement, while the neuropsychological approach emerged from a concern with the effects of cortical damage and psychopathology. Meier (80) proposes that neuropsychology is one of the three major avenues to the scientific study of brain-behavior relationships in man. Apart from clinical neuropsychology, which involves the use of objective, standardized psychological techniques in the assessment of cortical function, he proposes that physiological psychology and behavioral psychology complete the triad.

Historically, clinical neuropsychology dates from the attempt, by psychologists and neurologists, to define and test for "organicity." These were probably related, in turn, to attempts on the part of clinicians to distinguish between organic and functional psychoses and were influenced in large measure by the mental measurements approach. The shift from the generalized organicity model to a more specific delineation of neuropsychological function can in large measure be credited to Halstead (81), whose test battery was enlarged and investigated in a rather considerable number of studies by Reitan (82, 83, 84, 85), Benton (86) and other associates. A number of the studies on the use of the Halstead-Reitan in adults have been summarized by Klove (87).

The Halstead-Reitan includes ten measures ranging from the Categories test (in which subjects must demonstrate their understanding of the unifying principle involving four stimulus figures projected on the screen by selecting one of the images) to such subtests as speed of finger tapping and identification of shapes and the placement of these shapes in a form board, using only tactual cues. The ten tests are designed to assess a variety of cognitive, visual, spatial and tactual-kinesthetic functions. Performance on the neuropsychological battery has been related to localization of brain lesions, in some instances with remarkable precision (87).

While the use of neuropsychological techniques holds considerable promise for the study of normal aging, the literature on neuropsychological testing and normal aging is relatively sparse. Deficit as a function of age past 45 is reported (83, 88), but is modifiable by higher education and social class status (89). While older subjects do more poorly on complex problem-solving tasks, they do as well or better on tasks involving experience in learning (88, 89, 90, 91). Reitan suggests, too, that similarities between neuropsychological performance of normal aged and younger subjects with brain damage indicate that a relationship may exist between aging itself and brain damage. He (82) cautions that there is no causal relationship established between aging and brain damage, however. Hallenbeck (92), on the other hand, feels that age and organic brain disease show quite different patterns of neuropsychologic performance.

Clinical Studies of Cognition

It is noteworthy that in his extensive review of intelligence and psychopathology, particularly involving the Wechsler test of intelligence, Matarazzo (93) did not deal with the diagnosis of brain damage in the elderly. In their review of clinical assessment in aging, Schaie and Schaie (94) indicate that a comparison of Wechsler's subtest performance among the aged patients with and without "chronic diffuse brain damage" indicates that the patterns are quite different between the samples. The verbal-performance discrepancy is reversed among the aged from what might have been suspected from the hypothesis that older age performance is the same as that of brain damage in younger adults. Crook (97) also reports that the utility of psychometric assessment techniques is extremely limited in the impaired aged. While there is support for the position that many tests used for assessing performance among young adults are inappropriate for the aged (96), analyses of individual tests are not without controversy. Among the tests which have been reported to be useful in discriminating between young and old, as well as between brain-damaged and non-brain-damaged, is the digit subtest of the WAIS. On the other hand, the Schaies' (94) report that the trail-making test from the Halstead-Reitan battery is not felt to be valid, with many false classifications increasing with age. This belief is not shared by Ball and Reitan (91). In all it has been estimated that more than 60 standardized psychological tests have been employed during the past decade and most of these are "clearly inappropriate" for use with cognitively impaired older persons and in many instances for older cohorts in general (97). Overall and Gorham (95), using multiple discriminant analyses involving WAIS subtests, suggest that Similarities, Digit Symbol Picture Arrangement, and Object Assembly decline relative to Vocabulary among normal aged. However, brain damaged patients show a contrast between Similarities, Vocabulary and Object Assembly, on the one hand, and Comprehension, Arithmetic and Picture Completion, on the other, with the first three being more sensitive to organic brain syndrome than to age. This pattern suggests that it should be possible to develop psychometric, if not neuropsychological, batteries to assess performance of brain-damaged elderly.

A brief review of the factors which influence the examination of older persons using tests of cognition is in order. These include, at the outset, the validity of the measures employed. Although validity itself involves a complex set of variables, many tests of intelligence and cognitive ability were developed with academic or work (military) performance as the criterion, and the acquisition of academically related material has face validity. It is clear that measures appropriate for predicting the performance of children and young adults may be less so with respect to the performance of older adults and the aged. Differences in test-taking ability itself may represent a problem for older persons, who, characteristically, are more cautious (1) and less experienced than more schooled and test-wise young adults. This is, in part, a cohort problem, which could change as future generations of young adults age, but to a considerable extent the predictable ongoing changes in the education of children and young adults will eventually result in new cohort differences.

Anxiety about learning and of examination and laboratory situations may result in the greater tendency toward inhibition of responses among the aged, who could profit from repeated measures and adaptation to the assessment setting (46). A strategy of familiarizing older persons to testing is rarely, if ever, employed and most clinical data are analyzed after a single test session. Better instructions may be more important to older persons than younger persons (98) and performance speed is a particular problem (31) for the aged. Older persons may also be more distractible than the young and seem particularly susceptible to irrelevant stimuli (78, 99).

Fatigue is another important factor in performance which discriminates more against the aged than the young, and mode of presentation, i.e., visual, auditory, tactual, is also a consideration, particularly for those aged who are more likely to have sensory impairment (100, 101). Health appears to have a significant influence on performance, and the aged are more likely to suffer from health deficits and a variety of somatic variables ranging from drug problems to infections to endocrine and metabolic disorders, all of which are known to affect cognitive functioning, in some instances quite profoundly (102). Identification of affective states, particularly including the depressions, also appears to be an important consideration for psychometric evaluation, since such states have a strong influence on cognitive functioning and exacerbate measurement error (102).

These factors all act to complicate evaluation of cognitive functioning in patients and nonpatients alike and may play a determining role in our ability to assess a patient's current state as well as to plot change through the natural history of a disorder or to assess therapeutic efficacy of a treatment modality (103, 104).

CLINICAL ISSUES

As we have come to recognize that "senility" is a term best relegated to the lexicon of medical historians rather than to clinical use, it also becomes evident that the paucity of laboratory techniques for the assessment of the cognitively impaired elderly has emerged as a problem of substantial importance. Even the terminology of those clinical problems involving impaired cognition among the aged has been confusing. For example, the use of a term such as Acute Organic Brain Syndrome to describe a broad class of disorders, some of which take months to develop, and are in the aggregate characterized by reversibility rather than time of onset, still pervades our literature (105). Since the course of disease is a major component in the differential diagnosis of the organic brain syndromes, and since the level of cognitive functioning may be an important consideration in clinical care, regular assessment of cognitive functioning would seem to be valuable. Senile dementias of the various types may have different presentations at outset and differing responses to treatment as well as differing courses (102, 106). Efforts to develop new pharmacologic, as well as other, therapeutic strategies for patients with the senile dementias will require the separation of organically impaired patients into appropriate diagnostic categories based upon the etiology of their disorder since those treatments best suited for multi-infarct dementia may have little value for dementia secondary to primary neuronal degeneration (Alzheimer's variety) (104, 107, 108). Failure to discriminate between patient groups will thus risk serious error in research methodology (104), as well as clinical care (107).

Since the natural history of the senile dementias is still largely unknown, charting the clinical course may yield valuable epidemiologic data, as well as provide a more appropriate basal level against which to chart changes. Relatively recent data suggest that primary neuronal degeneration rather than cerebrovascular dysfunction is the source of most dementing illness in the aged (109, 110). In view of the growing activity in investigating this disorder and other associated disturbances, such as normal pressure hydrocephalus (111, 112), geriatric alcoholism, Wernicke's-Korsakoff's syndrome and Huntington's chorea, increased support is emerging for the contention that a stronger base of diagnostic laboratory and cognitive performance measures is needed. Of interest, too, is the contention (109) that Alzheimer's disease and senile dementia of primary neuronal degeneration are the same disorder emerging at different points in the life cycle, and that these disorders are not distinguishable neuropathologically from aging of the brain. This contention has rather dramatic implications for our society in view of the pattern of lengthening adult human life (4, 80).

A number of genetic studies raise some question about Terry and Wisniewski's (109) hypothesis, however, since early onset dementia of the classic Alzheimer's variety shows a different family morbidity record than does late onset dementia secondary to neuronal degeneration of unknown etiology (the Alzheimer's variant) (113, 114). There is controversy about this class of disorders and its course, and obviously more data are needed. Indeed, the data which address this issue could help us understand not only the disease process(es), but the issues of CNS pathology and brain functioning, as well as more about cognitive functioning in normal aging.

There may be some light on the horizon. Miller and Lewis (115), for example, have demonstrated that depression, which often may masquerade as one of the senile dementias (44, 102), may be distinguishable from other forms of cognitive loss by psychological testing. The role of cognitive evaluation is certainly changing and moving from global generalized measures of orientation, memory and information to more microanalytic techniques emerging from an array of cognitive and psychophysiologic laboratories and clinics. As we understand more about the aging process and the specific elements of cognitive performance which change with normal aging, we should significantly strengthen our ability to evaluate clinical problems in the aged and the effect of emerging therapies for this group of hitherto relatively ignored patients.

REFERENCES

1. BOTWINICK, J.: Intellectual abilities. In: J. E. Birren and K. W. Schaie (Eds.), *Handbook of the Psychology of Aging.* New York: Van Nostrand Reinhold Company, 1977, pp. 580-602.
2. BUSSE, E. W.: Theories of aging. In: E. W. Busse and E. Pfeiffer (Eds.), *Behavior and Adaptation in Late Life.* Boston: Little, Brown, 1969, pp. 11-32.
3. MYERS, GEORGE C.: Future age projections and society. Paper presented at World Conference on Aging: A Challenge for Science and Social Policy. Organized by L'Institute de la Vie. Vichy, France: April, 1977. (Proceedings in press.)
4. HAUSER, P. M.: Aging and world-wide population change. In: R. H. Binstock and E. Shanas (Eds.), *Handbook of Aging and the Social Sciences.* New York: Van Nostrand Reinhold Company, 1976, pp. 58-86.
5. STORRIE, M. and EISDORFER, C.: Psychophysiological studies in aging: A ten-year review. In: A. DiMascio (Ed.), *Psychopharmacology: A Generation of Progress.* 1977, pp. 1489-1497.
6. BERGER, H.: On the electroencephalogram of man: Twelfth report. *Electroencephalo. Clin. Neurophysiol.*, 19:394-397, 1965.

7. OBRIST, W. D.: Cerebral physiology of the aged: Relation of psychological function. In: N. R. Burch and H. Altshuler (Eds.), *Behavior and Brain Electrical Activity.* New York: Plenum Press, 1975, pp. 421-430.

8. OBRIST, W. D.: Cerebral ischemia and the senescent electroencephalogram. In: E. Simonson and T. H. McGavack (Eds.), *Cerebral Ischemia.* Springfield, Illinois: Charles C Thomas, 1964, pp. 71-98.

9. MARSH, G. R. and THOMPSON, L. W.: Psychophysiology of aging. In: J. E. Birren and K. W. Schaie (Eds.), *Handbook of the Psychology of Aging.* New York: Van Nostrand Reinhold Company, 1977, pp. 219-248.

10. SILVERMAN, A. J., BUSSE, E. W., and BARNES, R. H.: Studies in in the process of aging: Electroencephalographic findings in 400 elderly subjects. *Electroencephalo. Clin. Neurophysiol.,* 7:67-74, 1955.

11. OBRIST, W. D., BUSSE, E. W., EISDORFER, C., and KLEEMEIER, R. W.: Relation of the electroencephalogram to intellectual function in senescence. *J. Geront.,* 17:197-206, 1962.

12. WANG, H. S., OBRIST, W. D., and BUSSE, E. W.: Neurophysiological correlates of the intellectual function of elderly persons living in the community. *Amer. J. Psychiat.,* 126:1205-1212, 1970.

13. BUSSE, E. W. and WANG, H. S.: The multiple factors contributing to dementia in old age. In: *Proceedings of the Fifth World Congress of Psychiatry.* Amsterdam: Excerpta Medica. 1971, 274:818-825.

14. INGVAR, D. H. and GUSTAFSON, L.: Regional cerebral blood flow in organic dementia with early onset. *Acta Neurol. Scand.,* 46 (supplement 43), 42-73, 1970.

15. OBRIST, W. D., CHIVIAN, E., CRONQUIST, S., and INGVAR, D. H.: Regional cerebral blood flow in senile and presenile dementia. *Neurology,* 20:315-322, 1970.

16. WANG, H. S. and BUSSE, W. E.: EEG of healthy old persons—a longitudinal study: I. Dominant background activity and occipital rhythm. *J. Geront.,* 24:419-426, 1969.

17. LIBERSON, W. T.: Functional electroencephalography in mental disorders. *Dis. Nerv. Sys.,* 5:357-364, 1944.

18. WILSON, S.: Electrocortical reactivity in young and aged adults. Unpublished doctoral dissertation, George Peabody College for Teachers, 1962.

19. THOMPSON, L. W. and WILSON, S.: Electrocortical reactivity and learning in the elderly. *J. Geront.,* 21:45-51, 1966.

20. SURWILLO, W. W.: Timing of behavior in senescence and the role of the central nervous system. In: G. A. Talland (Ed.), *Human Aging and Behavior.* New York: Academic Press, 1968, pp. 1-35.

21. WOODRUFF, D. S.: Biofeedback control of the EEG alpha rhythm

and its effect on reaction time in the young and old. Ph.D. dissertation. University of Southern California, 1972.

22. MARSH, G. R. and THOMPSON, L. W.: Age differences in evoked potentials during an auditory discrimination task. *Gerontol.,* 12:44, 1972.

23. GERSON, I. M., JOHN, E. R., BARTLETT, F., and KOENIG, V.: Average evoked response (AER) in the electroencephalographic diagnosis of the normally aging brain: A practical application. *Clin. Electroencephalo.,* 7:77-91, 1976.

24. VISSER, S. L., STAM, F. C., VAN TILBURG, W., OP DEN VELDER, W., BLOM, J. L., and DeRIJKE, W.: Visual evoked response in senile and presenile dementia. *Electroencephalo. Clin. Neurophysiol.,* 40:385-392, 1976.

25. JOHN, E. R., et al.: Neurometrics. *Science,* 196:1393-1410, 1977.

26. MARSH, G. R. and THOMPSON, L. W.: Effects of age on the contingent negative variation in a pitch discrimination task. *J. Gerontol.,* 28:56-62, 1973.

27. McCALLUM, W. and WALTER, W.: The effects of attention and distraction on the contingent negative variation in normal and neurotic subjects. *Electroencephalo. Clin. Neurophysiol.,* 25: 319-392, 1968.

28. HARKINS, S. W., THOMPSON, L. W., MOSS, S. F., and NOWLIN, J. B.: Relationship between central and autonomic nervous system activity correlates of psychomotor performance in elderly men. *Exp. Aging Research,* 2(5):409-423, 1976.

29. ROLFWANG, H. P., MUNZIO, J. N., and DEMENT, W. C.: Ontogenic development of the human sleep-dream cycle. *Science,* 152:604-619, 1966.

30. EISDORFER, C.: Psychologic reaction to cardiovascular change in the aged. *Mayo Clinic Proceedings,* 42:620-636, 1967.

31. EISDORFER, C., AXELROD, S., and WILKIE, F.: Stimulus exposure time as a factor in serial learning in an aged sample. *J. Abn. Soc. Psychol.,* 67:594-600, 1963.

32. KAHN, E. and FISHER, C.: The sleep characteristics of the normal aged male. *J. Nerv. Ment. Dis.,* 148:477-494, 1969.

33. PRINZ, P. N.: EEG during sleep and waking states. In: B. E. Eleftheriou and M. F. Elias (Eds.), *Experimental Aging Research,* Vol. I. Bar Harbor, ME, 1976. pp. 136-163.

34. ELEFTHERIOU, B. E., ZOLOVICK, A. J., and ELIAS, H. F.: Electroencephalographic changes with age in male mice. *Gerontologia,* 21:21-30, 1975.

35. MICHALEWSKI, H. J., and THOMPSON, L. W.: The role of electroencephalographic techniques in the assessment of lifespan changes. In: A. Raskin and L. F. Jarvik (Eds.), *Geriatric Assessment.* Washington: Hemisphere, in press.

36. SHMAVONIAN, B. and BUSSE, E. W.: Psychophysiologic techniques in the study of the aged. In: R. Williams, C. Tibbits, and W. Donahue (Eds.), *Processes of Aging.* New York: Atherton Press, 1963.

37. WILKIE, F. L. and EISDORFER, C.: Serial learning and psychophysiological parameters. Paper read at the 29th Annual Gerontological Society meeting, New York, 1976.

38. EISDORFER, C., DOERR, H., and FOLLETTE, W.: Age and sex interaction with electrodermal level and response. Paper presented at the 17th annual meeting of the Society for Psychophysiological Research, Philadelphia, Pennsylvania, October 13, 1977.

39. LACEY. J. I. and LACEY, B.: Some autonomic-central nervous system interrelationships. In: P. Black (Ed.), *Physiological Correlates of Emotion.* New York: Academic Press, 1970, pp. 205-227.

40. MORRIS, J. D. and THOMPSON, L. W.: Heart rate changes in a reaction time experiment with young and aged subjects. *J. Gerontology,* 24(3):249, 1969.

41. NOWLIN, J. B., EISDORFER, C., and THOMPSON, L. W.: Unpublished manuscript, Duke University Medical Center, Durham, North Carolina, 1970.

42. POWELL, A. H., EISDORFER, C., and BOGDONOFF, M. D.: Physiologic response patterns observed in a learning task. *Arch. Gen. Psych.,* 10:192-195, 1964.

43. WILKIE, F. L. and EISDORFER, C.: Concurrent measures of autonomic activity in learning in the aged. Paper read at American Psychological Association, Washington, D.C., 1976.

44. POSTMAN, L.: Verbal learning and memory. In: M. R. Rosenzweig and L. W. Porter (Eds.), *Annual Review of Psychology,* Vol. 26. Palo Alto, California: Annual Reviews, 1975.

45. FROLKIS, V. V.: Aging of the autonomic nervous system. In: J. E. Birren and K. W. Schaie (Eds.), *Handbook of the Psychology of Aging.* New York: Van Nostrand Reinhold, 1976, pp. 177-189.

46. TROYER, W. G., EISDORFER, C., BOGDONOFF, M. D., and WILKIE, F.: Experimental stress and learning in the aged. *J. Abn. Psychol.,* 72:65-70, 1967.

47. EISDORFER, C., NOWLIN, J., and WILKIE, F.: Improvement of learning in the aged by modification of autonomic nervous system activity. *Science,* 197:1327-1329, Dec., 1970.

48. FROEHLING, S. D.: Effects of propranolol on behavior and physiological measures in elderly males. Unpublished doctoral dissertation. University of Miami, Florida.

49. HERR, J. J. and BIRREN, J. E.: Differential effects of epinephrine and propranolol on shuttle box avoidance learning in rats of different ages. Paper read at Gerontological Society Annual Meeting, Miami, Florida, 1973.

50. COHEN, D. and WILKIE, F.: Sex differences in cognition among the aged. In: M. Wittig and A. Peterson (Eds.), *Determinants of Sex-Related Differences in Cognitive Functioning.* New York: Academic Press, (in press).

51. WILKIE, F. L. and EISDORFER, C.: Sex, verbal ability and pacing differences in serial learning. *J. Geront.,* 32:63-67, 1977.

52. MACCOBY, E. E. and JACKLIN, C. N.: *The Psychology of Sex Differences.* Stanford, California: Stanford University Press, 1974.

53. ELIAS, M. F. and KINSBOURNE, M.: Age and sex differences in the processing of verbal and nonverbal stimuli. *J. Geront.,* 29:162-171, 1974.

54. BALTES, P. B. and SCHAIE, K. W.: Aging and IQ: The myth of the twilght years. *Psychology Today,* 7:35-40, 1974.

55. JARVIK, L. F. and FALEK, A.: Intellectual stability and survival in the aged. *J. Geront.,* 18:173-176, 1963.

56. JARVIK, L. F.: Discussion: Intellectual functioning in later years. In: L. F. Jarvik, C. Eisdorfer, and J. E. Blum (Eds.), *Intellectual Functioning in Adults.* New York: Springer Publishing Company, Inc., 1973, p. 67.

57. WILKIE, F. and EISDORFER, C.: Intelligence and blood pressure in the aged. *Science,* 172:959-962, 1971.

58. HORN, J. L.: Psychometric studies of aging and intelligence. In: S. Gershon and A. Raskin (Eds.), *Genesis and Treatment of Psychologic Disorders in the Elderly.* New York: Raven Press, 1975, pp. 19-43.

59. WECHSLER, D.: *The Management and Appraisal of Adult Intelligence.* 4th Edition, Baltimore: Williams & Wilkins, 1958.

60. BAYLEY, N. and ODEN, M. H.: The maintenance of intellectual ability in gifted adults. *J. Geront.,* 10:91-107, 1955.

61. RHUDICK, P. J. and GORDON, C.: The age center of New England study. In: L. F. Jarvik, C. Eisdorfer and J. E. Blum (Eds.), *Intellectual Functioning in Adults.* New York: Springer Publishing Company, 1973, pp. 7-19.

62. EICHORN, D. H.: The institute of human development studies, Berkeley and Oakland. In: L. F. Jarvik, C. Eisdorfer, and J. E. Blum (Eds.), *Intellectual Functioning in Adults.* New York: Springer Publishing Company, 1973, pp. 1-6.

63. OWENS, W. A.: Age and mental abilities: A second adult follow-up. *J. Ed. Psychol.,* 57:311-325, 1966.

64. OWENS, W. A., JR.: Is age kinder to the initially more able? In: *Proceedings of the Fourth Congress of the International Association of Gerontology.* Fidenza, Italy: Tipographia Tito Mattioli, 1957, p. 4.

65. EISDORFER, C. and WILKIE, F.: Intellectual changes with advancing age. In: L. F. Jarvik, C. Eisdorfer, and J. E. Blum (Eds.), *Intellectual Functioning in Adults.* New York: Springer Publishing Company, 1973, pp. 21-29.

66. HONZIK, M. P. and MACFARLANE, J. W.: Personality development and intellectual functioning from 21 months to 40 years. In: L. F. Jarvik, C. Eisdorfer, and J. E. Blum (Eds.), *Intellectual Functioning in Adults.* New York: Springer Publishing Company, 1973, pp. 45-58.

67. BAYLEY, N.: Development of mental abilities. In: P. Mussen

(Ed.), *Carmichael's Manual of Child Psychology,* Vol. 1. New York: John Wiley, 1970, pp. 1163-1209.
68. HORN, J. L. and DONALDSON, G.: On the myth of intellectual decline in adulthood. *Am. Psychol.,* 31:701-719, 1976.
69. HORN, J. L.: The structure of intellect: Primary abilities. In: R. H. Dreger (Ed.), *Multivariate Personality Research.* Baton Rouge: Claitor, 1972, 451-511.
70. HORN, J. L. and CATTELL, R. B.: Age differences in fluid and crystallized intelligence. *Acta Psychol.,* 26:107-219, 1967.
71. HORN, J. L. and KNAPP, J. R.: On the subjective character of the empirical base of Guilford's Structure-of-Intellect model. *Psychol. Bull.,* 80:33-43, 1973.
72. JARVIK, L. F. and COHEN, D.: A biobehavioral approach to intellectual changes with aging. In: C. Eisdorfer and M. P. Lawton (Eds.), *The Psychology of Adult Development and Aging.* Washington, D.C.: American Psychological Association, 1973, pp. 220-280.
73. EISDORFER, C. and WILKIE, F.: Stress, disease, aging and behavior. In: J. E. Birren and K. W. Schaie (Eds.), *Handbook of the Psychology of Aging.* New York: Van Nostrand Reinhold Company, 1977, pp. 249-275.
74. KLEEMEIER, R. W.: Intellectual changes in the senium. *Proceedings of the American Statistical Association,* 1:290-295, 1962.
75. BERKOWITZ, B. and GREEN, R. F.: Changes in intellect with age: Longitudinal study of Wechsler-Bellevue scores. *J. Genet. Psychol.,* 103:3-21, 1963.
76. SIEGLER, I. C.: The terminal drop hypothesis: Fact or artifact. *Exper. Aging Research,* 1:169-185, 1975.
77. CRAIK, F. I. M.: Age differences in human memory. In: J. E. Birren and K. W. Schaie (Eds.), *Handbook of the Psychology of Aging.* New York: Van Nostrand Reinhold Company, 1977, pp. 384-420.
78. BOYARASKY, R. E. and EISDORFER, C.: Forgetting in older persons. *J. Geront.,* 27(2):254-258, 1972.
79. ERICKSON, R. C. and SCOTT, M. L.: Clinical memory testing: A review. *Psychol. Bull.,* 84:6, 1130-1149, 1977.
80. MEIER, M. J.: Some challenges for clinical neuropsychology. In: R. M. Reitan and L. A. Davison (Eds.), *Clinical Neuropsychology.* Washington, D.C.: V. H. Winston & Sons, 1974, pp. 289-323.
81. HALSTEAD, W. C.: *Brain and Intelligence: A Quantitative Study of the Frontal Lobes.* Chicago: U. of Chicago Press, 1947.
82. REITAN, R. M.: Psychological changes associated with aging and with cerebral damage. *Mayo Clinic Proceedings,* 42:653-673, 1967.
83. REITAN, R. M.: The relationship of the Halstead Impairment Index and the Wechsler-Bellevue Total Weighted Score to Chronologic Age. *J. Geront.,* 11:4, 1956.
84. REITAN, R. M.: Certain differential effects of left and right

cerebral lesions in human adults. *J. of Comp. and Physiol. Psychol.*, 48:474-477, 1955.

85. REITAN, R. M.: The distribution according to age of a psychologic measure dependent upon organic brain functions. *J. Geront.*, 10:338-340, 1955.

86. BENTON, A. L.: The Revised Visual Retention Test: Clinical and Experimental Applications (3rd ed.), Iowa City (distr. by Psych. Corp. of N. Y.), 1963.

87. KLOVE, H.: Validation studies in adult clinical neuropsychology. In: R. M. Reitan and L. A. Davison (Eds.), *Clinical Neuropsychology*. Washington, D.C.: V. H. Winston & Sons, 1974, pp. 211-235.

88. REED, H. B. C. and REITAN, R. M.: Changes in psychology test performance associated with the normal aging process. *J. Geront.*, 18:271-274(a), 1963.

89. REITAN, R. M.: Differential reaction of various psychological tests to age. *Estratto del Volume dell'International Symposium on Medical-Social Aspects of Senile Nervous Diseases*, Venezia, 1957, pp. 20-21, Inglio.

90. REED, H. B. C. and REITAN, R. M.: A comparison of the effects of the normal aging process with the effects of organic brain damage on adaptive abilities. *J. Geront.*, 18:177-179, 1963.

91. BALL, T. J. and REITAN, R. M.: Effects of age on performance of the Trail Making Test. *Percept. Mot. Skills*, 36:691-694, 1973.

92. HALLENBECK, C. E.: Evidence for a multiple process view of mental deterioration. *J. Geront.*, 19:357-363, 1964.

93. MATARAZZO, J. D.: *Wechsler's Measurement and Appraisal of Adult Intelligence*. Baltimore: Williams & Wilkins, 1972.

94. SCHAIE, K. W. and SCHAIE, J. P.: Clinical assessment and aging. In: J. E. Birren and K. W. Schaie (Eds.), *Handbook of the Psychology of Aging*. New York: Van Nostrand Reinhold Co., 1977, pp. 692-723.

95. OVERALL, J. E. and GORHAM, D. R.: Organicity versus old age in objective and projective test performance. *J. Consult. Clin. Psychol.*, 39:98-105, 1972.

96. EISDORFER, C.: Intelligence and cognition in the aged. In: E. Busse and E. Pfeiffer (Eds.), *Behavior and Adaptation in Late Life*. Second Edition. Boston: Little, Brown and Company, Inc., 1977, pp. 212-226.

97. CROOK, T.: Issues related to psychometric assessment of treatment effects in the aged. In: A. Raskin (Ed.), *Proceedings of the Workshop on Problems in the Assessment of Psychiatric Symptoms and Cognitive Deficits in the Elderly*. U.C.L.A., Los Angeles, California, April, 1977.

98. PARSONS, O. A. and STEWART, K. D.: Effects of supportive versus disinterested interviews on perceptual-motor performance in brain-damaged and neurotic patients. *J. Consult. Psychol.*, 20: 260-266, 1966.

99. RABBITT, P.: An age-decrement in the ability to ignore irrelevant information. *J. Geront.*, 20:233-238, 1965.

100. WELFORD, A. T.: Fatigue and monotony. In: O. G. Edholm and A. L. Bacharach (Eds.), *The Physiology of Human Survival.* New York and London: Academic Press, 1965.

101. GRANICK, S., KLEBAN, M. H., and WEISS, A. D.: Relationships between hearing loss and cognition in normally hearing aged persons. *J. Geront.*, 31:434-440, 1976.

102. EISDORFER, C. and COHEN, D.: The cognitively impaired elderly: Differential diagnosis. In: M. Storandt, I. Siegler, and M. F. Elias (Eds.), *Clinical Gerontology.* New York: Plenum Press, 1978.

103. SALZMAN, C., KOCHANSKY, G. E., and SHADER, R. I.: Rating scales for geriatric psychopharmacology: A review. *Psychopharmacology Bull.*, 8:3-50, 1972.

104. EISDORFER, C. and STOTSKY, B. A.: Intervention treatment and rehabilitation of psychiatric disorders. In: J. Birren and W. Schaie (Eds.), *Handbook of the Psychology of Aging.* New York: Van Nostrand Reinhold Company, 1977, pp. 724-748.

105. EISDORFER, C. and FRIEDEL, R. O. (Eds.): *Cognitive and Emotional Disturbance in the Elderly: Clinical Issues.* Chicago: Year Book Medical Publishers, Inc., 1977.

106. HALL, P.: Cyclandelate in the treatment of cerebral arteriosclerosis. *J. Am. Geriat. Soc.*, 24:41-44, 1976.

107. LEHMANN, H. E.: The use of medication to prevent custodial care. In: C. Eisdorfer and R. O. Friedel (Eds.), *Cognitive and Emotional Disturbance in the Elderly: Clinical Issues.* Chicago: Year Book Medical Publishers, Inc., 1977, pp. 129-138.

108. RASKIND, M. and EISDORFER, C.: Psychopharmacology of the aged. In: L. L. Simpson (Ed.), *Drug Treatment of Mental Disorders.* New York: Raven Press, 1976, pp. 237-266.

109. TERRY, R. D. and WISNIEWSKI, H. M.: Structural aspects of aging of the brain. In: C. Eisdorfer and R. O. Friedel (Eds.), *Cognitive and Emotional Disturbance in the Elderly: Clinical Issues.* Chicago: Year Book Medical Publishers, Inc., 1977, pp. 3-10.

110. KAY, D. W. K.: The epidemiology and identification of brain deficit in the elderly. In: C. Eisdorfer and R. O. Friedel (Eds.), *Cognitive and Emotional Disturbance in the Elderly: Clinical Issues.* Chicago: Year Book Medical Publishers, Inc., 1977, pp. 11-26.

111. HAKIM, S. and ADAMS, R. D.: The special clinical problem of symptomatic hydrocephalus with normal cerebrospinal fluid hydronamics. *J. Neuro. Sci.*, 2:307-327, 1965.

112. KATZMAN, R. and KARASU, T. B.: Differential diagnosis of dementia. In: W. S. Fields (Ed.), *Neurological and Sensory Disorders in the Elderly.* New York: Stratton, 1975.

113. SJOGREN, T., SJOGREN, H., and LINDGREN, A. G. H.: Morbus

Alzheimer and morbus Pick. A genetic, clinical, and patho-anatomical study. *Acta Psychiat. Neurol. Scand.*, 82 (Supplement 82), 1952.

114. CONSTANTANIDIS, J., GARRONE, G., and D'AJURIAGUERRA, J.: L'heredite des demances de l'age avance. *Encephale*, 4:301-344, 1962.

115. MILLER, E. and LEWIS, P.: Recognition memory in elderly patients with depression and dementia: A signal detection analysis. *J. Abn. Psychol.*, 86:84-86, 1977.

5

Aging Research: A Review
and Critique

Ewald W. Busse, M.D.

Research in aging is a relatively new field. To provide a background for this paper, I shall offer definitions for terms widely used when discussing research. Selected theories of aging will be explained, and methods and techniques of investigation will be considered. My experience as a member of the President's Biomedical Research Panel emphasized that there are many intelligent individuals with serious misconceptions in regard both to aging and to research. In the late spring of 1976, during one of my appearances before the U.S. Senate Health Subcommittee, it became apparent that the deficiency in the understanding of categories or types of research led to misunderstandings. For example, there is considerable confusion regarding the meaning of basic research, applied research, clinical research, biomedical and biobehavioral research, etc. Senator Kennedy requested me to submit to this subcommittee those commonly used terms and their explanations. These definitions are included in the next section of this chapter. There is the mistaken notion that clinicians do not engage in basic research and that so-called basic scientists, simply by being designated basic scientists, never engage in applied research. In my opinion this assumption is highly erroneous.

Aging in mammals is a biologic term that is used to identify inherent biologic changes that take place over time and end with death. The terms *growth* and *development* usually represent biologic processes which are the opposite of aging. Some investigators prefer to define biologic aging as a progressive loss of functional capacity after an organism has reached maturity, while others insist that aging processes can be identified with the onset of differentiation. Still others contend that an attempt to separate aging processes and to identify them is not useful or possible. For operational purposes, I prefer to separate declines in functioning into primary aging (senescence) and secondary aging (senility). *Primary aging* consists of biologic processes which are apparently rooted in heredity. They are inborn and inevitable detrimental changes that are time-related but are etiologically relatively independent of stress, trauma, or acquired disease (infection, toxication, hostile environment). *Secondary* aging refers to defects and disabilities resulting from trauma and disease.

All of the aging processes are not recognizable in all people, and those that are present do not progress at the same rate. This operational definition of primary aging clearly has limitations. For example, it does not adequately distinguish between the so-called "normal" aging process and the diagnostic entities related to inborn errors of metabolism. Nevertheless, the ultimate question is whether or not science, through research, can provide the diagnostic skills and the techniques for prevention and intervention that will control both the primary and secondary aging processes.

DEFINITIONS

Definitions are primarily derived from theory and are influenced by the extent of knowledge and value systems. Hence, definitions are rarely acceptable to all individuals and groups. Shortcomings exist in definitions as presented, and their acceptance and, therefore, usefulness vary according to the situation. However, in the area of biomedical science, the public should have a better understanding of research. In addition to facilitating understanding, certain definitions make possible cost accounting and perhaps cost benefit studies. Bearing these factors in mind, the following definitions have been developed.

Research: Research is the careful or diligent search or examination based upon investigation or experimentation aimed at the discovery and the interpretation of facts that may result in the revision of accepted theories or laws in the light of new fact, or the practical application of such new or revised theories or laws.

Basic Research: Basic research is a systematic inquiry whose objective is to identify the components and functions of any unit (or mass) and to understand the sequence of events and to identify the factors that initiate or alter its functions, structure, size, or appearance. Basic research is not only concerned with normality (the usual) but also with abnormality (the unusual).

Applied Research: Applied research is a planned effort whose objective is to alter the composition, size, appearance, or functions of a unit or mass. This effort is directed toward achieving some positive value and is usually dependent upon knowledge derived from basic research.

Clinical Research: Clinical research is a type of applied research that is directed to the maintenance of health, the prevention and treatment of disease or trauma, and the restoration of functions that have been disrupted as the result of disability, pain, or discomfort. Clinical research is based on data derived from direct observations of the person.

Behavioral Research: Behavioral research encompasses not only those observable actions or responses of an individual or group but also those processes that transpire within the individual and the external influences that result in the observable actions and responses. Behavioral research may be basic, applied or clinical.

Social Research: Social research is concerned with all of the elements or factors inherent in a social environment which influence sociability, cooperativeness, and interdependent relationships. It is concerned with the structure and process of human society, the interaction of the individual and society, and the welfare of human beings as members of society.

Biologic Research: Biologic research is concerned with living organisms and the vital processes.

Biomedical: Biomedical relates to the information base that is derived from principles of physiology and biochemistry and other areas of scientific knowledge which are pertinent to clinical medicine.

Biobehavioral Research: Biobehavioral research is concerned with the relationship between observable actions or responses to a stimuli of an individual or a group: the factors that produce or alter such actions or responses and the influence of such actions and responses upon the vital processes of a living organism, particularly those which are detrimental or advantageous to the living organism.

THEORIES OF AGING

Although there is no unified theory of aging, there are numerous biologic theories, some social theories, and a few psychologic theories. The biologic theories are all decremental. This negative view of aging does not hold true for the social and psychologic theories.

Biologic Theories

Biologic theories are understandably primarily applicable to one of three components of the human body. Two of these components are cellular. The first is the nondividing and irreplaceable cells, and the second is cells capable of multiplying throughout the life span. The third component is the noncellular material of the body. Although most biologic theories are molecular or cellular, there are aging theories that relate to physiologic systems or to an organ or to a specific part of the body. It would be a lengthy, if not impossible, task to review all of the theories. Therefore, I have selected for review those theories which are historically interesting and/or worthy of continuing scientific attention.

One early biologic explanation of aging rested on the assumption that a living organism contained a fixed store of energy, diffusely or strategically located, that, not unlike a coiled watch spring, at some time would be unwound, whereupon life would end. This is a type of *exhaustion theory*. Although it has essentially disappeared, it has been replaced by some more sophisticated approaches consistent with our current scientific knowledge.

Another simple theory of aging relates to the accumulation of deleterious material. This particular theory continues to hold the interest of some scientists, particularly neuropathologists, who have yet to explain the origin and the significance of the accumulation of lipofucsin in neurons of the brain. There are other late-appearing accumulations within the nerve cells that require explanation, such as the hirano bodies. At the molecular and cellular level, the theory that aging constitutes a *deliberate biologic programming* process appears to have considerable validity. If deliberate biologic programming is present in the cell, it would be logical to assume that it is located in the genetic (DNA) portion of the cell.

It appears to be highly unlikely that normal human diploid cells are immortal. Normal human cells contain two sets of 23 chromosomes or a total of 46. Cancer cells are mixoploid cells and may have anywhere from 50 to 350 chromosomes per cell. In addition, the chromosomes within the mixoploid cell differ considerably in size and shape from the 46 chromosomes found in the normal diploid human cell. It is the mixoploid cell which appears to be immortal.

Based on the assumption or hope that immortality exists in the lower, simpler forms of life, it has been held that some animal cells are immortal if removed from the body's regulatory mechanisms. Carrell and Ebeling (1) in 1921 reported that cultured fibroblasts from chicken embryo heart tissue could be held in a state of continuous proliferation for many years. This finding, if true, would of course prove that biologic aging was not the result of intrinsic failures within the individual cell but was the result of disorganization of the entire organism. Unfortunately, Carrell's success and apparently that of other investigators were the result of errors in technique. Carrell and Ebeling fed the cell culture with a crude extract taken from chick embryos. This extract actually contained a very few but a significant number of new viable cells. The new cells permitted the culture to survive. It was found that if the extract was carefully prepared by removing all new cells, the cell colony would die.

Beginning in 1961, Hayflick and Moorhead (2) reported that normal human fibroblasts, when cultured, underwent a finite number of population doublings and then died. A number of years later Hayflick and co-workers reported that human fibroblast cultures derived from embryo donors as a group underwent significantly more population doublings, 40 to 60, than those derived from adults as a group, 10 to 30. Other experiments demonstrated that cells could be removed from the culture, stored in subzero temperatures for as long as 12 years, and when removed and returned to a culture medium, they would begin to divide. Hayflick reports that, regardless of the number of doublings reached by the population at the time the cells were preserved, the summated total number of doublings was about 50. The stored cells seemed to contain an inherent mechanism for remembering at what doubling level they were stored in the cold. Hayflick contends that this *in vitro* demonstration can be repeated *in vivo* by marking cells and injecting them into a host animal in which they can be withdrawn later and then reinjected into new host animals; a similar limit to the number of possible doublings can be demonstrated. It has been reported that a given number of doublings is not different in male or female cells. If this observation holds up, then it is evident that the differences in life expectancy between the male and female cannot be attributed to intracellular differences. These studies would substantiate the biologic theory of aging as a deliberate biologic programming that limits the number of times a cell capable of dividing can, in fact, do so.

Holliday and co-workers (3) doubt the validity of Hayflick's conclusions. They believe that, when a cell divides, some of the daughter cells are "committed to senescence," while the other cells would, under proper circumstances, be capable of continuous reduplication. Obviously the *commitment theory* of cellular aging is extremely complex and awaits much further study. Holliday and co-workers express the belief that the error theory which will be discussed in this paper may be compatible with the commitment theory in that aging of fibroblasts is accompanied by alterations or defects in genes, chromosomes, DNA replication, and repair.

The *error theory* of cellular aging proposes that, with senescence, alterations—not necessarily mutations—occur in the structure of the

DNA molecule. These errors are transmitted to messenger RNA and ultimately to newly synthesized enzymes. If the number of defective or inactive enzymes proceeds to a point at which synthesis within the cell is sufficiently defective that life cannot be sustained, the cell will die. Eventually, a sufficient number of cells will die or malfunction to the point that death of the organism will occur.

The *error theory* is often linked with the *mutation theory,* as it has been shown that chromosomal aberrations in the liver cells of normal mice increase linearly with age. Furthermore, exposure to ionizing radiation increases the number of chromosomal aberrations, leading to cellular malfunction, and eventual death.

The *cross-linkage* or *eversion theory* is primarily applicable to the noncellular material of the body. The investigation substantiating this theory rests on the study of collagen, the most abundant protein in the body. A collagen molecule is composed of three polypeptide strands. Each polypeptide strand contains four subunits that are held together by pairs of ester bonds. With the passage of time there is a switching of the ester bonds from within to between the individual collagen molecules. This switching is called cross-linking or eversion. Since collagen is a substantial component of connective tissue, as it ages, it renders the connective tissue less permeable, less elastic, and less capable of sustaining normal life.

The *immunologic theory of aging* is currently receiving considerable attention, since it may play an important role in the causation of senile dementia.

The Immune System and Normal Aging

The immune system as a primary defense mechanism of the body is essential for the preservation of life. The immune system is extremely complex and is widely dispersed throughout the tissues of the body. When a foreign substance is introduced into the body, the immune system can respond in two ways. The first is the humoral immune response which is characterized by the production of antibody molecules which specifically bind the introduced substance. The second is the cellular immune response. Cells are mobilized which can specifically react with and destroy the invader. The immunologic theory of normal aging advocated by Walford (4) and Burnet (5) holds that, with the passage of time, alterations transpire within the immune system. Surveillance is impaired and there is a decline in the protective mechanism. Furthermore, the system may be distorted so that it functions in a self-destructive, that is, autoaggressive, manner. The loss of cortical neurons characteristic of aging may be associated with specific brain-reactive antibody, as found in old mice (6). The protective mechanisms of the immune system reach a peak during adolescence and then decline in conjunction with the involution of the thymus. With the passage of years the body demonstrates an increased susceptibility to infection, and, in general, effective immunization cannot be induced in late life.

Walford and Burnet hold somewhat different points of views of the immune system and aging. Burnet considers the thymus gland the clock of aging, as its removal produces immunodeficiencies not unlike those associated with aging. Walford is concerned with autoimmune responses, but according to Kent (7), a critical issue is what comes first—immunodeficiency or autoimmunity.

There is evidence that prolonged survival in humans may be associated with an immunologic elite population. A cross-sectional longitudinal study of immunoglobulin serum levels at the Center for the Study of Aging and Human Development at Duke University found that, in elderly subjects, early death is likely in those who have relatively low levels of IgG and high levels of IgM. However, in many old people, both IgG and IgA increased with age. The immunoglobulin IgA is concentrated in the fluids of the respiratory and gastrointestinal system and here acts as a first line defense against invading organisms. IgM, although in some respects similar to IgG, is a much larger molecular structure than IgG, and is therefore likely to remain in the bloodstream. Serum IgG is a major defense against virus, bacteria, and fungi wherever they may be found in the body. IgM has a cleaning-up-of-debris function and appears to direct its effort to fighting disease in blood vessels. Why high IgM contributes to increased risk to life is not established.

There are two other major classes of antibodies (immunoglobulins): IgE and IgD. IgD is found in very low concentrations in humans. Its role is speculative. IgE is involved in the release of molecules like histamines associated with symptoms of allergies. Both require additional scientific attention (8).

Attempts have been made to determine the relationship between serum immunoglobulins and intellectual performance. Cohen and Eisdorfer (9) found no significant relationship between immunoglobulin level and the WAIS subtest scores in 23 women with a mean age of 73.2 years who reported that they were in good health. However, in 14 elderly men, age 74.2 years, Cohen and Eisdorfer report significant correlations between performance, both vocabulary and digit symbol, and heightened serum IgG and IgA.

Cohen and Eisdorfer found that among the men IgG was negatively correlated to both vocabulary and digit performance, and IgA was negatively correlated with vocabulary. The authors agree that these findings are difficult to explain, and the sex differences are particularly annoying. It is evident that much work needs to be done to understand the relationship of the central nervous system to the immune responses.

The progressive failure and perversion of the immune system with advancing age are thought to contribute to a number of diseases in late life, including the increasing incidence of cancer, amyloidosis, maturity-onset diabetes, and emphysema.

Amyloidosis is a condition that affects many people. *Amyloid B* is found in senile plaques. It is believed to be caused by a malfunctioning immune system and affects the connective tissue of nearly every part of the brain, as well as throughout the body. It is said to act like rust in a complicated machine, reducing the effectiveness of the body cells.

Maturity-onset diabetes occurs in a severe form in about 13 percent of people over the age of 75 and in a mild form in almost half of the population over 65. This, too, is considered to be an autoimmune phenomenon, and it is assumed that it is an autoimmune reaction to insulin and to the cells that produce it.

Emphysema is becoming an increasingly serious disease in the United States. It is generally associated with chronic lung infections and heavy smoking. An individual with an impaired immune system is even more vulnerable to the possibility of emphysema.

Psychologic Theories

According to Birren and Renner (10), there is no pressure on the field of psychology to produce a unifying theory or to explain how behavior is organized over time. They view the psychology of aging as predominantly a problem- and data-oriented area of research. Baltes and Willis (11) reach a number of conclusions, including "all existing theories (of psychological aging and development) are of the prototheoretical kind and are incomplete."

The psychologic theories that have appeared are often the extension of personality and developmental theories into middle and late life. Personality theories usually consider the innate human needs and forces that motivate thought and behavior and the modification of these biologically based energies by the experiences of living in a physical and social environment.

Personality and developmental theories of aging are to a remarkable degree influenced by the fact that as humans pass through their life experiences they become increasingly different rather than similar. Infants at six months of age are more similar than children at age 12. This divergence continues as a response to a large array of possible learning and living experiences. It is possible that this divergence phenomenon reverses in extreme old age, as very elderly people show considerable similarity in certain characteristics. However, this may result from the fact that they are a biologically special group and that very old people are treated by society in a relatively uniform manner.

Schaie (12) has recently advanced what he calls "a stage theory of adult cognitive development." His tentative scheme involves four or five possible adult cognitive stages. These sequential stages are denoted as acquisitive (childhood and adolescence), achieving (young adulthood), responsible and executive (middle age), and reintegrative (old age). He suggests that during the life span there is a transition from "what should I know?" through "how should I use what I know?" to "why should I know?" phase of life. He believes that numerous new strategies and techniques will have to be developed in order to test fully a stage theory, and that alterations in the theory will emerge.

Kalish and Knudtson (13) recommend the extension of the *concept* (*theory*) *of attachment* common in infant and child psychology to a lifetime conceptual scheme for understanding relationships and involvements of older people. They further state that the *concept* (*theory*) *of disengagement* is not functional, and that it should be eliminated. Attachment is a relationship established and maintained by "social bonds" and is distinguished from social contacts. Elderly people lose significant early objects of attachment. New attachments are often much weaker and frequently not mutual and therefore vulnerable. Kalish and Knudtson argue that an appreciation and understanding of attachments will provide a better approach to explaining the psychologic changes in elderly people. Relevant to the attachment concept is the finding by Lowenthal and Haven that, more than any other single factor, having a confidant appeared to discriminate between elderly persons who were institutionalized and those who could remain in the community (14).

Social Theories

The term *social,* in its broadest usage and as applied to human beings, "refers to any behavior or attitude that is influenced by past or present experience of the behavior of other people (direct or indirect) or that is oriented (consciously or unconsciously) toward other people. Normally the term is morally neutral (15)."

Social scientists are usually concerned with the social role or place (status) of the aged in society. Aging to a social scientist may refer not only to a decline in social usefulness but also to an alteration of status. Social theories relevant to the aging and elderly are affected by the structure of society and social change. One such theory holds that the status of the aged is high in static societies and tends to decline with rapid social change. According to another theory, the status of the aged is high in societies where there are few elderly, and the value and status of the aged decline as they become more numerous. A third theory holds that the status and prestige of the aged are high in those societies in which older people, in spite of physical infirmity, are able to continue to perform useful and socially valued functions. This last theory has a particularly pessimistic quality when applied to Western society, because early retirement and rapid social change are making it increasingly difficult for elderly persons to be involved in socially valued functions unless provision for their continued participation is rapidly developed.

Two social theories are frequently discussed by behavioral scientists. One is the *disengagement theory* targeted by Kalish in the previous section. The second is the *activity theory*. The disengagement theory maintains that high satisfaction in old age is usually present in those individuals who accept the inevitability of reduction in social and personal interactions. The activity theory holds that the maintenance of activity is important to most individuals as a basis for obtaining and maintaining satisfaction, self-esteem, and health. Elaborations and modifications on these theories appear in this chapter.

PROBLEMS IN AGING RESEARCH

The inconsistencies that have occurred in studies dealing with aging individuals and elderly persons have raised important methodologic as well as analytic problems for investigators. It is very possible that age differences are the result of differences in the environmental histories of the age groups (16). The cohort approach is based upon the proposition that position in the stream of historical environments, indexed by date of birth, differentiates one cohort from another with respect to broad classes of behavior. The fact that the environment is unstable means that the 65-year-old in 1965 has or has not experienced certain events that are characteristic of the 65-year-old in 1975. Furthermore, the response to the environmental stimulus in 1965 may be quite different from that in 1975 because the options for response may be quite different. On the other hand, it is well recognized by behavioral scientists that there is a tendency for behavior established in response to an environmental stimulus to persist over time. A behavior acquired in early childhood will continue despite subsequent environmental changes. Each successive cohort bears the stamp of those common environmental influences to which they have been exposed. This is referred to as a "period" effect.

Research: Scarce Resources and Abundant Human Needs

Biomedical research and training have been severely criticized for many reasons and for many years; this criticism has been accompanied by reductions in federal financial support for these activities. Basic research support has been particularly adversely affected.

There is no doubt that the economic situation plays a significant role in declining research support, since it has brought into the focus the concept of cost benefit. Although the United States remains the most affluent nation in the world, it is becoming increasingly evident that our resources are limited and that many are scarce or exhausted. In contrast, human needs are great and human wants seemingly inexhaustible. Our society is now confronted with the fact that we must be more realistic in understanding and achieving compromises between human wants and natural and economic resources. Inasmuch as resources are in short supply, we cannot afford inefficiency or waste. Therefore, we cannot afford investments, whether they be in research, production, or services, that will not at some reasonable point in time contribute to satisfying basic human needs. This situation is further complicated by the multiplicity of human wants, the wide variation in individual values and preferences, the geographic distribution of our population, the resources within various segments of the United States, and the differing social values which are held by minority groups. When one considers all of these factors, it is understandable that any decision as to how economic resources should be allocated will only partially satisfy the wants of most people and will completely fail to meet the wants of some demanding groups and outspoken individuals.

A number of influential public and political leaders say that many scientists are engaged in aimless research in order to satisfy personal satisfactions without regard for the needs of the nation and rights of others. The continuing furor over recombinant DNA contains many of these elements of suspicion. Furthermore, one U.S. Senator has repeatedly proclaimed that many tax-supported research projects are used to increase the personal affluence of the investigator and have no relevance to human problems.

This negative view of basic research is abetted by the conviction that the product of basic research is largely dependent upon serendipity, and that it is therefore impossible to estimate the value or the intervening time before the return on the investment. Furthermore, it has become customary for scientists to defend basic research by presenting illustrations of the slow, complicated, and finally fortuitous emergence of discoveries from basic research that have great import to medical progress. There is no doubt that historical scientific reports, such as that concerned with chlorpromazine as an unpredictable therapeutic innovation, are fascinating and essentially accurate. However, the fact that such unrelated events have resulted in breakthroughs does not necessarily imply that no steps can be taken which will improve the linkage of basic research to applied research.

Serendipity in Research

Serendipity, according to Webster's *Seventh New Collegiate Dictionary,* is "the gift of finding valuable or agreeable things not sought for. Therefore, serendipity transpires with the occurrence of an unexpected or unintentional event (accidental event), and the individual in the event possesses sagacity."

The word *serendipity* is one of a number of words invented by Horace Walpole, an eighteenth century English author, art critic, and sometime politician. Walpole concocted the word after reading what he called a "silly fairy tale" called "The Three Princes of Serendip." Actually, an intelligent king deliberately and carefully educated his three sons so that by using their perceptual and cognitive skills and an interdisciplinary approach they could solve problems and explain mysteries (17).

Wisdom is defined by the dictionary as common sense. Wisdom requires that an individual accumulate a broad spectrum of accurate information derived from intellectual efforts and from a diversity of life experiences. A wise individual is able to integrate all types of information with social and individual values; consequently, the wise individual arrives at decisions that are not disparate from customary individual and social values and are understood and accepted as reasonable by the common person. Hence, wisdom is common sense. A biobehavioral scientist must have common sense.

In attempting to justify adequate support for basic research, it is my belief that too much emphasis has been placed on serendipity. Such emphasis implies that all basic research is unpredictable, and that only by accident will any worthwhile discovery be made. It is my contention that wisdom—a prerequisite of serendipity—can be recognized and that high quality basic research is predictable. It will generate new knowledge and will provide the sources of bits of information which are necessary to be pieced together in order to understand an event or a unit. Serendipity is a looked-for bonus. The value of the bonus does vary considerably, but the high value discoveries that are made are alone sufficient to justify the cost of the basic research.

In addition to serendipity and wisdom as important ingredients of basic research, we should strive for improved accountability by the use of a systematic analysis of scientific events which lead to technologic innovation and beneficial application. This type of analysis is found in the 1968 report, *Technology in Retrospect and Critical Events in Science*.* Five diversified scientific achievements are considered in Volume I. Of the key events documented as essential to the scientific-application process, approximately 70 percent were non-mission research, 20 percent mission-oriented research, and 10 percent development and application. Most of the nonmission research (76 percent) was done in universities and colleges, while industry did 54 percent of the mission-oriented research and 83 percent of development and application.

Not infrequently, the accusation is made that there is an unnecessary delay between new discoveries and practical application. It is possible that delays are the result of failure to recognize potential application. However, if the application is recognized but not utilized, one is confronted with several questions: Did the scientist withhold the information for selfish reason? Was it presented by the scientist to others who rejected it because they failed to see its application? Was the idea believed to be too expensive? Was the idea suppressed or ignored for social or political reasons? Additional studies need to include a close look at the factors that intervened between the laboratory breakthrough and the application of the new knowledge. Such careful study should be of great interest to the body politic, since it seems to believe that our current procedures are far too soft and chancy and the transfer of technology is too slow. Perhaps such critics

---

* Illinois Institute of Technology Research Institute, National Science Foundation, Dec. 15, 1968.

are correct. Only a carefully conducted investigation will give the answers.

On the other side of the coin is the premature application of incomplete new knowledge. Such premature implementation is often dangerous to the people involved and proves to be very costly because there is no cost benefit factor—only cost failure. The scientist has an attitudinal characteristic that is not understood and certainly not often appreciated by the nonscientist.

The competent basic scientist often has an inherent dislike for targeted research, as he knows that the desire to find "the answer" is likely to result in a biased, if not invalid, outcome. The investigator who is sure he knows the answers before he starts to find the supporting evidence to confirm his theory or hypothesis can either emerge as a misguided and unreliable scientist or, even worse, a deliberate fraud. No wonder that when a scientist is asked, "What are you trying to prove?" he will answer, "I am not trying to prove anything."

Basic and applied research demands a scientist be open-minded with limited predetermined objectives. This is in contrast to the politician who has predetermined objectives.

LONGITUDINAL STUDIES

Longitudinal studies can deal with individuals, families, institutions, or communities to determine how specific changes occur with the passage of time. Such studies have certain scientific advantages over cross-sectional approaches.

To appreciate the limitation of cross-sectional studies, one should recall that cross-sectional studies resulted in an erroneous view of the growth and decline of intelligence with age. The cross-sectional study utilized measures of intelligence which were obtained for different groups of people at varying ages. These measures plotted as a function of age increased up to the late teens when a slow decline set in, which leveled off between 25 and 45 years. In late life, that is, at 60 to 65 years of age or over, it was assumed that all normal individuals showed a decline in intellectual functioning. It is true that earlier studies of intelligence included other methodologic errors, but longitudinal studies have made it very clear that, for a substantial proportion of the population, intelligence will continue to increase well into mid-adulthood and that a decline in intelligence thereafter is influenced by health and socioeconomic factors.

Properly designed longitudinal studies are particularly helpful in following the interaction between a number of life changes. Of particular interest in the field of aging is the relationship between the onset of acquired disease, the influence of social stresses, and the importance of life-styles, motivation, and expectations.

In the United States there are two aging-research centers that have a heavy commitment to longitudinal research. One is the Gerontological Research Center in Baltimore, which is the intramural branch of the National Institute on Aging. The Duke University Center for the Study of Aging and Human Development is the second locus for longitudinal research concerned with the problems of aging. There are two long-term investigations under way at Duke. The First Longitudinal Study is officially designated as a study of "The Effect of Aging Upon the Nervous System—A Physiological, Psychological, and Sociological Study of Aging (18)." Cross-sectional studies were begun in 1950. These studies indicated that it would be necessary to conduct a longitudinal study to test certain hypotheses and answer specific questions. Up until this time most of the studies of the aging processes had been carried out utilizing, for subjects, patients who were institutionalized or receiving medical services, and/or assistance from social agencies. The First Longitudinal Study was begun in 1955 with a panel of 267 noninstitutionalized persons age 60 to 94. Eleven observations by panelists over a period of 21 years have been completed. During the two days of intensive examination, 788 pieces of information were observed and recorded. Of these, 336 were medical; 109 psychiatric or neurologic; 109 psychologic; and 234 social. This study, like most longitudinal studies, is limited by the fact that advantaged persons tend to be more likely than others to participate in such research. As analysis of the old longitudinal study progressed, it became evident that it was the most logical way to get a better understanding of certain changes that seem to have their onset in middle life. In addition, the Duke investigators were cognizant of the inconsistencies that can develop in aging research which are attributable to the interaction between the aging individuals and a changing environment. Therefore, a second longitudinal study was designed utilizing Schaie's cross-sequential approach (19). This cross-sequential design included four, six-year cohort groups and an overall six-year time of measurement. This second longitudinal study became quickly known as the Adaptation Study, as many of the observations were concerned with stressful events in the environment. The Adaptation Study was begun in 1968 utilizing a stratified random sample of 502 persons age 45 to 69 at the time of the beginning of the study and separated into cohorts. The subjects were drawn from a membership list of a major health insurance association in the Durham area. The details of the complicated design of the Adaptation Study have been published by Palmore (20).

Longitudinal studies on humans and on animals are essential if one is to identify genetic (aging) and environmental factors and their interactions that affect behavior in late life. The scientific value of a longitudinal study is very much dependent upon the research design and requires a reasonable knowledge of the biologic sciences, including genetics, as well as the behavioral and social sciences.

Neuropathology of the Aging Brain

There is a long list of pathologic findings in the aged brain. One of the earliest observations that continues to be of great significance is the gradual loss of neurons. Evidence is accumulating that the neuronal loss is not evenly distributed throughout the brain. The counting of neurons in more circumscribed areas has revealed that variation occurs in the cortex and in the brain stem (21). Age changes are complicated by the recent work demonstrating that there are alterations within the synapses of the brain, and that a decline in dendrites further disrupts the neuronal networks (22, 23).

Within the cell body of the neuron occurs neurofibrillary degeneration, granulo-vacuolar degeneration, lipofuscin accumulation, lewy bodies, and hirano bodies. Changes in the neuropile include senile plaques, amyloid deposits, shrinkage in the dendritic arbor, and a decrease of extracellular space. Glial changes include corpora amylacea and myelin remodeling. There are also arteriosclerotic and other vascular lesions (24). The two age-related lesions most frequently assumed to be a major cause of senile dementia are neurofibrillary changes and senile plaques. Normal neurons contain thin threads of fibrillary material in the cytoplasm. Alzheimer, therefore, assumed that the change seen in the aged brain was a degeneration of the normal neural fibers. However, modern electron microscopic studies reveal that in affected cells the preexisting filaments are not affected: The pathologic change is a new class of fibrillary material made up of paired helical filaments (PHF). Very little more is known about neurofibrillary degeneration other than the fact that it is common in Alzheimer's disease and senile dementia, found in lesser numbers in the normal aged brain, and is also excessive in such conditions as mongolism, "punchdrunk" boxes, postencephalitic Parkinsonism, and the amyotrophic lateral sclerosis-Parkinsonism dementia complex found in the indigenous population of Guam.

As to senile plaques, also called neuritic plaques, they are composed of three elements: degenerative neuronal processes, nonneuronal cells, and amyloid. The classical senile plaque is composed of a central core of amyloid surrounded by degenerative neurites and reactive cells. Atypical plaques known as amyloid or compact plaques are made up of a central core alone. The primary mechanism of these pathologic changes is unknown, but in man they do not appear to be associated with a localized vascular defect. In the body there are two types of amyloid, A and B. Amyloid A is a protein of unknown origin. In contrast, the amyloid believed to be associated with aging is Amyloid B, which consists of a complex of light chains of immunoglobulins. This fact is one of the major reasons for the theory that the immune system is involved in senile dementia.

The occurrence of neurofibrillary tangles and senile plaques in other disorders, such as Down's syndrome, has resulted in a recent study which indicates that a correlation exists within families between Alzheimer's disease, Down's syndrome, and hematologic malignancies (25). This finding, if substantiated, would focus more attention upon chromosome (21).

Another relatively new important observation is the fact that there is a sevenfold increase in aluminum in the brain of patients with Alzheimer's disease. At this point it is unknown whether the large amount of aluminum is a primary contributing factor or whether it accumulates as a secondary phenomenon. It is possible that there are certain populations which are at high risk. It even has been speculated that the use of antacids for gastric distress can be dangerous, since they often contain aluminum hydroxide.

EEG Changes

EEG changes in adulthood and particularly those that occur in late life have occupied a substantial part of my interest and work. I will briefly review certain observations which are pertinent to both research and clinical psychiatry.

Alpha activity is associated with maturation of the brain, appearing after three-and-a-half to four years of age and progressing to adult characteristics at between 12 and 16 years. The amount of alpha activity is maximum during a state of relaxed wakefulness, decreases during arousal, and disappears in sleep. The absence or rarity of alpha activity may have no pathologic meaning.

A common characteristic of EEG changes after the age of 65 years is the progressive slowing of the dominant alpha frequency and the appearance of slow waves in the theta or delta range. Elderly subjects in good health are found to have a mean occipital frequency which is almost a full cycle slower than that found in healthy young adults. A slight slowing of the alpha index is not pathognomonic for any particular brain disorder (see Figure 1). However, a nonspecific moderate to severe slowing is characteristically found in brain disorders, whether they are classified as degenerative or vascular in origin. Since a good correlation has been demonstrated between EEG frequency and cerebral oxygen consumption or blood flow, the slowing of the dominant frequency in the majority of elderly people may indicate a depression of cerebral metabolism.

Residents of institutions for the aged are found to have EEG slowing that highly correlates with measures of psychologic impairment. Unfortunately, this correlation is not nearly as consistent in subjects remaining in the community. It is possible that those who live in the community are actually adjusting at a borderline level and may be vulnerable to stress which would precipitate the appearance of organic brain disease. Throughout adult life, fast waves are more frequent in women than in men and tend to increase in females.

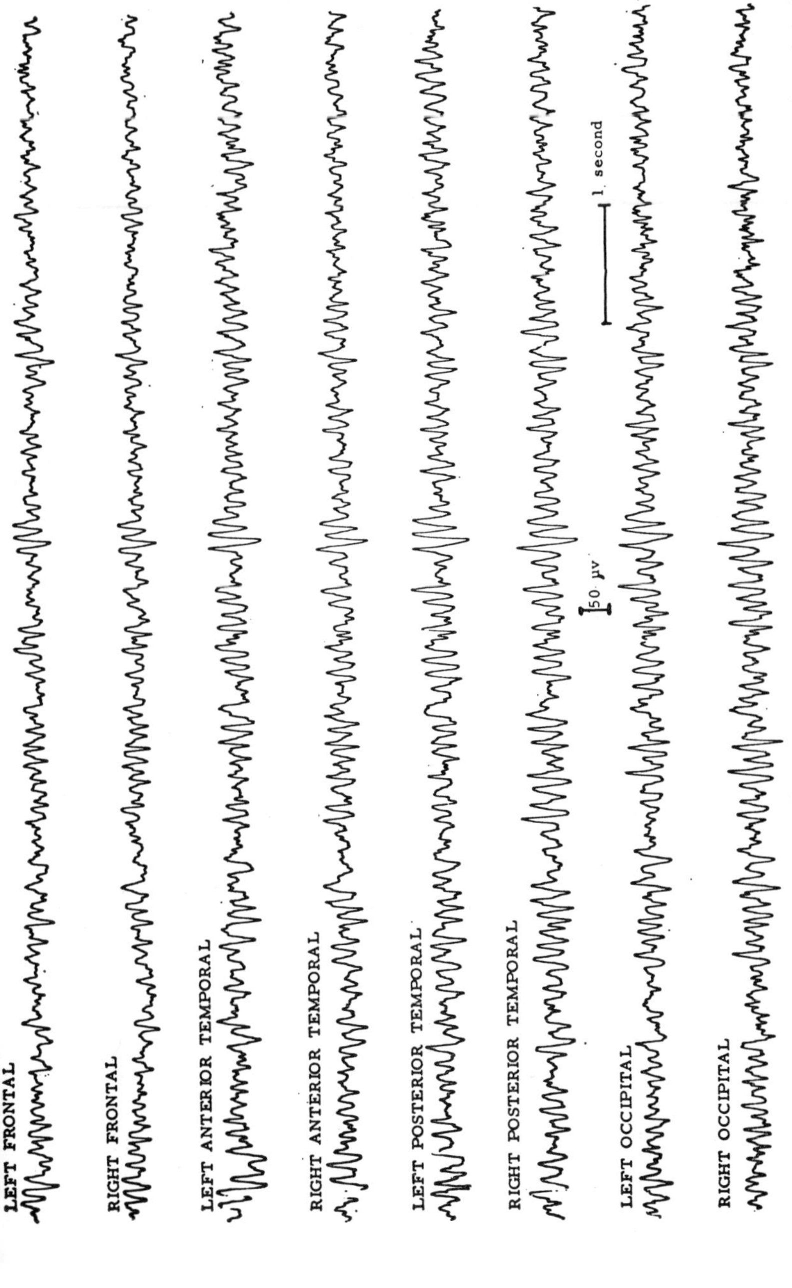

FIGURE 1. Normal EEG, male, age 76. Dominant alpha frequency (alpha index 9-1 over parietal-occipital leads). Rare scattered slow waves (theta).

Fast activity is present in 23 percent of females age 60 to 79 years but in only 4 percent of elderly males (see Figure 2).

Focal abnormalities of EEG, slow waves and sharp waves over the temporal areas of the brain, have been repeatedly observed in 30 to 40 percent of apparently healthy elderly people. Occasionally, the slow waves (delta) are polymorphic; that is, the slow waves appear to have a superimposed activity. Polymorphic slow waves are suspected of being associated with localized brain damage, but our studies of cerebral blood flow do not confirm a focal vascular pathology (26). The left anterior temporal area is primarily involved (75 to 80 percent). In approximately 25 percent of temporal foci, the mid- and posterior temporal leads are active. Bilateral focal patterns are found in 18 to 20 percent, and in 4 to 5 percent the disturbance is found on the right. This finding was first reported by Busse, et al. in 1955 (27). Since that date the observation of the frequent occurrence of a left-temporal focus in old people has been reported by other investigators. A study of healthy volunteers between the ages of 20 and 60 reveals that only 3 percent of normal adults under the age of 40 years have temporal lobe EEG changes. This percentage increases, so that in the 20 years between 40 and 60, 20 percent of the subjects show temporal lobe irregularities. After age 60, the severity of the focal disturbance tends to stabilize, but new foci are more likely to appear in women; hence a higher percentage of women have the change as compared to men (28).

In spite of over 20 years of study, the exact origin of these foci, as well as their significance, is not clear. The localized EEG abnormality is usually episodic in nature and is composed of high-voltage waves in the delta and theta range, occasionally accompanied by focal short waves. The disturbance is found in the waking record, is maximum in the drowsy state, and disappears in sleep (29). In 75 to 80 percent of the cases the abnormality is at a maximum in, or completely confined to, the left side of the brain. It is not related to handedness, and although it is evidently episodic in nature, it is unrelated to seizures. Numerous attempts have been made to relate temporal foci to localized cerebral vascular insufficiency and transient ischemic attacks. No consistent relationship has been established. Furthermore, the anterior temporal focal disturbances in senescent

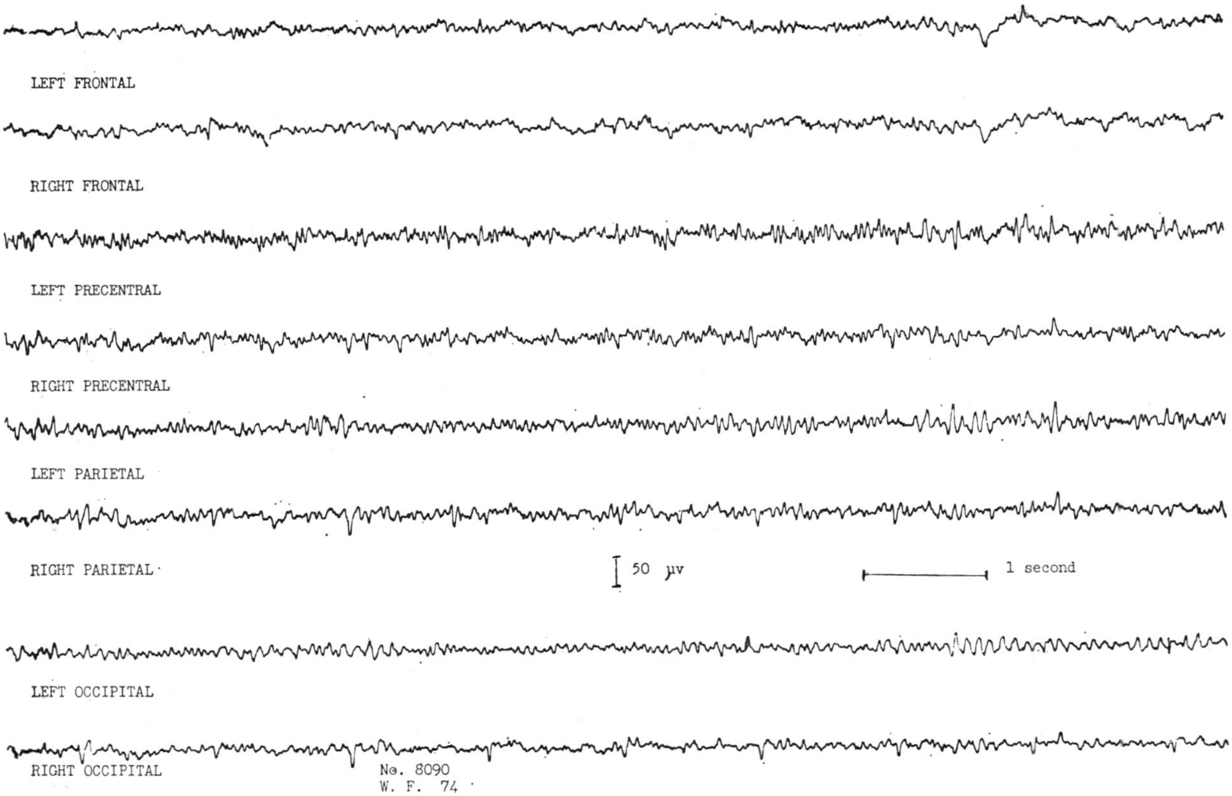

LEFT FRONTAL

RIGHT FRONTAL

LEFT PRECENTRAL

RIGHT PRECENTRAL

LEFT PARIETAL

RIGHT PARIETAL

LEFT OCCIPITAL

RIGHT OCCIPITAL

No. 8090
W. F. 74

1 second

50 μv

FIGURE 2. Fast EEG, white female, age 74. Fast waves in all leads. Maximum in the parietal leads. Fast waves common (25-35 percent) in elderly women but rare in men (5 percent or less).

EEG's have not been consistently correlated with any clear alteration in psychologic function, social adjustment, chronic disease, or longevity. Obrist (30) indicates, however, that when a focal alteration "involves adjacent areas or is associated with a more diffuse disturbance, organic brain syndrome is probable"* (see Figure 3).

Averaged Evoked Potential (AEP)

This particular method of studying the physiologic changes in the brain is an EEG-derived bioelectric response of the central nervous system elicited by a brief stimulus. The phenomenon is usually referred to as the averaged evoked potential (AEP), and sometimes it is called the cerebral evoked response (CER). I prefer the latter. The characteristics of this bioelectric measure are influenced by the type of stimulus and the area of the central nervous system being affected; consequently, studies differentiate accordingly. Visual stimulus or visual evoked response may be referred to as VER; auditory stimulus as AER; somatosensory evoked response as SER.

These complicated studies have been made possible only by the utilization of computer capabilities. Those interested in a more detailed and yet understandable review of the origin and the composition of these interesting responses should consult Beck and Dustman's publication of 1975 (31). The measured response is usually divided into two parts, an early and a late component, and at least eight subcomponents are also observed for age changes. It appears that this type of research will be extremely useful in understanding the physiologic basis for learning, memory, and the value of pharmaco-

---

* Brief explanation of EEG classification:
Normal includes alpha 8-12 c/sec and beta (low voltage fast)—15-35 c/sec at low amplitude.
Diffuse slow includes theta (4-7 c/sec) and delta (1-3 c/sec).
Diffuse fast—above alpha frequency usually 15 c/sec or more exceeding 15 microvolts and present 50 percent of the time or more, (not gamma) (26).
Focal disturbance includes: (a) focal slow, (b) amplitude asymmetry, (3) focal sharp waves.
Focal only—localized abnormality with normal activity in other parts of the brain.
Total foci include focal only and a focal abnormality accompanied by a diffuse disturbance.

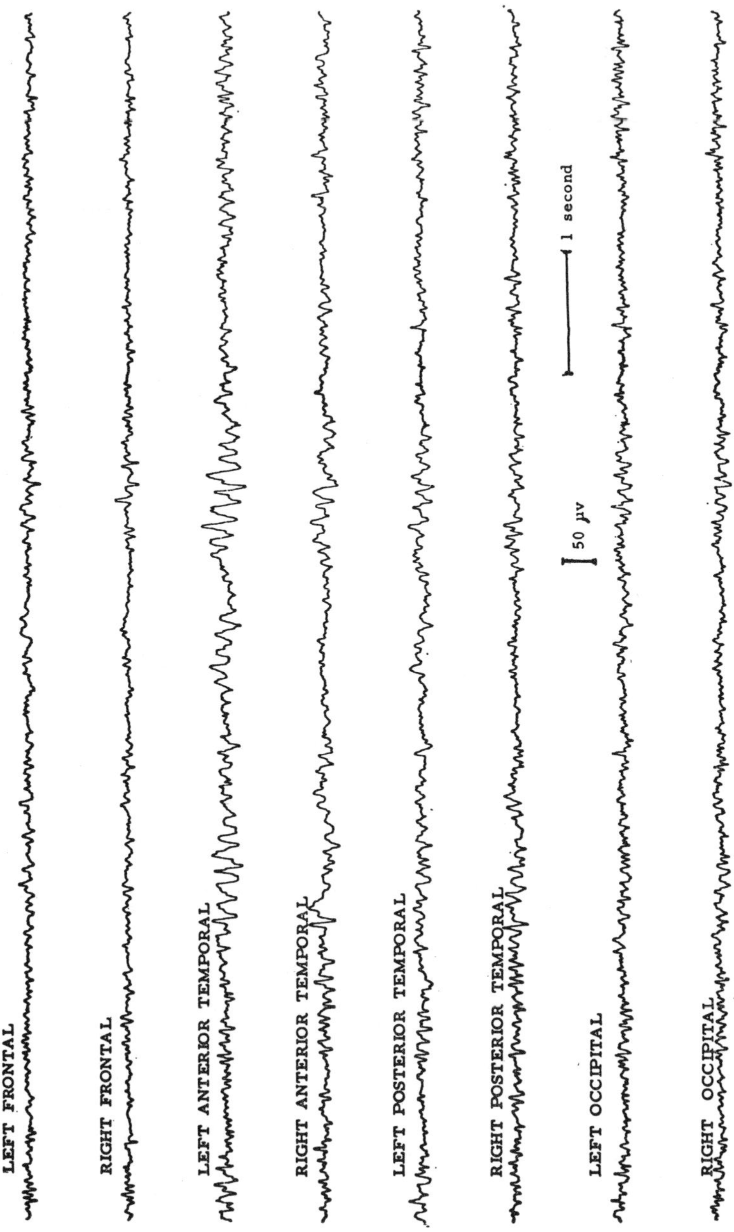

FIGURE 3. Focal EEG, female, age 77. Maximum—left anterior temporal. Note spread on left and reflection in right temporal leads. Minimal mental impairment.

logic agents in improving the functioning of the brain. At the present time, one aspect of AEP seems to have received particular attention, the so-called late positive component (LPC). Furthermore, it appears that the visual stimulation results in a response that is most sensitive to age changes (32).

Sleep

During the past 15 years, considerable advancement has been made in our understanding of the physiologic changes during sleep, although the functions of sleep in a large degree remain a mystery. Four major stages of sleep have been identified. Stage I, commonly known as rapid eye movement sleep (REM) after the first REM appearance in a night of sleep, is the stage that is most likely to be associated with dreams. Four to five REM episodes occur during a night's sleep, and these REM periods become progressively longer during the sleep period. Sleep patterns and sleep requirements change throughout the life span (33). In advanced age, the REM periods become more equal in duration, and Stage IV, the deepest stage of sleep, virtually disappears.

Elderly people require a longer period to fall asleep, their sleep is lighter, and they experience more frequent awakenings. It is important that people in the latter part of their life span recognize that the process of going to sleep lengthens and that, as part of their normal aging changes, they will be aware of more frequent awakenings. Throughout adult life, women sleep differently than men. Women spend more time in bed, sleep more, and awaken during the night less often than do men.

A variety of sleep complaints occur in the elderly, and these are reflected in their utilization of sleeping pills. In one study of apparently well-adjusted community subjects over the age of 60, up to 40 percent occasionally used sleeping pills, and 10 percent habitually took medication to induce or assure sleep. In elderly subjects who are free of physical pain, those who used sleeping pills excessively were found to have many other neurotic complaints and to be poorly adjusted socially (27). Recent studies indicate that sleep changes are more pronounced in persons with organic brain disease (34).

The Surviving Spouse: Why Do Women
Live Longer Than Men?

Since 1900, the percentage of the United States population age 65 and over has more than doubled, from 4.1 percent in 1900 to an estimated 10.3 precent in 1975, while the actual number of aged persons has increased sevenfold from 3,000,000 to over 21,000,000 (8.9 million males and 12.8 million females) (35). There has also been a clear reversal in life expectancy trends for men and women. In 1900, in the United States there were 98 old women to every 100 old men. Women have had longer life expectancies from 1900 onward (36). During the two-year period 1900 to 1902, life expectancy for white females below age 20 was lower than for males of a like age but slightly higher for females through the adult years.

By 1964, the longevity of the young female had improved remarkably and had considerably surpassed that of the young male. Apparently this was not the result of selective immigration, that is, more men than women coming into the country, but a shift in health as related to sex.

Women are outliving men. In fact, there are about 138.5 older women per 100 older men. Life expectancy for women is still increasing faster than for men. During the next years, although it is unlikely that the percentage of the population of older people in the population will increase significantly, their actual number will go over 27,000,-000 (37). Assuming that the current life expectancy trends continue, by the year 2000 the ratio of elderly women to men will be approximately 149 women to 100 men.

In the United States, the high mortality of males as compared to females appears to be a complex interaction between genetically determined physiologic differences, socioeconomic factors and cultural values, and expectations and environmental conditions that may be more dangerous to the man than to the woman.

Waldron (38) presents data to indicate that 40 percent of the excess male mortality is due to arteriosclerotic heart disease. An additional one-third is due to the male having a higher rate of suicide, fatal motor accidents and other accidents, cirrhosis of the liver, carcinoma of the lung, and emphysema. Thus, these conditions account for 75 percent of the causes of the male mortality. It is clear that cultural behavioral patterns which are more prevalent among men than women contribute to arteriosclerotic heart disease, as well as habits of excessive smoking and drinking and a higher risk behavior found so often in men as compared to women. Johnson, in a recent review of sex mortality differentials in the United States, concludes that data do not indicate a "purely biological" explanation but are most consistent with a social stress theory (39).

Genetic factors undoubtedly play a role, but the interaction of such factors with the environment must be kept in mind. It is true that in many species males have a higher mortality rate than females, particularly in insects and in other Arthropoda. However, a higher female mortality appears to be just as common in many birds and mammals. For example, in mallard ducks it appears that the female mallard suffers a much higher natural mortality than the male (40).

Human males do have a higher fetal mortality, as well as a higher mortality during the first year of life. Prior to the development of the fetus there are male/female differences, as the male-producing Y-carrying sperm is claimed to be smaller, with a head resembling an arrowhead, and having a longer tail and being much speedier in its movements. The X-carrying female-producing sperm has a larger round head, a shorter tail, and moves at a comparatively sluggish pace. The difference in speed of motility is believed to account for the greater number of male fetuses as opposed to female fetuses (41).

The genetic differences between the male and female cannot be ignored, as the female does have the possible advantage of having two X chromosomes, one in effect backing up the other. The male Y chromosome is smaller than the X chromosome. However, at least 150 detrimental traits are X-linked, while only one has been proven to be Y-linked. It is also likely that sex hormones play a role, but no consistent information regarding the impact of male/female hormones upon longevity is available at this time. More is known about the detrimental effects of hormones than the positive ones, since sex hormones are implicated in atherosclerosis, carcinoma, and high blood pressure.

Sexual Behavior and Attitudes

Our society is currently engaged in a major change in regard to the value and place of sexual activity in the young adult and middle-aged adult. Our society is moving from an attitude that sex is primarily for procreative purposes to one that it is a highly valued recreative pursuit. Sexual permissiveness is permeating the adolescent population, but clearly observable changes are not as yet evident in our elderly population. The adult child is often upset by observing the flirtatious behavior of an elderly parent. Many elderly persons are aware that this bothers their adult children and deliberately avoid such anxiety-producing behavior when in their presence. It is also possible that the taboo against sex in old age served the selfish interests of the middle and younger generation. The stereotype of the elderly as an asexual group, or as incapable of competing with them in many aspects of living, is fostered by younger people.

In 1972, Weiss and Butler (42) expressed the belief that elderly women and their sexual needs and rights are being neglected by the women's liberation movement. Nearly six years have passed, and little has changed. Sexual activity of an elderly male is likely to be sanctioned, and it is permissible for him to marry a younger woman. In contrast, women who show an interest in sexuality are seen as depraved or "grasping for lost youth." Sexual interest by an older female involving a younger male is not socially condoned. These observations are substantially accurate, but no effort is made to understand the resisting forces that prevent the sexual liberation of an elderly woman.

The male-female ratio in the population has been noted, and marriage in late life will be considered. Under these circumstances the surviving male has the opportunity to expand his sexual choices, while the elderly woman is being restricted by the reality of male-female imbalance.

Because of the increased number of females, a few physicians and social scientists have advocated that polygamy be permitted after the age of 60. One author (43) believes that a man should have the right to marry two to five women in the same age group. According to these advocates of polygamy, plural marriages have many advantages, including the reestablishment of a family constellation, a method of insuring a better diet, improving the economic status of the participants, reducing illness, providing better care while ill, sharing housework, and avoiding depression and loneliness. It also is believed that the aging male will respond to the extra stimulation and function appropriately.

The aging male and female undergo important anatomic and physiologic sex changes. The pioneering investigations of Masters and Johnson (44) can be divided into two categories. The first category consists of laboratory observations related to the anatomic and physiologic changes in old age, and the second category is composed of data derived from interviews with a larger but self-selected group of aged subjects. Laboratory observations were conducted on 35 men whose ages ranged from 51 to 89 years. Sociosexual interviews were carried out with 212 men beyond the age of 50 years. As to the study of females, 61 menopausal and postmenopausal subjects were utilized. In this grouping, the youngest was 41, and the oldest 78. Thirty-four of the participants were considered to be postmenopausal.

Masters and Johnson cautioned that in many instances the number of women was insufficient to provide biologic data of statistical significance.

In aging men, with the passage of time, the usual nipple erection that accompanies the act of ejaculation declines so that the majority, if not all, of males after the age of 60 do not demonstrate nipple erection at the time of ejaculation. Under the age of 60, the correlation of these two events is expected. It is evident that most, if not all, physiologic processes are slowed with the passing of time. Consequently, it takes the aging male a longer period of time to achieve erection. For the male 60 or over full penile erection is frequently not attained until just before ejaculatory experience. However, the maintenance of penile erection over long periods of time without ejaculation is also an achievement of old age. Masters and Johnson point out that a slowing process is inevitable, and this slowing should be recognized as normal by both the male and his female partner. Probably the most important change in the male sexual function associated with the aging process is the reduction both in the frequency of ejaculation and the need to ejaculate (44). A male in his middle and late sixties often finds that his demand for ejaculatory release of sexual tension levels out to about once a week, while he may enjoy sexual intercourse twice a week or more. Again, the reduced demand for ejaculatory release should be accepted without reservation by both husband and wife.

The aging process also has obvious physiologic influences on the sexual response cycle of the female. Production of vaginal lubrication is the exact physiologic counterpart of the male erection. Consequently, vaginal lubrication may be delayed in onset and in full development. These changes develop relatively rapidly in the postmenopausal woman. In addition to the delay in the response, there is also a reduction in the amount of lubrication. Not infrequently, the postmenopausal woman reports that she is more easily distracted from the sexual response cycle, and the lubricating process may be slowed or even terminated in situations where previously stimuli may not have interfered with the response.

After the menopause the mucosal lining of the vagina usually becomes very thin and atrophic; hence the vaginal wall is vulnerable to the trauma associated with the sexual act. Local irritation and bleeding may occur. Aging usually brings a loss of some of the fatty integument of the external genitalia with the constriction of the vaginal outlet. Hence, there are other factors that may contribute to distress or pain during intercourse.

Few postmenopausal women experience painful tonic contractions of the uterus accompanying orgasm. In younger women the uterus contracts rhythmically with orgasm. This pattern is not dissimilar to the contractions observed during the first stage of labor. However, in advanced years the rhythm of the contractions may be lost and a spasm can occur which is experienced as a severe lower abdominal pain. This type of spastic uterus response accompanying orgasm reflects a state of sex steroid starvation. Consequently, sex steroid replacement is particularly useful in such cases.

The existence or absence of the male climacteric continues to be a subject of debate. If it occurs it is, in my opinion, quite rare and difficult to distinguish from a depression. The testes of the aging male show little change in normal structure. If the clinician elects a trial on hormone replacement for the elderly male, one must exercise considerable caution, as prostatic hypertrophy is common in elderly men, and testosterone frequently accentuates this condition. Furthermore, testosterone is definitely contraindicated if a neoplasm of the prostate is suspected, as this hormone accelerates the development of a carcinoma. Another complication in males is the possible development of polycythemia. Therefore, if testosterone is given to a male, regular hemoglobin and red cell determinations are important and attention must be given to the possibility of prostatic changes.

The first Duke Longitudinal Study has been previously described in this paper. Many reports related to sexual behavior and attitudes based upon data derived from the investigation have appeared in journals. The reports concerned with the frequency of sexual activity have remained relatively consistent over the past 19 years. The sexual changes that do occur provide useful information to clinicians but may reflect cohort differences rather than age changes. A publication in 1954 (45), which was actually based upon a cross-sectional analysis, reported that the amount of sexual activity was correlated with socioeconomic status; that is, the better the socioeconomic status of the subjects, the more likely was the continuation of sexual activity. Since then, it has become evident that the variable of physical health must be given primary attention, as physical health is an important determinant regardless of socioeconomic status. Individuals who live in poverty or near poverty are not as likely to be in good health as those who are better off. Consequently, there are several factors that interact to influence the continuation or termination of sexual activity.

Sexual activity between marital partners tends to be maintained until after the age of 75. Approximately 60 percent of married couples between the ages of 60 to 74 years of age remain sexually active. After the age of 75 coitus declines to less than 30 percent of married couples. The continuation of sexual activity is dependent upon several interrelated factors, including the availability of a sexual partner. Among the married, the physical and mental health of the partner is important, as are the patterns of sexual interest and activity that have been established in early adulthood. Only 7 percent of the elderly subjects without a wife or husband continued to have sexual relations in old age. This small percentage drops rapidly with advancing age. A larger number of men, four of five in good health, express a continuing interest in sexual activity (46). Verbalized interest in sex is found in about a third of elderly women—this loss of interest by the female may be a direct result of the lack of stimuli, since the older woman lives in a predominantly women's world.

Two-thirds of men 65 years and over live with wives, but only one-third of women over 65 have husbands. Most older men are married, while most older women are widows. There are almost four times as many widows as widowers. It should be noted that about two-fifths of the older married men have wives under 65 years of age. There are at least 35,000 marriages a year in which the groom and/or the bride is 65 years of age or over. The number of marriages among elderly people has been steadily increasing.

The marital status of the aged group—that is, 75-plus years—reflects the social tradition for men to marry younger women. Twice as many aged men as women are married, and only one-third of the men have wives over 75. About one-half have wives between 65 and 74 years of age, and a fifth have wives under 65 years of age.

Of men 75 years or older, 33.9 percent are living with their wives. In contrast, of 75-plus women, only 17.8 percent are living with their husbands. Of these women who are 75 years or older, 3 percent have husbands under 65 years of age; roughly 20 percent have younger husbands between the ages of 65 and 74; and the remainder have husbands their own age or older. Each year approximately 2,000 women aged 75 or older marry, and 6,000 men 75 years or older go to the altar. Both of these groups are usually moving out of widowhood. Of these 8,000 marriages, over 4,000 are involved with partners under age 75.

The difference in marital status for older patients is of significance to the physician, as it has been reported that the hospital admission rates and stays of the unmarried exceed those of the married (47).

The single woman who is seeking to marry finds the probability of her achieving marriage is very much influenced by her previous marital status (48). At age 35, a never-married female has a 50 percent chance of marrying; a widow, a 67 percent chance; and a divorcee, a 94 percent chance. At age 40, the single never-married has a 20 percent chance of marrying; a widow, 50 percent; and a divorcee, 84 percent. Five years later, that is, at age 45, a single woman has a 12 percent chance of marrying; the widow, 34 percent; and the divorcee, 69 percent. No national figures are available regarding the marrying possibilities of the never-married single, the widow, or divorced elderly person. However, it appears that regardless of the age, the divorcee has the best chance of being remarried. One would doubt that this finding is based upon the desirability of the woman as determined by such factors as appearance and economic status; it may merely be the result of effort.

Many women, particularly those in late middle-age, realize that they in all likelihood will outlive their husbands. Many such women begin to indulge in fantasy and behavior of a sort that Neugarten labels "rehearsal for widowhood" (49). This preparation for widowhood, when approached sensibly and realistically, can be of considerable benefit but, when the relationship is far from congenial, the wife may begin to develop plans and behavior which are quite divergent from the interest and even well-being of her husband.

It is evident that during the latter part of life sexual activity is, as earlier, influenced by physical and psychosocial factors. It is likely that the health of the elderly will gradually improve, and the rapid change in social attitudes and expectations will be reflected in a definite increase in sexual activity among the elderly.

REFERENCES

1. CARRELL, A. and EBELING, A. H.: Age and multiplication of fibroblasts. *Journal of Experimental Medicine*, 34:599-623, 1921.
2. HAYFLICK, L. and MOORHEAD, P. S.: The serial cultivation of human diploid cells. *Experimental Cell Research*, 25:585-621, 1961.
3. HOLLIDAY, R., HUTSCHTSCHA, L. I., TARRANT, G. M., and KIRKWOOD, T. B. L.: Testing the commitment theory of cellular aging. *Science*, 190:136-137, October, 1977.
4. WALFORD, R.: *The Immunological Theory of Aging.* Copenhagen: Munksgaard, 1969.
5. BURNET, F. M.: An immunological approach to aging. *Lancet*, 2: 358, 1970.
6. NANDY, K., FRITZ, R. B., and THREATT, J.: Specificity of brain-reactive antibodies in serum of old mice. *Journal of Gerontology*, 30:269-274, 1975.
7. KENT, S.: Can normal aging be explained by the immunologic theory? *Geriatrics*, 32:112-138, May, 1977.

8. *Immunology—Its Role in Disease and Health,* DHEW Publication No. (NIH) 77-940, National Institute of Allergy and Infectious Diseases, Bethesda, Maryland, 1977.

9. COHEN, D. and EISDORFER, C.: Behavioral-immunologic relationships in older men and women. *Experimental Aging Research,* 3:225-229, May, 1977.

10. BIRREN, J. E. and RENNER, V. J.: Research on the psychology of aging. In: J. E. Birren and K. W. Schaie (Eds.), *Handbook of the Psychology of Aging.* New York: Van Nostrand Reinhold Company, 1977, pp. 3-38.

11. BALTES, P. B. and WILLIS, S. L.: Toward psychological theories of aging and development. In: J. E. Birren and K. W. Schaie (Eds.), *Handbook of the Psychology of Aging.* New York: Van Nostrand Reinhold Company, 1977, pp. 128-150.

12. SCHAIE, K. W.: Toward a stage theory of adult cognitive development. *Journal of Aging and Human Development,* 8:129-138, 1977-78.

13. KALISH, R. A. and KNUDTSON, F. W.: Attachment versus disengagement: A life-span conceptualization. *Human Development,* 19:171-181, 1976.

14. LOWENTHAL, M. F. and HAVEN, C.: Interaction and adaptation: Intimacy as a critical variable. In: B. L. Neugarten (Ed.), *Middle Age and Aging.* Chicago: University of Chicago Press, 1968, pp. 390-400.

15. GOULD, J. and KOLB, W. L.: *Dictionary of the Social Sciences.* New York: Free Press of Glencoe, 1964.

16. MADDOX, G. L. and WILEY, J.: Scope concepts and methods in the study of aging. In: R. H. Binstock and E. Shanas (Eds.), *Aging and the Social Sciences.* New York: Van Nostrand Reinhold Company, 1976, pp. 3-34.

17. REMER, T. G.: *Serendipity and the Three Princes.* Norman: University of Oklahoma Press, 1965.

18. BUSSE, E. W.: The Duke Longitudinal Study I—Senescence and Senility. Presented at the Workshop Conference on Alzheimer's Disease and Senile Dementia and Related Disorders, NIH, Bethesda, Maryland, June 1976 (to be published).

19. SCHAIE, K. W.: A general model of the study of developmental problems. *Psychological Bulletin,* 64:92-107, 1965.

20. PALMORE, E.: Design of the adaptation study. In: E. Palmore (Ed.), *Normal Aging II.* Durham: Duke University Press, 1974, Appendix A, pp. 291-296.

21. BRODY, H.: Aging of the vertebrate brain. In: M. Rockstein (Ed.), *Development and Aging in the Nervous System.* New York: Academic Press, 1973, pp. 121-133.

22. SCHEIBEL, M. E., LINDSAY, R. D., TOMIYASU, U., and SCHEIBEL, A. B.: Progressive dendritic changes in aging human cortex. *Experimental Neurology,* 47:391, 1975.

23. BONDAREFF, W. and GEINISMAN, Y.: Loss of synapses in the

dentate gyrus of the senescent rat. *American Journal of Anatomy*, in press.

24. WISNIEWSKI, H. M. and TERRY, R. D.: Neuropathology of the aging brain. In: R. D. Terry (Ed.), *Neurobiology of Aging*. New York: Raven Press, 1976, pp. 265-280.

25. HESTON, L. L. and MASTRI, A. R.: The genetics of Alzheimer's disease. *Archives of General Psychiatry*, 34:976-981, August, 1977.

26. DONDEY, M. and GAUCHES, J.: Formulation of an EEG semiology. In: Antoine Remond (Ed.), *Handbook of Electroencephalograpy and Clinical Neurophysiology*. Amsterdam: Elsevier Scientific Publishing Company, 1977, Vol. 22, Part A, Section 2, pp. 11A-25 — 11A-40.

27. BUSSE, E. W., BARNES, R. H., SILVERMAN, A. J., THALER, M. B., and FROST, L. L.: Studies of the processes of aging. X. Strengths and weaknesses of psychic functioning in the aged. *American Journal of Psychiatry*, 111:896-901, 1955.

28. BUSSE, E. W.: Brain wave changes in late life. *Clinical Electroencephalography*, 4:153-163, 1973.

29. BUSSE, E. W. and OBRIST, W. D.: Significance of focal electroencephalographic changes in the elderly. *Postgraduate Medicine*, 34:179-182, 1963.

30. OBRIST, W. D.: Problems of aging. In: Antoine Remond (Ed.), *Handbook of Electroencephalography and Clinical Neurophysiology*. Amsterdam: Elsevier Scientific Publishing Company, Vol. 6, Part A, Section 6, 6:6A275-6A292, 1976.

31. BECK, E. C. and DUSTMAN, R. E.: Developmental electrophysiology of brain function as reflected by changes in the evoked response. In: J. W. Prescott, M. S. Read, and D. B. Coursin (Eds.), *Brain Function and Malnutrition*. New York: John Wiley & Sons, 1975.

32. MARSH, G.: Electrophysiological correlates of aging and behavior. *Special Review of Experimental Aging Research: Progress in Biology*. Bar Harbor: Experimental Aging, Incorporated, 1976, pp. 165-178.

33. WILLIAMS, R., KARACAN, I., and HURSCH, C. J.: *EEG of Human Sleep—Clinical Implications*. New York: John Wiley & Sons, 1974.

34. FEINBERG, I., BRAUN, M., and SCHULMAN, E.: EEG sleep patterns in mental retardation. *Electroencephalography and Clinical Neurophysiology*, 27:128-141, 1969.

35. NEUGARTEN, B. L.: The future and the young-old. *The Gerontologist*, 15:9, 1975.

36. RILEY, M. W. and FONER, A.: *Aging and Society*. New York: Russell Sage Foundation, 1968, p. 28.

37. U.S. Department of Labor, Bureau of Census. *Statistical Abstract of the U.S.*, Table 6, 1971, p. 81.

38. WALDRON, I.: Why do women live longer than men? *Journal of Human Stress*, 2:2-29, 1976.

39. JOHNSON, A.: Recent trends in sex mortality differentials in the United States. *Journal of Human Stress*, 3:21-32, 1977.
40. DONNELLY, J.: Duck wings tell a story. *Wild Life in North Carolina*, 18-19, December, 1974.
41. ROSENFELD, A.: If Oedipus' parents had only known. *SR World*, 49-52, September 7, 1974.
42. WEISS, L. M. and BUTLER, R. N.: Neglected by women's lib. *The National Observer*, July 29, 1972, p. 20.
43. KASSELL, V.: Polygyny for aged could add spice to life. *Geriatric Focus*, 5:1, June, 1966.
44. MASTERS, W. H. and JOHNSON, V. E.: Sex over sixty. *Geriatrics —Medical World News*, 74-76, 1971.
45. BUSSE, E. W., BARNES, R. H., SILVERMAN, A. J., THALER, M. B., and FROST, L. L.: Studies of process of aging: VI. Factors that influence the psyche of elderly persons. *Am. J. Psychiatry*, 110: 897-903, 1954.
46. PFEIFFER, E.: Geriatric sex behavior. *Medical Aspects of Human Sexuality*, 3:19-28, July, 1969.
47. BROTMAN, H. B.: Who are the aged, a demographic view. Read before the 21st Annual University of Michigan Conference on Aging, Ann Arbor, August 5, 1968.
48. KLEMER, R. H.: Problems of widowed, divorced, and unmarried women. *Medical Aspects of Human Sexuality*, 3:26-34, April, 1969.
49. NEUGARTEN, B. L.: Personal communication re two studies: (1) One hundred middle-aged women; and (2) One hundred middle-aged men and women, fifty each.

BIBLIOGRAPHY

BUSSE, E. W. and PFEIFFER, E. (Eds.): *Behavior and Adaptation in Late Life*. Boston: Little, Brown and Company, 1977.
BINSTOCK, R. H. and SHANAS, E. (Eds.): *Handbook of Aging and the Social Sciences*. New York: Van Nostrand Reinhold Company, 1976.
FINCH, C. E. and HAYFLICK, L. (Eds.): *Handbook of the Biology of Aging*. New York: Van Nostrand Reinhold Company, 1977.
TERRY, R. D. and GERSHON, S. (Eds.): *Neurobiology of Aging*. New York: Raven Press, 1976.
MALLETTA, G. J. (Ed.): *Survey Report on the Aging Nervous System*. U.S. Department of Health, Education, and Welfare, National Institutes of Health, Publication No. (NIH)74-296.

6

Death and Dying

Thomas H. Holmes, M.D.

The boast of heraldry, the pomp of pow'r,
And all that beauty, all that wealth e'er gave,
Await alike the inevitable hour:
The paths of glory lead but to the grave.

From Gray's "Elegy in a Country Churchyard."

Death is omnipresent. It permeates culture and influences and molds fashions in attitudes, values, and behavior in explicit and implicit ways. Death is the subject of some of the world's great paintings, music, architecture, and literature. It is a major concern of medicine and the law. Myriad economic facets are implicated in its thrust. Death is a central theme of religion. It predicts the future. By the process of *differential mortality*, it determines the genetic composition of succeeding generations, that is, death of the young throughout human history has exerted a major influence on natural selection and the evolution of mankind. Thus, death has a dual role in determining both the biology and the sociocultural environment of man.

Despite its universality, as well as man's continuous experience with it, death still embodies much of the unknown. Biologically, death tends to occur prematurely. Most bodily systems are still reasonably intact and capable of functioning at the time of death, despite the age of the individual.

Another biological dimension that is poorly understood is the mechanism by which death is achieved. Certainly the cardiovascular system is the system of sudden death, and the lethal effect of trauma, poisons, and lack of oxygen on bodily mechanisms is reasonably well understood. However, this leaves the mechanisms of death in most instances unexplained. This is especially true of most chronic diseases, a notable exception being disorders of the heart.

This leads to an examination of dimensions of two questions: 1) What accounts for the time of onset of death? and 2) What are some of the psychophysiologic mechanisms by which death is achieved?

CULTURAL EXPECTATIONS OF DEATH

As part of the process of acculturation, intuitive knowledge about death is acquired by members of the society. At least five categories can be identified where the cultural expectation of death is high: 1) individuals during time of crisis; 2) those with disease; 3) those who live dangerously; 4) the very old or very young; and 5) those who are considered sinful.

These cultural expectations of death appear to have broad relevance. They provide a universe of discourse for formulating "voodoo death" in primitive societies, as written about by Cannon (1), and death in contemporary Western society. Like the medicine man with his bone pointing, the modern physician has his own techniques for communicating to the patient and the family that the time has come to die. Compliance by the involved person is not unusual.

Crisis

The cultural expectation of death is high during time of crisis. Data generated by the systematic use of the Schedule of Recent Experience (SRE) (2, 3) indicate that most, if not all, illnesses have their onset or exacerbation in a setting of high life change. Of relevance to time of death are the studies of heart disease, athletic injuries, fractures, accidents in children, burns, other injuries, and serious suicide attempts (4). Reasoning from these morbidity studies of the time of onset of diseases involved frequently as cause of death, one can infer that life changes also account, in part, for the time of occurrence of death from these diseases.

Two studies have been done that support this inference. Rahe and Romo (5) did a retrospective study of time of coronary heart disease deaths using the SRE. Townes, et al. (6), using the SRE, followed a small number of families prospectively from the time of diagnosis of leukemia in a child to his death. Both studies indicate that death occurs in a setting of increasing life change or a life crisis.

Mortality experience of prisoners of the Japanese during World War II documents not only the immediate impact of the crisis on the death rate, but also that the effect may be long lasting. During the first year of imprisonment, the death rate was three times that ordinarily expected. By the second year, the death rate was eight times the expected rate (7). Liberation after the war and rehabilitation to health did not alter the mortality experience. Six years later the same high death rate in these people persisted (8).

Clinical experience also supports the inference that death occurs in unique life situations composed of salient events and emotional states. Engel (9, 10), using an intuitive approach, documents the occurrence of sudden death in settings of anniversaries, loss, danger, threat, or triumph, coupled with strong emotional reactions such as hopelessness, helplessness, relief, or pleasure.

Hackett and Weisman (11, 12, 13) report a series of patients with "predilection to death. . . ." These patients predicted their own death in the near future as appropriate and reasonable—and were free, for the most part, from conflict, tension, anxiety, or depression.

"Blind alley behavior" is another reaction to a life crisis which culminates slowly in death. Here the individual's perception is that for a variety of reasons he or she has gone as far in life as possible. There is no way left to go and it is too late to retrace the steps to another route, or to start over. The individual retires to a state of relative hibernation and either chronic invalidism or death. Stewart Wolf (14) has called this state, which is similar to Hackett's predilection to death category, "the end of the rope" syndrome.

Disease

The cultural expectation of death is high for people who are sick or who have disease. When the correlation of morbidity rates to death rates per unit of time are observed, the relationship is very small, but positive. The total number of illnesses experienced per day by over 215 million Americans generates only a very small number of deaths. Most sick people on any given day do not die!

It is only when the relationship of selected diseases to death is examined that the correlation is salient. In the United States, the total number of deaths from cancer, diabetes, anemia, and diseases of the gastrointestinal tract, the heart, the nervous system, and the genitourinary system account for about 85 percent of the deaths experienced by males 45 to 65 years of age (15, 16). These diagnoses have many of the aspects of "Hex words" (11), since death so often closely follows the assignment of the patient to the category.

This cultural expectation of death is well based in other clinical facts. Bruce and his co-workers (17) studied prospectively 5,459 males of whom 2,532 were without heart disease, 592 had hypertension, and 1,586 had coronary artery disease with histories of angina pectoris, coronary occlusion with myocardial infarction, or cardiac arrhythmia with arrest and resuscitation. It is not surprising that of the 140 deaths, 118 of them occurred in males previously diagnosed as having coronary artery disease. Nor is it surprising that the more serious the disease, the higher the death rate. In serious disease the annual rate was 97.9 per 1,000 men; in moderately serious disease the rate was 25.3 per 1,000 men; and for mild disease 6.6 deaths per 1,000 men. The mortality rate was four times as great in the serious disease category as in the mild disease category.

In historical perspective, types of diseases which result in almost certain death change over time (18). Ushered in by the industrial revolution, tuberculosis, along with other infectious diseases, ravaged and decimated the Western world. The death rate was estimated as high as 500 per 100,000 population in urban areas. As a consequence of social evolution and natural selection by differential mortality resulting from infectious diseases, resistance to the "selecting" diseases emerged. Between 1800 and 1900, the death rate was reduced by half, and it has been steadily declining until recently. This helps account for the fact that tuberculosis is a cohort disease. That cohort of the population born between 1880 and 1920 has produced most of the tuberculosis morbidity and mortality experienced in the United States since 1880. As this cohort has aged, the ages of onset and of death have paralleled the progression. The death rate from infectious disease in the older population is still of epidemic proportions and accounts for the fact that pneumonia is still one of the ten leading causes of death.

An urban-industrial life-style has become the modern mode, replacing the old rural-agrarian way of life. As this has transpired, the social and biological evolution which has emerged has largely eliminated the infectious diseases as a cause of death. Now attempts at coping with the problems of the urban-industrial life-style have generated a new set of causes of death. Cancer, cardiovascular-renal disease, and diabetes constitute the new fashion in death.

Living Dangerously

The cultural expectation of death is high for people who live dangerously. Accidents and injuries account for a high proportion of deaths, despite safety engineering, accident prevention, education, and antibiotics. Death from accidents and injuries is an epiphenomenon of living dangerously. The settings in which the activities commonly associated with injury or death occur include: the home; the streets and highways; the light airplane; the sports arena for participants in racing, football, baseball, mountain climbing, hunting; and the field of combat for both civilians and armed service personnel.

The available evidence suggests that accidents and injuries occur when, in the midst of many life changes, the individual is preoccupied with things other than the immediate activity and acts impulsively. This behavior, occurring in an environment where lethal, high energy sources abound, enhances the occurrence of an accident with injury and the probability of death.

Aging

The cultural expectation of death is high for the very young and the very old. Aging is a biological process by which man approaches the life expectancy of species homo sapiens of 100 ± 15 years. The physiological age of an individual (15, 16) can be defined as his current distance from that age of 100. When life expectancy is short, the physiologic age is advanced. There is a close correlation between advancing age and death rate for adults. The rate is relatively high for infants and children, and low during mid-adolescence. There are more deaths in the first year of infancy than are seen to accumulate in the same population followed until it is age 30. The age-specific death rate for adults, that is, the rate for cohorts in the population, doubles every 8.5 years beginning in early adulthood and continuing through senescence. For example, as a cohort in the general population age 40 progresses to age 48.5, the death rate of that cohort doubles. This biologic constant of the increase in risk of death has been called by Hardin Jones "the force of mortality" (15, 16).

The biology of aging involves genetically regulated metabolic and enzyme functions and the integrity of the cardiovascular system. These phenomena are strongly influenced by a variety of environmental and demographic factors, which in turn influence the rate of aging (15, 16). The following are associated with a reduced rate of aging and time of death, their converse with accelerated aging and time of death: 1) rural habitat, 2) habitat in Sweden, Norway, or the Netherlands, 3) married, and 4) female gender. Constitutional factors associated with a longer life span (younger physiologic age) include: 1) normal weight and serum lipoprotein level, and 2) longevity of forebears, i.e., parents and grandparents lived to be 80 or older.

As the aging process advances, the progressive deterioration of integrity of the bodily systems generates a state called disease by modern medicine. These diseases, defined by their signs and symptoms, are correlated with physiologic age, and, in general, are correlated in adults with chronological age as well (15, 16).

The gradual disappearance of the major and minor infectious diseases (15, 16) has contributed to reduction in rate of aging and increase in longevity. The tendency to survive accidental injury, as well as tuberculosis, pneumonia, influenza, and bronchitis, is *increasing* at the same logarithmic doubling of the death rate as the general tendency to die.

People in 1950 were aging less rapidly than people in 1900 (15, 16). A person in 1950 at age 71 had the same physiological age as a person in 1900 at age 56, i.e., he has aged less rapidly and a total of 15 years has been added to his useful life. This is calculated to be a gain in human efficiency of about 10 percent.

Sin

The cultural expectation of death is high for sinners. "For the wages of sin is death" certainly expresses the powerful Christian sentiment about the relationship of morality and death. The converse, "the good die young," is a cultural apology for the conviction that infants, though "conceived in sin," have not had enough experience in their short lives to be personally sinful. The great American morality plays, the cowboy stories of a past generation, the police stories of the current generation have a consistent theme: the good guys always win, crime and sin do not pay.

The Judeo-Christian mandate, "Thou shalt not kill," is translated by the Law into rubrics regulating man's aggressive and destructive behavior. These often reflect society's requirement of an "eye for an eye and a tooth for a tooth"; or as Gilbert and Sullivan's Mikado decrees, "Let the punishment fit the crime." Although there currently exists controversy over whether or not the death sentence is cruel and inhumane punishment, a powerful and vocal segment of society insists that execution of criminals who have committed specified homicidal acts is the requisite of justice. A few prisoners who have admitted their crime of murder insist that punishment by execution is appropriate and should be consummated.

A prominent moral value placed on illness in the Western world holds that illness is tantamount to sinfulness, or even weakness. Since it is "sinful" to smoke cigarettes, death from lung cancer is sinful; since it is sinful to overeat (gluttony), it is sinful to be obese and die of the consequences; since it is sinful to abuse alcoholic beverages, it is sinful to die of cirrhosis of the liver or bleeding esophageal varices. In caricature, even the upwardly mobile, ambitious businessman, who is often unethical if not immoral, and aggressively insensitive to the rights of the other person, must play the ultimate price of reaping the bitter gall of empty success: loneliness, dissatisfaction, disease, and death.

THE PSYCHOPHYSIOLOGIC MECHANISMS OF DYING

The previous section defines five categories in which the cultural expectation of death is high: crisis, disease, danger, age, and sin. The dynamic interaction of these forces helps determine the time of death. This section examines some of the psychophysiologic mechanisms by which death comes about. The cultural set provides the stimuli; the psychophysiologic mechanisms provide the response which culminates in death. The logic of this section is inferential by method and the inferences are often intuitive.

Suicide

Suicide is the problem-solving behavior for hopelessness. Hopelessness is defined as that state in which the individual's perception is that there is no answer to the situation. There is nothing the individual can do and nothing anyone else can do. The present is intolerable and the future seems bleak, dark, empty, meaningless. Living is purposeless.

There seems to be general agreement that four dynamic factors contribute to the emergence of hopelessness: 1) a sense of importance; 2) a sense of guilt, i.e., of having done those things which should not have been done and/or having left undone those things which should have been done; 3) a sense of anger, i.e., the conscious, willful intent to attack, injure, destroy; and 4) a sense of deprivation or of loss.

The epidemiology of suicide indicates that old age, male gender, chronic disease, recent alcohol intake, plans for the act, selection of a lethal method, and writing a note account for much of the variance. On the other hand, gesture suicide occurs in young females who, after recent alcohol intake, impulsively apply a non-lethal method, often in the presence of others. Here the probability of death is low.

Reasoning from clinical observations of patients with serious suicide intent the following sequence seems evident. When the high intensity of the intolerable affect of hopelessness is established, it occurs to the patient that committing suicide is the only possible solution. This conscious decision is often followed by temporary relief of the hopelessness, and may be followed by plans for the successful execution of the act. The completion of the self-destruction does, indeed, alleviate the problem.

Fainting

Fainting is a common cause of sudden death, even in the absence of structural heart disease. Graham, et al. (19) have determined that fainting is the consequence of diphasic or go-stop behavior. Their clinical studies define a hyperdynamic cardiovascular response followed immediately by a hypodynamic cardiovascular phase during which the faint occurs. Anxiety, apprehension, tension, and other intense action-oriented behaviors, such as the excitement of those who only watch sports activities from the sidelines, are characteristic "coping behaviors," occurring simultaneously with the hyperdynamic cardiac response. This behavior is mobilized to adapt to some critical event in the immediate present. Venapuncture in the blood bank caricatures the stimulus. Once the critical event is passed and survival no longer depends on active coping, the hypodynamic cardiovascular phase promptly ensues. As vagal activity replaces sympathetic, there is a drop in pulse rate and systolic and diastolic blood pressure. Loss of consciousness occurs with the reduced blood flow to the brain. Lethal epiphenomena of the faint are asystole, arrhythmia, apnea, and convulsions.

Death by Coronary Occlusion and Myocardial Infarction

Here the point of departure is an older individual with disease, atherosclerosis of the coronary vessel, whose life-style is to approach problems with a go-stop behavior. As described by Friedman and Rosenman (20), this behavior includes tension and an intense drive under pressure toward a goal. Once the deadline is achieved, there is a letdown, at which time the death occurs—from thrombosis of the coronary vessel and myocardial infarction.

Physiologically, during the action-oriented, "go" behavior a hyperdynamic state of the cardiovascular system occurs: pulse rate, cardiac output, and diastolic and systolic blood pressure increase (21). Simultaneously, blood viscosity and hematocrit increase and bleeding time and clotting time decrease (22). Circulating adrenal hormones and free fatty acid increase. Once the deadline is achieved, a hypodynamic cardiac state accompanies the letdown or relief or "stop" behavior, and there is a decrease in pulse rate, cardiac output, diastolic and systolic blood pressure, and circulating hormones. Under these circumstances there is a dramatic decrease in coronary circulation of blood ready to clot when it encounters the atherosclerotic plaque and narrow arterial lumen. This state seems ideal for the propagation of a blood clot and its lethal consequences.

Arrhythmias

Although a variety of cardiac arrhythmias are compatible with life, they often are the mechanism that so disrupts the function of the heart that death is the outcome. A number of investigators (23-27) have established the participation of these rhythmic dimensions of cardiac dysfunction that may accompany adaptive behavior: paroxysmal auricular fibrillation, nodal rhythm, ventricular tachycardia, and ventricular fibrillation. These phenomena have been observed to occur during action-oriented behavior, during the letdown or stop phase following action, and during prolonged periods of non-action-oriented behavior such as withdrawal, helplessness, depression. These psychophysiological reactions, especially in association with progressive structural disease of the heart, are probably commonly involved in the mechanism of death.

Irving and Bruce (28) have made direct observations of the occurrence of ventricular fibrillation with resuscitation immediately following exercise. Patients with serious coronary heart disease were observed during and after maximal exercise testing on a treadmill. Exertional hypotension or a decrease in or limited increase in systolic blood pressure was observed *during* or shortly after the exercise (go phase of the behavior). The reduced perfusion pressure further limited blood supply to the already overburdened cardiac muscle. This alteration in the environment of the neural and muscular components of the heart appears to set the stage for arrhythmia at the termination of exercise which culminates in death.

Kidney Function, Water and Electrolyte Balance

Life situations, emotions, behavior patterns, and the renal excretion of fluid and electrolytes may set the stage for the occurrence of death (29). Action-oriented behaviors were associated with excretion of water, sodium, and potassium. The range of behaviors included preparation for violent action such as anger, tempestuous and aggressive behavior, and feelings of excitement, apprehension, tension, anxiety. Such changes, along with hormonal changes associated with action behavior, may contribute to altered neural and cardiac muscle states that may lower the threshold to arrhythmias and heart failure.

Non-action-oriented behaviors were associated with fluid and electrolyte retention. The range of behaviors included listlessness, inactivity, and feelings of despair, hopelessness, and depression. Many of these behaviors fit into the attitude of being overburdened, having too much to do, carrying a heavy load, having too much responsibility, and wanting others to help (30). In the presence of certain types of heart disease, this reaction may contribute to progressive, intractable heart failure and ultimately death.

Death Associated with Infectious Disease

In a prospective study of 109 patients hospitalized for tuberculosis, the relationship of emotional state, behavior, course of pulmonary tuberculosis, and the urinary excretion of 17-ketosteroids (17-KS), as an index of resistance to infections and inflammation, was investigated (31). In general, minimal tuberculosis occurred in younger, anxious, action-oriented females who had moderately elevated 17-KS excretion. Acute, exudative, bilateral, far advanced tuberculosis occurred in older males who were withdrawn, non-action-oriented, overwhelmed, depressed, and who had reduced resistance as exhibited by low 17-KS excretion.

Those patients whose disease improved rapidly or moderately exhibited mood and behavior and 17-KS excretion which rapidly approached normal. Those whose disease progressed and those who died continued to show withdrawn, depressed, overwhelmed behavior associated with widely fluctuating or decreasing urinary steroid levels.

Comment

Action-oriented behavior, non-action-oriented behavior, and the sequential occurrence of action-non-action, or go-step behavior appear to be the critical coping or adaptive techniques, the epiphenomenon or byproduct of which is sudden death.

Respiratory System Function and Death and Dying

During a 15-year period in my laboratory, the interrelationships of respiratory function, feeling state, behavior, and social status in many patients with advanced diffuse obstructive pulmonary disease were studied and compared and contrasted with subjects with normal pulmonary systems (32). The high mortality rate of the subjects with advanced pulmonary disease provided prospective data (33) of death and dying behavior in these patients. In a sample of 40 such subjects followed for four years, 29 died (72 percent). Ten of the remaining 11 subjects, however, were able to live outside the hospital. Characteristics of the sample under observation relating to the cultural expectation of death include age and constitutional factors, disease, and life crisis. Dying behavior and death in these patients were evaluated and formulated within a universe of discourse provided by acute experiments and natural history observations in a large number of patients and normal subjects. Two distinct patterns of adaptive or coping behavior were documented: 1) action-oriented behavior, and 2) non-action-oriented behavior. Both patterns occurred in response to crisis situations requiring adaptation.

The action-oriented behavior was characterized physiologically by respiratory hyperventilation: increased minute ventilation and alveolar ventilation, and decreased alveolar carbon dioxide. Metabolically, increased oxygen consumption and carbon dioxide production occur. Psychologically, the action orientation includes attitudes of something must be done, anger, anxiety, and tension. This integrated behavior is often associated with dyspnea or shortness of breath.

The non-action behavior was characterized physiologically by respiratory hypoventilation: decreased minute volume and alveolar ventilation, and increased alveolar carbon dioxide. Metabolically, decreased oxygen consumption and carbon dioxide production occur. Psychologically, this non-action-oriented behavior includes withdrawal, non-participation, sleep, depression, and a hibernation-like state. This psychophysiologic state is also often associated with dyspnea or shortness of breath. In subjects with a normally functioning respiratory system, this coping behavior falls well within the physiological range of the organism and is well tolerated.

In subjects with advanced obstructive pulmonary disease, either of these coping styles can have ominous consequences. The hyperventilation is inadequate to keep up with the increased carbon dioxide production and oxygen conusmption. Also, during hypoventilation, and despite the lowered level of metabolism, the embarrassed respiratory system is unable to keep up with the reduced carbon dioxide production. The result of either the hyperventilation-action pattern or the hypoventilation-non-action pattern of adaptation in the presence of advanced obstructive pulmonary disease is acidosis. As the chronic disease progresses, decreased appetite and relative starvation contribute metabolic acidosis to the clinical picture. When the body's reserves of buffer ultimately are depleted, the uncontrolled acidosis establishes an internal environment incompatible with life.

The occurrence of dyspnea is not only highly uncomfortable but is often so disturbing as to enhance the anxiety or depression and set up a vicious circle which perpetuates the disability and discomfort.

These patients learn to adapt by frequent use of a variety of mental mechanisms, prominent among which are denial, repression, withdrawal, and non-participation. They learn to avoid situations which provoke emotions because they know that increasing discomfort and disability will ensue. Techniques of management such as group therapy or dynamic interviews are not only poorly tolerated, but usually avoided after initial exposure. Power struggles or interpersonal conflicts with staff are particularly devastating.

As the disease progresses with age, activity is curtailed, interpersonal and social relationships are restricted, and the quality of life is diluted as sources of satisfaction disappear. When they approach the end of the road or the blind alley of chronic invalidism, these patients utilize a variety of adaptive techniques. Depression with feelings of hopelessness is prevalent, although suicidal preoccupation is seldom identified. Preoccupation with dying, however, is common, and the achievement of death is often considered by the patient as a goal which is both relevant and appropriate to the situation.

Although fear is expressed by some of these patients as the time of death approaches, many find the process comfortable. The main source of distress, however, is not the prospect of death, but continues to involve power struggles and conflicts with staff and family. The maintenance of vigilance and control by the patient in these interperpersonal and social relationships assumes critical importance for the patient. This is especially salient when the staff and family and friends protest the patient's decision to die and seek to interfere with or modify the dying behavior. In such situations the patient may withdraw into increased depression or become aroused, hostile, angry and even abusive. The source of discomfort is seldom the prospect of death but the interpersonal situation. The psychological distress, combined with the physiological distress, places the patient's survival in serious jeopardy by engendering respiratory decompensation. When free from such conflicts, many of these patients describe the dying process as a normal event in man's history and are quite comfortable with the situation and the prospects.

It was not always possible to establish the mechanisms by which death occurred in these patients. In some cases, however, where it was possible to monitor respiratory and metabolic processes during dying behavior, one pattern did emerge. Despite the occurrence of occasional action-oriented behavior and hyperventilation, the predominant trend was that of respiratory hypofunction with decreased ventilation, oxygen consumption, and carbon dioxide production. Respiratory quotient fell, indicating the prominent role of fat metabolism and its contribution to the acidosis already engendered by the progressive respiratory failure. The terminal event seemed to correlate with a precipitous fall in the already reduced blood pH.

Psychologically, these patients were inactive, nonparticipating, sometimes withdrawn, sometimes with an undercurrent of depression and hopelessness. However, some of these patients described themselves during the experience as relaxed, calm, comfortable. There was little spontaneous complaint of shortness of breath.

This pattern of quiet, calm, insulated behavior, with a physiological pattern of respiratory hypofunction and preeminence of fat metabolism, we have labeled hibernation behavior. Death, when it does appear, occurs as an epiphenomenon or byproduct of this style of adaptation.

During this study of patients with diffuse obstructive pulmonary disease, data which predicted outcome were examined. The Berle Index (34), a predictive index of psychosocial assets, was used to compare the deceased with the living at 18 months and at four years from beginning of observations. The following respiratory variables were used to compare the two groups: percent vital capacity, percent maximum breathing capacity, pH of the blood, and partial pressure in arterial blood of oxygen and carbon dioxide.

Comparison of the physiologic variables revealed that both the living and the dead had had significant impairment, and the biologic state of the two groups was not significantly different. The exceptions were an elevated partial pressure of arterial carbon dioxide among the 16 patients who died compared to the 24 living at 18 months, and a higher percent vital capacity among the 11 living patients compared to the 29 patients who were dead by the end of four years of observation.

In contrast, the psychosocial assets as measured by the Berle Index clearly distinguished the two groups at both 18 months and four years. The survivors at both times of comparison had significantly more assets than the ones who had died.

Another comparison was made between the two groups by combining the quantity of psychosocial assets with a physiologic variable. The percent maximum breathing capacity was chosen as the variable most representative of functional respiratory capacity. When this number was combined with the score of the Berle Index, the total obtained discriminated even more significantly between the living and the deceased. The greater the biological and psychosocial assets, the greater the probability of survival.

SUMMARY

The evidence suggests that death is a byproduct or epiphenomenon of man's goals and the techniques used in their achievement. The mechanisms are of learned behaviors which often have adaptive value.

The time of occurrence is determined by man's expectation of death for himself or the culture's expectation of death for him—or both in concert!

> *To every thing there is a season, and a time*
> *to every purpose under the heaven:*
> *A time to be born, and a time to die; . . .*
>
> *Ecclesiastes*, III, 2

REFERENCES

1. CANNON, W. B.: "Voodoo" death. *Psychosomatic Medicine*, 19: 182-190, 1957.
2. HOLMES, T. H. and RAHE, R. H.: The social readjustment rating scale. *Journal of Psychosomatic Research*, 11:213-218, 1967.
3. HOLMES, T. H. and MASUDA, M.: Life change and illness susceptibility. In: J. P. Scott and E. C. Senay (Eds.), *Separation and Depression: Clinical and Research Aspects*. Washington, D.C.: American Association for the Advancement of Science (Publication #94), 1973, pp. 161-186.
4. PETRICH, J. and HOLMES, T. H.: Life change and onset of illness. *Medical Clinics of North America*, 61:825-838, 1977.
5. RAHE, R. and ROMO, M.: Recent life changes and the onset of myocardial infarction and sudden death in Helsinki. In: E. K. Gunderson and R. H. Rahe (Eds.), *Life Stress and Illness*. Springfield, Ill.: Charles C Thomas, 1974, pp. 105-120.
6. TOWNES, B. D., WOLD, D. A., and HOLMES, T. H.: Parental adjustment to childhood leukemia. *Journal of Psychosomatic Research*, 18:9-14, 1974.
7. BERGMAN, R. A. M.: Who is old? Death rate in a Japanese concentration camp as a criterion for age. *Journal of Gerontology*, 3:14-17, 1948.
8. COHEN, B. M. and COOPER, M. Z.: *A Follow-Up Study of World War II Prisoners of War*. Veterans Administration Medical Monograph. Washington, D.C.: Government Printing Office, 1954.
9. ENGEL, G. L.: A life setting conducive to illness. The giving up-given up complex. *Annals of Internal Medicine*, 69:293-300. 1968.

10. ENGEL, G. L.: Sudden and rapid death during psychological stress. *Annals of Internal Medicine*, 74:771-782, 1971.
11. HACKETT, T. P. and WEISMAN, A. D.: "Hexing" in modern medicine. *Proceedings of the Third World Congress of Psychiatry*, pp. 1249-1252, 1961.
12. HACKETT, T. P. and WEISMAN, A. D.: The treatment of the dying. In: J. Masserman (Ed.), *Current Psychiatric Therapies*, Vol. II. New York: Grune & Stratton, Inc., 1962, pp. 121-126.
13. WEISMAN, A. D. and HACKETT, T. P.: Predilection to death: Death and dying as a psychiatric problem. *Psychosomatic Medicine*, 23:232-257, 1961.
14. WOLF, S.: The end of the rope: The role of the brain in cardiac death. *Canadian Medical Association Journal*, 97:1022-1025, 1967.
15. JONES, H. B.: A special consideration of the aging process, disease, and life expectancy. *Advances in Biology and Medical Physics*, 4:281-336, 1956.
16. JONES, H. B.: The relation of human health to age, place, and time. In: J. E. Birren (Ed.), *Handbook of Aging and the Individual*. Chicago: University of Chicago Press, 1959, pp. 336-363.
17. IRVING, J. B., BRUCE, R. A., and DeROUEN, T. A.: Variations in and significance of systolic pressure during maximal exercise (treadmill) testing. *American Journal of Cardiology*, 39:841-848, 1977.
18. HOLMES, T. H.: Infectious diseases and human ecology. *Journal of the Indian Medical Profession*, 10:4825-4829, 1964.
19. GRAHAM, D. T., KABLER, J. D., and LUNSFORD, L.: Vasovagal fainting: A diphasic response. *Psychosomatic Medicine*, 23:493-507, 1961.
20. FRIEDMAN, M. and ROSENMAN, R. H.: *Type A Behavior and Your Heart*. New York: Alfred A. Knopf, 1974.
21. STEVENSON, I. and DUNCAN, C. H.: Alterations in cardiac function and circulatory efficiency during periods of life stress as shown by changes in the rate, rhythm, electrocardiographic pattern and output of the heart in those with cardiovascular disease. *Research Publications Association for Research in Nervous and Mental Disease*, 29:799-817, 1950.
22. SCHNEIDER, R. A.: The relation of stress to clotting time, relative viscosity and certain other biophysical alterations of the blood in the normotensive and hypertensive subject. *Research Publications Association for Research in Nervous and Mental Disease*, 29:818-831, 1950.
23. STEVENSON, I. P., DUNCAN, C. H., WOLF, S., RIPLEY, H. S., and WOLFF, H. G.: Life situations, emotions, and extrasystoles. *Psychosomatic Medicine*, 11:257-272, 1949.
24. STEVENSON, I. P., DUNCAN, C. H., and WOLFF, H. G.: Circulatory dynamics before and after exercise in subjects with and with-

out structural heart disease during anxiety and relaxation. *Journal of Clinical Investigation,* 28:1534-1543, 1949.

25. DUNCAN, C. H., STEVENSON, I. P., and RIPLEY, H. S.: Life situations, emotions, and paroxysmal auricular arrhythmias. *Psychosomatic Medicine,* 12:23-37, 1950.

26. STEVENSON, I., DUNCAN, C. H., and RIPLEY, H. S.: Variations in the electrocardiogram during changes in emotional state. *Geriatrics,* 6:164-178, 1951.

27. RAHE, R. H. and CHRIST, A. E.: An unusual cardiac (ventricular) arrhythmia in a child: Psychiatric and psychophysiologic aspects. *Psychosomatic Medicine,* 28:181-188, 1966.

28. IRVING, J. B. and BRUCE, R. A.: Exertional hypotension and post-exertional ventricular fibrillation in stress testing. *American Journal of Cardiology,* 39:849-851, 1977.

29. SCHOTTSTAEDT, W. W., GRACE, W. J., and WOLFF, H. G.: Life situations, behavior patterns, and renal excretion of fluid and electrolytes. *Journal of American Medical Association,* 157: 1485-1488, 1955.

30. GRACE, W. J. and GRAHAM, D. T.: Relationship of specific attitudes and emotions to certain bodily diseases. *Psychosomatic Medicine,* 14:243-251, 1952.

31. CLARKE, E. R., ZAHN, D. W., and HOLMES, T. H.: The relationship of stress, adrenocortical function, and tuberculosis. *American Review of Tuberculosis,* 69:351-369, 1954.

32. DUDLEY, D. L.: In collaboration with C. J. Martin, M. Masuda, H. S. Ripley, and T. H. Holmes, *Psychophysiology of Respiration in Health and Disease.* New York: Appleton-Century-Crofts, 1969.

33. DUDLEY, D. L., VERHEY, J. W., MASUDA, M., MARTIN, C. J., and HOLMES, T. H.: Long-term adjustment, prognosis, and death in irreversible diffuse obstructive pulmonary syndromes. *Psychosomatic Medicine,* 31:310-325, 1969.

34. BERLE, B. B., PINSKY, R. H., WOLF, S., and WOLFF, H. G.: A clinical guide to prognosis in stress diseases. *Journal of American Medical Association,* 149:1624-1628, 1952.

7

Mental Health and Community Support Systems for the Elderly

Bennett S. Gurian, M.Sc., M.D.
and
Marjorie H. Cantor, M.A.

INTRODUCTION

There are over 600 community mental health centers in the United States, yet fewer than four percent of the clients served are 65 years of age or older. Of the one million persons living in nursing homes, about one-half have identifiable symptoms of mental illness, yet they receive little, if any, active therapeutic intervention. Half the inpatient population of our mental hospitals is made up of persons over 65 years of age (1, 2). Despite our current level of knowledge, most institutionalized elderly persons receive custodial care, are overmedicated, are deprived of human rights without truly giving informed consent, and rarely return to an independent life in the community. Major studies of the prevalence of mental illness among the elderly living in their own homes in large urban communities indicate that 15

184

to 30 percent have need for psychiatric intervention (3). Yet funding has not been available for appropriate programming to meet these needs, nor have there been adequate numbers of well-trained professionals interested in providing the direct services (4, 5).

Therefore, when we describe the components that constitute a system of community supports for the mental health needs of elderly Americans, we are, to an extent, speaking theoretically.

The Community Mental Health Center Act of 1963 (PL. 88-164) placed emphasis on both caring for persons with mental illness within their own communities, and on consultation and education as primary prevention services for those with relative mental well-being. The debate over the definition of mental illness adds to the difficulty faced by those responsible for policy development and program planning. Some policy makers maintain that the mental health network should concern itself solely with those who manifest the symptoms of a disease entity included within the APA *Diagnostic and Statistical Manual* (DSM II) and that all other problems should be left to the other human service providers. Others contend that there are not, in fact, discrete entities of health and illness. In their view, mental health is best conceptualized as a continuum ranging from dysfunctional to functional, with great variability in between.

The elderly, perhaps more than those of other age groups, present a multiplicity of problems requiring a comprehensive approach throughout all stages of our intervention. Mental health programs ought not compromise the quality of orthodox psychiatric diagnosis and treatment, but should provide this in concert with social and medical services in a truly comprehensive way. A discussion of community support systems impacting on the mental well-being and mental illness of older persons is therefore best described with language evolved by other disciplines as well as that of psychiatry.

SUPPORT SYSTEMS

Concept of Support

Gerald Caplan, a psychiatrist, defines "support system" as "an enduring pattern of continuous or intermittent ties that play a significant part in maintaining the psychological and physical integrity of the individual over time" (6). This broad conceptualization emphasizes the consistency and the availability of the relationship, be it of long-term or occasional support. It also is inclusive of both formal ties (organizational, either under government or voluntary auspices) and informal ones (familial or significant others).

Robert S. Weiss, a sociologist, comments that "although no systematic information is available on helping people in crisis, unsystematic observation suggests that almost the only useful form of help is *support*. Support is furnished by a helper (who may or may not be a professional), who is accepted as an ally by the distressed individual. It consists of the communication, sometimes nonverbal, by the helper that the helper's training, experience, and understanding are at the service of the distressed individual as the latter struggles to regain equilibrium" (7).

Social Support System*

Our holistic approach requires that we think of an elderly person not only in intrapsychic terms but as a functioning element of a natural setting. This underscores our need to understand the relationship of mental health services to other support systems, most importantly to those constituted of relatives, friends, and neighbors. The whole social support system is seen as enabling older persons to meet three major needs: socialization, the carrying out of tasks of daily living, and assistance during times of illness or crisis (8). Operationally, the system includes all activities and services remaining after one separates out programs dealing with income maintenance and employment, physical health, formal education, and housing (9).

---

* The portions of the chapter pertaining to the social support system of the elderly, the nature of its functioning and the role of formal components are the work of Marjorie Cantor. This material evolved from research undertaken while she was Director of Research at the New York City Department for the Aging. (See bibliography for further references.)

A SYSTEMS VIEW OF THE SUPPORT STRUCTURE

If one can envision an older person as being at the core of a series of subsystems which usually operate independently but at times intersect, the concept of a broad-based social support system becomes clearer. At the outermost reaches of such a schema are the political and economic entities which determine the basic entitlements available to all older people; these impact significantly on their well-being in the areas of income maintenance, health, housing, safety, education and transportation. Somewhat closer to the older person in terms of social distance, though still far from playing a central role, are the governmental and voluntary agencies that carry out economic and social policies by providing the actual services mandated under laws such as the Older Americans Act, Social Security, Medicare, etc. These organizations in the two outer rings are clearly the formal part of the support system. As Sussman has noted, like all bureaucratic organizations, they attempt to function instrumentally and objectively in accordance with an ideology of efficiency and rationality (10).

Still closer, and standing somewhere between formal organizations and primary group members, are the representatives of non-service, formal or quasi-formal organizations, capable of performing a helping function in such roles as those of postmen, storekeepers, bartenders, building superintendents, friendship delegates from unions or visitation groups from churches. This network has been labeled "tertiary," inasmuch as it resembles the informal network but springs from and is related to formal organizations.

Closest to the daily life of an older person are the individuals who comprise the *informal support system*—kin, friends, and neighbors. It is precisely these "significant others" with whom older people have the most frequent interaction both instrumentally and affectively.

In line with such a system approach it is possible to view social networks from a variety of theoretical foci. Some researchers, such as Lowenthal (11), stress issues of isolation and interaction; others, such as Litwak (12, 13), concern themselves with role differentiation, both as between formal and informal network elements and among various types of primary groups. Our interest is with social networks as support systems and, in particular, with the ways in which the various elements of such systems operate to enhance the ability of older people to remain independently in the community (8, 9).

INFORMAL SUPPORT SYSTEM

In recent years there has been increased interest in whether the demise of the traditional extended family has been accompanied by a decrease in supportive interaction between older people and their relatives and friends and by a resultant shift to bureaucratic organizations for the provision of an increasing proportion of assistance.

Research seems to indicate that, although family structure continues to change, an informal support network of relatives, friends and neighbors still exists. The amount and nature of interaction with the elderly undoubtedly varies in different areas and sociological strata, but, on the whole, evidence exists of a solid core of informal social support, particularly in time of crisis (8, 9, 10, 13, 14, 15, 16). Particularly noteworthy is the evidence of reciprocity in patterns of exchanges, with older people helping children as well as children looking after elderly parents.

Models of Informal Support

What determines to whom an older person will most likely turn when in need of social support assistance? From the point of view of the elderly, are there some supportive tasks most appropriately belonging to kin, others logically falling within the support sphere of friends and neighbors, and still others which should be assumed by formal organizations? Do older people perceive potential support givers according to a hierarchal model regardless of task? To what extent is the choice of friend, neighbor or formal organization, rather than an adult child, an issue of compensation or replacement and thus dependent on the availability of a particular supportive element?

One can think of the support system as operating according to several alternative models (9). The first is *additive*: Each support element performs randomly chosen tasks which added together increase the social supports available to the elderly person. The second is *asymmetrical*: One element dominates all forms of support; no other element is either involved or considered appropriate. Research findings to date support neither of these two models.

The third model—*the task-specific model* of Litwak—places the emphasis on the nature of the task and the characteristics of the various support elements. The kinship system is seen as most appropriately carrying traditional tasks involving long-term history and intimacy. Given the geographic dispersion of many children, however, only those tasks not requiring proximity or immediacy may be appropriate for kin. Neighbors can be expected to assist with tasks requiring speed of response, knowledge of and presence in the territorial unit. Friends are uniquely able to deal with problems involving peer group status and similarity of experience and history.

Fourth is the *hierarchical-compensatory model,* in which the function of support giving is generally ordered according to the primacy of the relationship of the support giver to the elderly recipient rather than to the nature of the task. This model postulates an order of preference in the choice of the support element. Relatives are generally seen by the elderly as the most appropriate support givers, followed by significant others and lastly by formal organizations, though when the originally preferred element is absent, other groups act in a compensatory manner as replacement.

In all of these models four basic factors operate, although to different degrees: the nature and extent of the support network, the nature of the tasks involved, the proximity and availability of various support elements, and the characteristics and cultural traditions of the elderly. In all conceptualizations the role of formal organizations is seen as secondary with respect to the more personal, idiosyncratic social support tasks, becoming involved only when the level of technical skill or the time involvement is beyond the resources of the informal support elements (9). Research indicates that in highly dense urban areas older people tend to be neighborhood-bound, and functional friends most frequently live in the neighborhood (8). The more important distinctions appear to be between kin (primarily children), non-kin (friends and neighbors), and formal organizations (or their representatives) (8).

Choice of Support Elements: Hypothetical Cases

To learn more about the preferences of old people for support agents in typical life situations, the New York City Department on the Aging, in its study, *The Elderly in the Inner City*, developed a series of ten hypothetical critical incidents, covering a broad spectrum of instrumental and affective needs (14, 15).

For each situation respondents were asked to choose whom other than a spouse they would most likely turn to for assistance. The choices were ordered according to the principal components of the support system, from child, other relative, friend, neighbor, to the representative of a formal organization. In addition, a "no one or myself" option was included (see Table 1).

Relatives, preferably children, are clearly the support element of first choice. In all situations except one, kin are either clearly preferred or the choice is divided between kin and either "no one— myself" or a friend/neighbor. The fact that in some situations no one or a friend/neighbor is seen as almost as appropriate a choice as child/relative suggests that the nature of the task is being taken into consideration.

With respect to health-related tasks, including emergency assistance, the longer range commitment of daily bathing, and giving medicine and transportation to a doctor, the role of family is clear: close to 45 percent of the respondents prefer help from a child/relative. However, there is a small but steady proportion of approximately 25 percent of the respondents who would turn to a friend or neighbor, probably because there are no available chlidren. Only a small proportion see a role for the formal organization in personal health services.

In the area of financial assistance, the importance of the role of the family is affected by the strong desire of older people to remain financially independent and avoid becoming a burden on children. Thus, the responses are equally divided between approximately one-third who would turn to kin and another third who would turn to no

TABLE 1

Whom Would You Turn to in Various Situations Other than Spouse

(in percents)

Types of Assistance	KIN			NON KIN			Formal Organization	No One	N/A	Total
	Child	Relative	Total	Friend	Neighbor	Total				
Instrumental Health										
1. Suddenly feel sick or dizzy	28.9	13.4	42.3	11.4	13.3	24.7	14.6	17.9	2.0	100.0 (N = 1552)
2. Accident, need someone to help, to come in every day to bathe you and give medicine	30.7	15.1	45.8	12.8	8.4	20.2	14.3	15.8	3.7	100.0 (N = 1552)
3. Help going to doctor	28.9	13.3	42.2	15.7	11.5	27.2	10.9	18.9	1.7	100.0 (N = 1552)
Financial										
1. Do not have enough money for big medical bill	24.6	9.7	34.3	6.4	2.1	8.5	20.6	35.3	2.4	100.0 (N = 1552)
2. Need to borrow few dollars until check comes	27.5	12.3	39.8	13.8	5.0	18.8	6.0	36.0	1.0	100.0 (N = 1552)
Other Tasks of Daily Living										
1. Need new light bulb in ceiling	19.9	6.9	26.8	5.7	8.5	14.2	17.1	41.7	1.0	100.0 (N = 1552)
2. Look after apt., when in hospital	31.6	17.8	49.4	13.7	11.5	25.2	4.8	18.0	3.1	100.0 (N = 1552)
3. Fill out a form	32.6	12.2	44.8	13.0	8.0	21.0	4.7	28.8	1.1	100.0 (N = 1552)
Affective										
1. Talk about problem concerning child or someone in family	24.3	17.6	40.9	18.9	7.9	26.8	4.4	26.0	2.5	100.0 (N = 1552)
2. Feel lonely and want to talk	24.3	13.5	37.8	27.3	12.8	40.1	1.7	19.5	2.3	100.0 (N = 1552)

Source: Marjorie Cantor. Neighbors and Friends: An Overlooked Resource in the Informal Support System. Paper presented at Thirteenth Annual Meeting, Gerontological Society, San Francisco, California, 1977.

one. About 20 percent of the respondents recognize a role for the formal organization in this situation in providing money for expensive medical care.

In the case of the three tasks of daily living inquired about—looking after apartment when ill, filling out a form, and needing a new light bulb in the ceiling—the family is seen as the most appropriate source of help in the first two, which involve intimacy and personal knowledge. With respect to putting in a new light bulb—clearly impersonal and time-limited—40 percent of the respondents would take care of it themselves rather than bother kin (who are, however, the next most frequently mentioned support choice).

The final area tapped was that of the need of affective assistance, including the desire for a confidant. The discussion of a family problem is appropriately seen as remaining within the network, or perhaps as being shared with friends/neighbors. Thus 41 percent of those queried indicate turning to family; 27 percent, friend-neighbor network, and 26 percent, keeping the problem to themselves. The reluctance to turn to formal organizations here persists, even though the required knowledge may not be present within the informal support network; this attitude undoubtedly is reflected in the national statistics which indicate that only four percent of the population served by the mental health clinics are elderly.

The one area in which a substantial proportion of respondents would turn to friends or neighbors is for relief of loneliness. The proportions choosing friends and kin are roughly equal, and there are fewer persons who would turn to no one in such circumstances.

The foregoing suggests that elderly persons, in expressing preference with regard to avenues of social support, are guided by some underlying principals regarding the priority of the support giver and the nature of the task. First and foremost is the central role played by children and other kin almost irrespective of task. Within this general framework there are some variations, particularly when money is involved or when the task merely involves socialization or can easily be accomplished on one's own. The reluctance to become a financial burden on one's children is clearly apparent, and it is prevalent among all groups of older people, regardless of the financial status of their children.

Need for Formal Community Supports

In addition to the hierarchical aspects of the informal support system, the compensatory nature of its functioning is also clear (9). Among respondents who have a child seen often enough to permit caregiving, from 50 to 80 percent, deepnding on the task, select kin, usually a child, above all other potential support givers. As the child becomes increasingly geographically removed, however, the support function begins to be shared by other relatives, friends, neighbors, and even, in some cases, formal organizations.

In the area of socialization and the provision of day-to-day companionship, friends and neighbors play a highly significant role. Friends and neighbors are likewise helpful for short-term emergency service, such as shopping in inclement weather or help when one is ill. But their most important function appears to be as compensatory support elements when kin and children are non-existent or unavailable.

The available evidence suggests that much more attention should be given by practitioners of all disciplines to the well organized and functioning network of informal support available to the elderly.

Reliance on the informal support system in no way negates the acceptance by the elderly and their families of the role of government and other formal organizations in the provision of broad-based economic, health, education and transportation entitlements. The empirical data appear to support the theory of shared functions between formal organizations and primary groups according to the nature of the task involved and the competence of the structures (12). In situations involving unpredictable and idiosyncratic needs, where fast and fiexible decision-making is involved or where knowledge based on everyday socialization is the more useful, the primary group is the appropriate avenue of social support. Formal organizations are best able to handle tasks requiring the application of technical knowledge uniformly and impartially to large aggregates of people. Contrary to Parson's belief that a complete separation of formal and informal organizational functions is necessary, Litwak argues that it is in the best interest of older people that the two subsystems operate at some midpoint of social distance, close enough to cooperate but not so close as to conflict. The well-being of an older person will be in direct relationship to the extent that he possesses social support assistance both from formal organizations and primary groups (12, 13).

FORMAL SUPPORT SYSTEM

If it is in the best interests of older people to possess both strong informal and strong formal support systems, to what extent are the components of the formal system in place in the area of mental health? Perhaps most importantly, are there recommendations which would strengthen the formal services, link them to the informal network and thereby more effectively meet the mental health needs of the elderly?

Principles Underlying Mental Health and the Elderly (17)

1) The elderly are a heterogenous group, representing the whole economic, social, and ethnic spectrum of American society.

2) The overwhelming majority of persons 65 years of age or older live in the community in their own homes. Only about four percent are institutionalized at any one moment. Of those living in the community, about 80 percent are totally mobile; about 11 percent have limited mobility but require medical care at home; only about 16 percent are totally unable to carry on usual major activities.*

3) There is a range of mental illness requiring a range of services. Like younger people, the elderly may suffer with psychoses, neuroses, personality and situational disturbances, as well as organic mental syndromes.

4) Active pyschiatric intervention is the appropriate and effective approach to mental health services for the elderly.

5) Evaluation—socioeconomic, physical, and psychiatric—should be comprehensive and diagnosis accurate.

6) Services should focus on strengths and resources as well as on illness.

7) Services should address the needs of the consumer, not the

---

* There is some overlapping between these groups.

provider. Mental health services for the elderly should be geared specifically to the needs of the aged population.

8) Service delivery should be structured to provide continuity of care. The elderly should not be confused by cumbersome bureaucratic procedures. They should be able to receive comprehensive mental health care from a single agency provided by as few persons as possible.

9) Mental health services for the elderly are best offered as an integral part of a coordinated and well managed general human services delivery system. Because older people are mainly neighborhood bound, services must be easily accessible or otherwise transportation must be provided. Above all, mental health services must be made acceptable and not intimidating to older people.

10) Formal services should become aware of and utilize the informal support network. An important role of the informal network, particularly the family, is as a linking and facilitating mechanism to formal services.

11) Services are best provided in a setting where there is interdisciplinary training and a wide range of services, such as a teaching hospital.

12) Governmental recommendations and regulations should be sufficiently flexible to permit service facilities to adapt to specific local conditions.

Barriers to Utilization of Mental Health Services

Some of the major forces which have tended to limit the provision of mental health services to the elderly rest with the attitudes of the elderly themselves; some are imposed by society and the organization and delivery of services.

1) The elderly have preconceptions about aging which inhibit them from seeking mental health care. They tend to think of age as a kind of disease and believe it is best to be taken care of at home by the family. They tend to regard identification as psychiatrically ill as humiliating. They tend to deny such illness, perhaps because they associate any illness with death, but largely because they fear relocation and loss of family connections. They value their independence;

asking for help in situations of mental distress appears to be a compromise of freedom.

2) Caregivers are apt to have their own anxieties regarding old age (18). They may identify the elderly patients with their parents in uncomfortable ways. They often believe that mental illness in the elderly is untreatable.

3) American culture emphasizes the value of youth at the expense of the aged: "Old" in the United States is usually equated with decreased value. The elderly are perceived as people who do not contribute to the gross national product and who drain the social services budget.

4) Although community mental health centers have been in operation for over ten years, special services for the elderly have been made a low priority item through oversight and ignorance. The limited funds (and hence personnel) available for mental health programs go for "attractive" patients, those believed to have a good chance of being cured. Mental health care providers are often at a low level of skill and knowledge with respect to the aged. Little evaluative research is undertaken regarding the complex problems of the elderly.

5) Such resources as exist are not used properly or in proportion to need. Fifty percent of the population in state hospitals is over the age of 65, whereas the elderly constitute only four percent of those persons who use psychiatric outpatient facilities.

6) Existing services are generally poorly publicized and, in a practical sense, often unavailable. The elderly do not really know about them, and, even if they wish to take advantage of them, they often cannot go to the facility because they are afraid, physically immobile, or unable to afford the transportation costs.

7) Mental health care services for the elderly have been a low priority budget item. Medicare and Medicaid do not provide sufficient coverage.

8) The current federal funding policy encourages the release of elderly patients from mental institutions into inappropriate community settings. Nursing homes receiving Medicaid funds are often unprepared to meet the needs of the mentally disabled. Medicare sets limitations on outpatient coverage.

CURRENT SOLUTIONS

The above material paints a gloomy picture of the mental health care of older people. There have been, however, some attempts by individual psychiatrists and by mental health facilities to address the needs of this population.

Several models of specialized mental health services have been evolved in recent years in Community Mental Health Centers. One such model will be described in some detail.

The Massachusetts Mental Health
Center Geriatric Team

The Massachusetts Mental Health Center (MMHC), located in Boston, has been a Community Mental Health Center since 1967. In 1969 it received a grant from the National Institute of Mental Health which enabled it to begin a special geriatrics unit (19). As the federal matching grant declined over the years, the state Department of Mental Health assumed financial responsibility, and now it supports the program fully.

From the beginning, the MMHC has worked with an Area Board selected to represent the community. Since 1973 there has been a geriatric sub-committee. The Board provides advocacy, support, lobbying capability, and the means to locate resources and to reach the community through educational programs. The geriatric unit draws on university resources through MMHC's affiliation with Harvard Medical School and local schools of nursing, occupational therapy and social work.

Though its original mandate was to provide consultation and education, the geriatric team responded to the needs of the elderly by expanding its services to become the most comprehensive community-focused program of mental health services for the elderly in Massachusetts. The program's success can, in part, be measured by the very small number of old persons in the area who have required full-time hospitalization and by the large number receiving services in the community.

The special geriatric services are seen as augmenting the existing services offered to all adults by the MMHC. These special services include: screening, diagnosis and treatment of the elderly in their own homes (20) and in nursing homes, crisis intervention, various forms of psychotherapy, family therapy (21), drug evaluations, advocacy, information, and referral. A geriatric psychiatric day treatment center provides an alternative to full-time institutional care. There are also a mobile mental health unit for isolated elderly persons in the community and scheduled weekly gatherings of elderly living in public housing and in need of socialization. Indirect services include client-centered consultation, program and administrative consultation, workshops, seminars, continuous in-service training, and group therapy leadership training for the staffs of long-term care facilities in our catchment area, as well as consultation to any other community agency serving the elderly on issues involving mental health and aging. A regional medical-psychiatric geriatric program has been established as a collaborative model project with the state Department of Public Health, providing long-term comprehensive care for patients with both medical and psychiatric illness, as well as research and program evaluation.

The MMHC is an example of a large-scale, comprehensive, community-focused approach on the part of a mental health facility. Most community mental health centers have not evolved such a program of special services for the elderly, but some have begun to address the problem of serving the elderly in various more limited ways, such as retraining staff members and hiring persons with special skills.

Other Formal, Mental Health Related Support Systems

There are in the community a variety of other formal services for the aging which could and do have implications for the provision of mental health care.

In 1965, two major pieces of federal legislation—the Social Security Act (including Medicare and Medicaid provisions) and the Older Americans Act—set forth in broad outlines the services mandated for the elderly, defined the role of state and local governments, promulgated standards of performance and provided upward of 50 percent of the cost of the various programs encompassed in these Acts. The day-to-day administration of the aging services rests within designated state and area agencies on aging.

These agencies provide little direct service to the elderly, but contract out for the provision of services to community-based voluntary agencies. In this way, although planning, coordination, evaluation and distribution of funds are functions of centralized government, the actual service provision is neighborhood-oriented. This attempt at decentralization of service flows from the belief that if services for older people are effectively to reach those who are inclined to use them, such services must be as diverse and embedded in as many organizational contexts as there are preferences, attitudes, patterns, and values regarding aging among the older population.

Among the specific services funded through the Older Americans Act, the Social Security Act, and the Comprehensive Employment Act of the Department of Labor are recreation, nutrition and continuing education programs, homemaker and home chore services, counseling, escort and shopping assistance, transportation, employment, information and referral, protective and legal services. In addition, local housing authority, departments of public welfare, police and firemen, and public libraries are also deeply involved on a day-to-day basis with older people. Many such programs and individuals provide mental health services to elderly, although they are neither mandated nor consumer-identified as such resources. They have become a major source of referrals for elderly who need either the more sophisticated or more intensive therapeutic intervention of a mental health clinic, center or hospital.

With respect to the provision of supportive services in the home, the United States lags far behind comparable industrialized countries. For example, the provision of direct personal services in the home, such as homemakers, housekeepers, home meals, home repairs, and so on, is in short supply and virtually unavailable from the formal governmental or social agency sector, unless the client has a public assistance income.

One hopes that the passage of National Health Insurance will result in more direct services in the home, but at the present time the major care of older people in times of illness or crisis rests with the informal social support system of family, friends and neighbors.

RELATIONSHIP BETWEEN FORMAL AND INFORMAL SUPPORT SYSTEMS

The question is how best to construct a comprehensive formal support which does not replace, dominate, or substitute for the informal system, but instead builds upon it. The complementary nature of the two systems is well illustrated by an analysis of the characteristics predictive of an old person's turning to social agencies for help. In addition to expected personal deficiencies, such as poor health, limited functional ability, criminal victimization, and reduced sense of personal mastery over the environment, the lack of available help from children and the absence of knowing even one neighbor well are significantly related to reliance on the formal support system for help.

For persons moving into the frailer middle stage of aging—those 75 to 80 years of age—the services of the formal support structure loom more importantly. Particular attention should be given to services in the home, counseling for the clients and their families on future alternatives to independent living, and transportation to medical and social service facilities. Even in this group, however, informal supports and relationships still play a great role.

As old people reach the age of greatest frailty, illness and functional incapacity—85 and above—the balance tips toward a greater assumption of responsibility for their welfare by society. In this stage it is likely that few families, even with assistance, could supply the kinds of specialized services needed by the oldest and frailest. In all of this, the crucial goal is the manipulation of the environment and social structure in order to help older people live out their lives in the greatest dignity and with the fullest utilization of their capacities for independent living.

RECOMMENDATIONS

On the basis of our experience with the elderly, we feel the responsibility to depart somewhat from the typical format of a scientific paper and offer the following extensive recommendations.

1) Change Medicare to:

(a) treat mental illness, acute and chronic, with the same coverage as physical illness, acute and chronic;

(b) cover the services, not merely of physicians, but of related mental health professionals;

(c) cover such items as prosthetics and drugs prescribed for patients not in hospitals;

(d) cover comprehensive evaluation and some treatment as outpatients;

(e) make mental health consultation and in-service education to nursing homes reimbursable;

(f) eliminate the monthly premium charge and the 20 percent co-insurance feature under part B supplementary medical insurance;

(g) eliminate the deductible requirements for hospitalization and physician's services;

(h) include the installation and costs of a telephone in an elderly person's home as an added benefit upon the prescription of a doctor;

(i) provide major revisions in coverage for psychiatric disorders, especially with regard to the 190-day lifetime limitation on treatment in mental hospitals.

2) Change Medicaid to:

(a) restrict reimbursement for nursing home care to those who require it for medical-psychiatric reasons so that the health dollar is not used to support housing needs;

(b) provide for overseeing that Medicaid is implemented in the spirit of the legislation; example: to insure that states reallocate funds saved through Medicaid for improved health care (Long Amendment);

(c) increase limits of coverage for outpatient care per year.

3) Develop special mental health services for such subgroups of the aged as ethnic groups, special langauge groups, "young" old and "old" old, the blind, and the hard-of-hearing.

4) Build special geriatric mental health services into existing com-

munity structures, such as nursing homes, general hospitals, home care agencies, and boarding homes.

5) Adapt such existing mental health facilities as community mental health centers, state and private mental hospitals, and Veterans Administration hospitals to include special geriatric mental health services.

6) Stop the inappropriate discharge of the elderly from institutions into unprepared communities.

7) Find ways to increase the utilization of existing legislation designed to benefit the elderly, such as Titles III and IV of the Older Americans Act and Title XX of the Social Security Act, as part of mental health programs.

8) Improve protective services related to providing mental health care for the incompetent elderly and enhancing their access to health care.

9) Enforce regulations which protect the aged from poor care, overmedication, inappropriate placements, and so on.

10) Organize services at local levels to provide maximum continuity of care, as the elderly move within the system.

11) Consumers and providers together should determine the specifics of the needed services to the elderly based on their own, often unique, local conditions.

12) Mental health services for the elderly should include outreach to diagnosis of, support and education for, and maximum involvement of their families and friends.

13) Apply research findings more swiftly. The National Institute on Aging should sponsor joint meetings of researchers, planners, and clinicians. The Administration on Aging should sponsor research and demonstration projects to show the benefits of establishing working relationships between academicians and health planners in the community.

14) Data collection and reporting systems should be standardized. The National Institute on Aging should form a data bank based on the standardized collection and reporting systems.

15) Coterminous boundaries for all human services at all government levels should be established.

16) The system should give its mental health workers advance-

ment for skill and productivity as well as a high degree of control and responsibility for their own work.

17) Every community mental health center should provide interdisciplinary training and opportunities for career development in geropsychiatry.

SUMMARY

Utilizing the concepts, findings and language of several academic disciplines, this chapter has dealt with community support systems in a broad theoretical fashion.

Based on this perspective, several conclusions are drawn and recommendations for change are made. Underlying all recommendations are three basic concepts: 1) Enlightened policy is based on an understanding of how the elderly consumer views and uses available supports. 2) Both the formal psychiatric services and the informal mental health services in any community are best delivered as part of a well-managed human service system. 3) The best care is preventive care; our energies need to be continuously directed toward gaining a better understanding of the causes of mental illness in later life so that we can work toward a healthier personal, social, and political life for all older people.

REFERENCES

1. KRAMER, M. TAUBE, C., and STARR, B.: *Patterns of Use of Psychiatric Facilities by the Aged*: Current Status, Trends, and Implications, Psychiatric Research Report 23, APA, Part III, Chapter 9, February, 1968.
2. United States Department of Health, Education, and Welfare, *Patients in Mental Institutions*, PHS Publication No. 1818, Part II, Washington, D.C., 1968.
3. LOWENTHAL, M. F., BERKMAN, P. L., et al.: *Aging and Mental Disorders in San Francisco*. San Francisco: Jossey-Bass, 1967.
4. WEINTRAUB, W. and ARONSON, H.: A survey of patients in classical psychoanalysis: Some vital statistics. *Journal of Nervous Mental Disorders*, 146:98-102, 1968.
5. GARFINKEL, R.: The reluctant therapist. *Gerontologist*, 15:136-137, 1975.
6. CAPLAN, G.: *Support Systems and Community Mental Health*: Lectures on Concept Development. New York: Behavioral Publications, 1974, p. 7.

7. WEISS, R. S.: Transition states and other stressful situations. In: G. Caplan and M. Killilea (Eds.), *Support Systems and Mutual Help—Multidisciplinary Explorations.* New York: Grune & Stratton, 1976, p. 215.

8. CANTOR, M.: Life, space and the social support system of the inner city elderly of New York. *Gerontologist,* 15:23-27, 1975.

9. CANTOR, M.: *Neighbors and Friends: An Overlooked Resource in the Informal Support System,* presented at the Thirtieth Annual Meeting, Gerontological Society, San Francisco, California, November, 1977.

10. SUSSMAN, M. and SHANAS, E. (Eds.): *Family, Bureaucracy and the Elderly.* Durham, North Carolina: Duke University Press, 1977, pp. 3-19.

11. LOWENTHAL, M. F. and ROBINSON, E.: Social networks in isolation In: R. Binstock and E. Shanas (Eds.), *Handbook of Aging and Social Sciences.* New York: Van Nostrand, 1976.

12. LITWAK, E.: Extended kin relations in an industrial democratic society. In: E. Shanas and G. Strieb (Eds.), *Social Structure and the Family.* New Jersey: Prentice Hall, 1965.

13. LITWAK, E.: *Towards the Multifactor Theory and Practice of Linkages Between Formal Organization.* Final Report, Grant Number CRD-4 25-C 1-9, United States Department Health Education and Welfare, Washington, D.C., June 1970.

14. CANTOR, M.: *The Formal and Informal Social Support System of Older New Yorkers,* presented at Tenth International Congress of Gerontology, Jerusalem, Israel, June, 1975.

15. CANTOR, M.: *The Configuration and Intensity of the Informal Support System in a New York City Elderly Population,* presented at Twenty-Ninth Annual Meeting, Gerontology Society, New York, 1976.

16. MAYER, MARY: *Kin and Neighbors Differential Roles in Differing Culture,* presented at Twenty-Ninth Annual Meeting, Gerontological Society, New York, 1976.

17. GURIAN, B.: *Current and Anticipated Need for Mental Health Services and Service Facilities to Meet the Mental Health Care Needs of the Elderly,* position paper prepared at the request of the Committee to Study the Mental Health and Illness of the Elderly, Appointed by the United States Department of Health, Education and Welfare, 1977.

18. GURIAN, B.: Psychogeriatrics. *Bulletin New York Academy of Mediciine,* 49:1119-1123, 1973.

19. GURIAN, B., and SCHERL, D.: A community focused model of mental health services for the elderly. *Journal of Geriatric Psychiatry,* 5:77-86, 1972.

20. GURIAN, B.: The psychiatric house call. *American Journal Psychiatry,* in press.

21. GURIAN, B.: Psychogeriatrics and family medicine. *The Gerontologist,* 15:308-310, 1975.

BIBLIOGRAPHY

BUSSE, E. W. and PFEIFFER, E.: *Mental Illness in Later Life*. American Psychiatric Association, Washington, D.C., April, 1973.

BUTLER, R. and LEWIS, M.: *Aging and Mental Health*. St. Louis: Mosby and Co., 1972.

COHEN, E. D.: *The Contingency Plan—Community Mental Health Center Program for the Elderly*. Center for the Study of Mental Health and Aging, 1975.

GAITZ, C. M. and VARNER, R. V.: *Community Based Comprehensive Geriatric Services—A Multidisciplinary Mental Health Model*. Texas Research Institute of Mental Sciences, Houston, 1975.

HOWELLS, J. G.: *Modern Perspectives in the Psychiatry of Old Age*. New York: Brunner/Mazel, 1975.

KNEE, R. I.: *Financing Mechanisms Affecting Mental Health Services and their Delivery*. Service Conference, NIMH Center for Aging, June 1, 1976.

KOBRYNSKI, B.: The mentally impaired elderly—whose responsibility? *The Gerontologist*, Vol. 15, No. 5, Pt. 1, 1975.

NORRIS, E. L. and LARSEN, J. K.: Critical issues in mental health service delivery: What are the priorities? *Hospital and Community Psychiatry*, Vol. 25, No. 8, August 1976.

PFEIFFER, E.: *Program Proposal for Geriatric Services*, in connection with Study Commission for Mental Health Services, State of North Carolina, January 18, 1974.

REDICK, R.: Statistical Note 107—*Patterns of Use in Nursing Homes by the Aged Mentally Ill*. Department of Health, Education and Welfare, NIMH, Division of Biometry, June 1974.

Community Mental Health Center Amendments of 1975, Title III, Public Law 94-63, National Council of Community Mental Health Centers, Washington, D.C., 1975.

The Financing, Utilization, and Quality of Mental Health Care in the United States (Draft Report), Office of Program Development and Analysis, NIMH, U.S. Department of Health, Education and Welfare, April, 1976.

Adult Day Care in the United States: A Corporative Study, (Executive Summary of Final Report). Julius Pellegrino, Jr., Project Officer, National Center for Health, Service Research Division of Health of Health Services Evaluation, September 2, 1975.

Improvements Needed in Efforts to Help the Mentally Disabled Return to and Remain in Comunmity. Draft of Report to Congress of the United States, Department of Health, Education and Welfare, Housing and Urban Development, Labor Department, and Management and Budget, 1970.

8

Aged Patients, Their Families and Physicians

Charles M. Gaitz, M.D.

Focusing attention on the aged patient is comparatively unusual, even for gerontologists. We are much more inclined to devote energy and resources to study diseases and social phenomena, filling the literature with observations about aging processes, social, cultural and political factors, and many other aspects of aging whose relevance I do not minimize. Researchers and caregivers tend to give more attention to the *aged* than to *individuals* who are old. This approach leads us to a heavy reliance on environmental manipulation and to the fond hope that when such necessities as adequate housing and income are provided, health problems will disappear or at least be minimized. This is true to some extent, but it is an incomplete consideration of the aged patient.

Old persons are survivors, people with the inner strengths and resources to cope with living. Therapists often fail to realize this; they overlook the reality that, with only minimal treatment, older persons often can mobilize their own resources and return to a satisfactory level of functioning. Elderly persons with psychiatric disorders rarely require the intensive efforts commonly associated with the treatment of disturbed young persons. One may argue that this is so because treatment objectives differ, but I submit that the difference lies in older persons' capacity to adjust and to accommodate to changing circumstances. It is these qualities that account for good therapeutic results once therapists overcome their own resistance to treating elders.

On Becoming a Patient

It is easy to understand why persons as they age are likely to become patients (in the sense of undergoing treatment for disease or injury). Elderly persons are likely to hurt. Hurt, in the sense used here, means "to suffer or cause to suffer physically or mentally; make or be painful." Even cursory examinations reveal that old people have a combination of physical and mental problems that cause pain and suffering. Although these problems may be of recent origin, they often have antecedents in early life. Yet aged persons are reluctant to ask for help; they may need encouragement to accept treatment and a role as a patient. Their disorders, always a combination of physical and mental problems, represent the prototype of psychosomatic illnesses. Their treatment, instead of reflecting this logical conclusion, is often limited and fragmentary. Let us now look more closely at some of the factors associated with patienthood in old age, a time when changes in physical health status and in social roles are especially dramatic.

Changes in Physical Health Status

Elderly persons have an increased likelihood, with advancing age, of suffering impairment of some organ systems. This is well documented in the geriatric literature. Nowlin (1), for example, writes of the "linear decline in the function of various tissues and organ systems associated with chronological aging." Verwoerdt (2) describes a healthy individual as one who is able to maintain an inner steady state regardless of changing external circumstances. With advancing age the capacity for homeostasis declines gradually, the range of adjustment and adaptation becoming smaller and narrower.

Studying the health status of elderly persons in six western countries, Shanas (3) found that physical capacity is independent of culture. In all these countries, about 75 percent of the elderly are ambulatory and report only minimal incapacity for personal care. Only a small percentage are bedfast at home or require institutional care. Longitudinal studies (4, 5) fail to demonstrate the inevitability of serious decline in functional capacity.

Demonstrating organic or systemic impairment, however, may be misleading. Even when such conditions are found, a much more critical measure is the degree of disability associated with them. Adjustment depends on an individual's ability to meet demands of a particular life situation; it is much more important, therefore, to know whether a person can walk to a food market than it is to determine how long it takes for his pulse rate to return to normal after exercise in a laboratory, or whether he can jog for three or 30 minutes. Physical disease influences mental status. The severity and duration of physical symptoms are important subfactors, but the discovery of impaired function in one or more physiological systems does not preclude a good adjustment and satisfying life experiences.

Loss of cognitive functioning is not a necessary concomitant of growing older, although research indicates a trend toward gradual decline (6, 7). Most authors, however, stress the influence of other factors in addition to age, such as education, health, and level of intelligence (8). Speed of responding and memory are two probable areas where decline may be first realized, and this is even more likely to occur in the very old, those 75 and older.

Changes in Social Roles

Social relationships and roles also change as one ages. Just as life themes change from adolescence to early adulthood, and then to full maturity, older age brings another set of changes. Parenting evolves into grandparenting, and each "typical" household returns to its original dyad. Emphasis on career roles becomes less important or perhaps nonexistent in the case of retirement, which brings not only changes in major life goals, but changes in social contacts, interactions, and time structuring. Again the aging individual is required to make adjustments, to keep a balance between inner harmony and changing external circumstances, and these at a time when physical and mental resources for adjustment are declining.

Social and role changes may be experienced as either good or bad, more likely as both. Retirement from the work force, for example, may bring a devastating loss of status and decline in income. It may also be relief from years of forced involvement with boring, emotionally unrewarding activity. Similarly, the "empty nest" may mean a major role loss and loneliness, but it may also signal freedom from responsibilities for the first time in years and money for personally expressive and rewarding forms of leisure.

As life-cycle studies show, changes, with their potential for satisfaction or frustration, occur at all stages of life. Adaptation is as necessary and as possible in old age as at other times. Typically, however, old persons must adapt to losses associated with former sources of pleasure and satisfaction. Sometimes these are personal, like lost relationships with relatives and friends; sometimes they are material, like loss of income. When these events are many and frequent, they may well force an elderly person into patienthood.

In very old age, a person's adjustments may revolve around autonomy. Because of physical and mental frailties, it may be necessary to relinquish control to others. The lifelong capacity to cope effectively with stresses may diminish late in life, when remaining mental and physical strengths are unequal to coping with intense and frequent demands for adjustment. The cumulative effects of losses or other stresses, occurring during a short time span, may lead to decompensation and illness.

PSYCHIATRIC DISORDERS IN OLD AGE

The emotional problems of an aged person may have their roots in the past, or they may be of recent onset and related to conditions of late life. Since elderly persons are more likely to have physical health problems than younger ones, it is especially important to explore a possible connection between physical and mental status. Many factors must be understood to determine why an elderly person enjoys good mental health, just as one must have clear evidence of mental illness. Chronological age has nothing to do with cure or remission;

it also does not imply that an illness in old age must last until death.

The manifestations and symptomatology of psychiatric disorders in old age are quite similar to those of earlier life. There may have been long periods of remission. When elderly persons are unable to cope with stresses of late life, the disorder may recur. Physiologic and metabolic changes associated with aging may contribute to frailty. Such elderly persons, when subjected to additional physical or emotional stress, are likely to manifest various psychiatric syndromes, including acute organic brain syndrome.

As for the psychiatric syndromes, we see patients with typical neurotic and psychotic disorders. Affective disorders, especially depression, are likely to occur in older patients. Psychosomatic disorders are common, particularly hypochondriasis. The tendency of elderly persons to have physical disorders may explain why hypochondriasis is a common manifestation of emotional conflict. Grief reactions are a response to a series of losses of spouse, relatives, friends, or children. Like others, aged persons respond to these tragedies, as well as to losses associated with social-role changes and health, with typical psychiatric syndromes. Thought disorders, particularly those manifested by paranoid delusions, are frequent, and they sometimes represent denial of infirmities, inadequacies, and diminished mental competence.

Psychiatric symptomatology is not age-determined. Prevalence may differ among age groups, but all of the neuroses and psychoses, the personality disorders, sexual deviations, alcoholism, and other conditions are manifested by elderly persons. Qualitative differences may exist, but these are minor. Symptoms of organic brain syndrome, for example, are alike in young and old patients.

In working with old people, it is perhaps even more important than with younger ones to realize that the signs and symptoms of physical disease may mimic psychiatric disorders. Changes in behavior are often associated with physical disorders. When evaluating behavioral changes, a diagnostician must be especially concerned with careful differential diagnosis and thorough evaluation so that remediable physical conditions can be recognized and treated. It is not always easy to differentiate between changes that may be associated with aging and those associated with illness. Whether aging brings inevitable and significant changes, or whether these changes constitute illness, is a conundrum and the subject of a continuing discussion. Suffice it here to say that some of the altered states, particularly the behavioral ones, commonly observed in older people resemble the behavior of persons with depression. For example, while some observers regard a life-style of disengagement as normal for older persons, others equate disengagement with a mood disorder. Accommodation to reduced physical capacity may result in symptoms that could be labeled as symptoms of depression.

Several years ago we undertook a study to determine the relationship of leisure and mental health, with particular interest in comparing various age groups. We found that depression-like symptoms increased in groups of persons aged 65 years and older (9). However, psychiatrists must distinguish between changes associated with "normal aging" and a condition which would warrant a diagnosis of depression. Implications for management abound. Improvement of a patient's quality of life and satisfaction does not derive solely from treatment in a medical setting; on the other hand, it is unlikely that providing better housing, a more stable income, and opportunities for more activity and social interaction represent adequate management of a severely depressed person. These steps may relieve the despair and frustration associated with aging, but they will not have any effect on a person with a profound depression.

Compared to younger persons, the elderly people in our study more frequently reported symptoms and complaints characteristic of depression. They saw themselves as more physically impaired, and a larger percentage reported themselves as less happy. They also tended to report fewer positive and negative experiencs, a pattrn that suggests apathy. A measure of total leisure participation revealed that the elderly group had lower participation scores, independent of health status. Such as data by no means prove that depression is an inevitable concomitant of chronological aging. They do emphasize, however, the need for caution in diagnosing depression in the elderly and in expecting response to the usual therapeutic modalities for depression. The issue is complex and places responsibility for careful differential diagnosis and thorough evaluation on physicians and therapists.

Our study (10) provided further information leading to a conclusion that, in measuring mental health of persons living in a community, age and ethnicity are factors independent of each other. The patterns shown by age cohorts were independent of ethnicity and, in turn, the ranking of measures for ethnic groups was the same in each age group. Age was not a significant factor in the total number of symptoms reported, but older age groups reported more somatic symptoms than younger age groups. Anglos reported more symptoms than either the Blacks or Mexican-American groups, but this probably represents a difference in mode of expression of distress rather than a genuine difference in mental health status.

Symptoms Commonly Presented by Elderly Patients

Symptoms generally fall into three spheres: cognitive, emotional, and somatic. Table 1 lists some of the more common manifestations and complaints and illustrates an overlap among the three major categories.

Common Precipitating Stresses and Strains

Table 2 shows the potential interaction of some common precipitating stresses and strains associated with disorders observed in elderly persons. Psychological, physiological, and environmental factors interact, and the result is often mental illness.

Components of Disorder

Goldfarb (11) has provided a formulation showing a sequence of events and states that contribute to the development of mental disorders in old age. These are summarized in Table 3. By identifying some of the components of a dynamic sequence, Goldfarb presented in graphic form an approach to understanding psychiatric disorders and behavioral changes. In his long and distinguished career, Goldfarb always emphasized the multifactorial aspects of development of illness and the need to attend to them.

Mental Decline

Mental confusion is the very stuff of geriatric medicine. Four features make it bulk so large: its great prevalence (it accounts

TABLE 1

Symptoms Commonly Presented by Elderly Patients

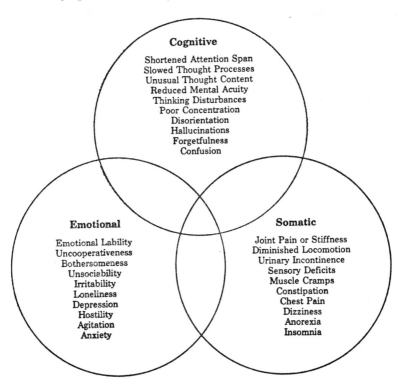

Cognitive

Shortened Attention Span
Slowed Thought Processes
Unusual Thought Content
Reduced Mental Acuity
Thinking Disturbances
Poor Concentration
Disorientation
Hallucinations
Forgetfulness
Confusion

Emotional

Emotional Lability
Uncooperativeness
Bothersomeness
Unsociability
Irritability
Loneliness
Depression
Hostility
Agitation
Anxiety

Somatic

Joint Pain or Stiffness
Diminished Locomotion
Urinary Incontinence
Sensory Deficits
Muscle Cramps
Constipation
Chest Pain
Dizziness
Anorexia
Insomnia

Source: Linden, M. E.: Retirement and the Elderly Patient: Problems and Practical Therapy. Scientific Exhibit, American Geriatrics Society, Miami Beach, April 16-17, 1975.

TABLE 2

Common Precipitating Stresses and Strains

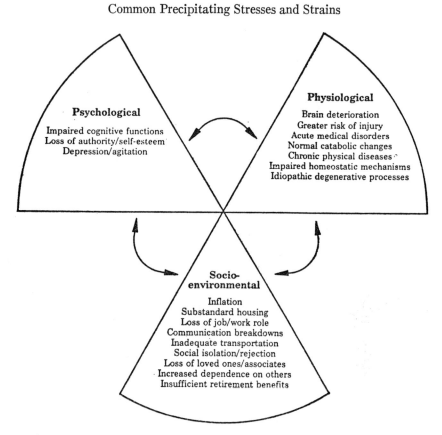

Source: Gait, C. M. and Varner, R. V.: Community-based Comprehensive Geriatric Services: A Multidisciplinary Mental Health Model. Scientific Exhibit, American Psychiatric Association, Anaheim, California, May 5-6, 1975.

TABLE 3

Components of Disorder: Psychodynamic Sequence

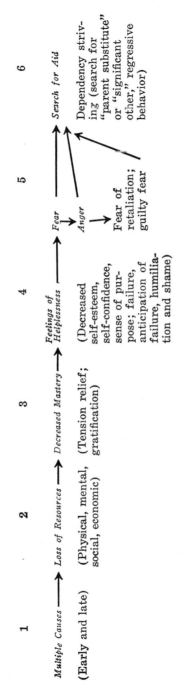

1	2	3	4	5	6
Multiple Causes →	*Loss of Resources* →	*Decreased Mastery* →	*Feelings of Helplessness* →	*Fear*	*Search for Aid*
(Early and late)	(Physical, mental, social, economic)	(Tension relief; gratification)	(Decreased self-esteem, self-confidence, sense of purpose; failure, anticipation of failure, humiliation and shame)	*Anger* → Fear of retaliation; guilty fear	Dependency striving (search for "parent substitute" or "significant other," regressive behavior)

1. Multiple causes or initiating factors that occur either early in life and are reinforced or modified with aging, or occur late in life and are peculiar to old age, several of which may combine forces and some of which may be necessary but insufficient alone, result in

2. an absence or loss of resources for minimally adequate functioning, so that

3. there is decreased mastery of problems, challenges, and adjustments posed by internal changes (biologically determined drives or acquired needs), external changes and threats, with resulting

4. feelings of helplessness or actual powerlessness, and consequent

5. fear with accompanying or subsequent anger, with consequent

6. "rationally" or "irrationally" aimed and elaborated search for aid which becomes patterned in terms acceptable to the individual in terms of his personality organization based upon his past, his present, and his expectations; and contingent on his perception of what is acceptable to and likely to work in "his world," as well as by the social response it receives. In this search there are observable constellations of motivated personal action which range from apathy through pseudoanhedonia, display of helplessness, somatization, hypochondriasis, depression, and paranoid states to the most open and manipulative behavior. In predisposed persons there may be a physiologic shift to a new and relatively inefficient homeostatic level with depressive states, which are then revealed by altered appetite, bowel function, sleep, and other vegetative signs.

From Goldfarb, A. I. (Feb.) 1968. Clinical perspectives. *Psychiatric Research Report 23.* Reproduced with permission of American Psychiatric Association.

for just under half of all admissions to geriatric wards), the large variety of diseases which can provoke it, its socially disabling effects when long continued, and the very large demands it makes on medical and social resources (12).

Organic brain syndrome is central to a discussion of psychiatric illness in the elderly. The condition is, of course, not unique to any single age group, but it is prevalent enough in older groups that some examiners almost routinely include a diagnosis of senile dementia, cerebral insufficiency, or cerebral arteriosclerosis when examining old patients. This practice is not based on fact but on the stereotype of old people as unvaryingly demented. Even in the presence of other psychiatric disorders, the tendency is to diagnose organic brain syndrome. As a consequence, other conditions which might respond to different treatment modalities are left undiscovered. Subjected to stress, elderly persons are especially susceptible to decompensation, which may surface as organic brain syndrome or other psychiatric disorders, especially depression.

Organic brain syndrome may be acute or chronic, the determining factor being reversibility. A long list of medical conditions and stresses of all types have been associated with acute brain syndrome; with proper treatment, the condition is reversible. Table 4 shows some of the more common problems associated with organic brain syndrome. We still have more questions than answers about the disease, but even when the condition appears to be chronic, the quality of life of those unfortunate patients can be much improved.

Ultimately, adequate treatment will depend on better diagnosis and an understanding of the etiology of the condition. Much can be done meanwhile, even with limited knowledge. Recognition that elderly persons may be particularly susceptible to delirium, for example, is a signal to offer additional support when they have to be cared for in intensive care units or in other settings likely to evoke anxiety and fear.

Personality traits tend to become accentuated as one gets older, but this is not consistently so. People may become more suspicious, argumentative, irritable, and demanding, but they are just as likely to "mellow" with age. Even patients with clear evidence of organic

TABLE 4

Some Somatic Conditions Underlying OBS

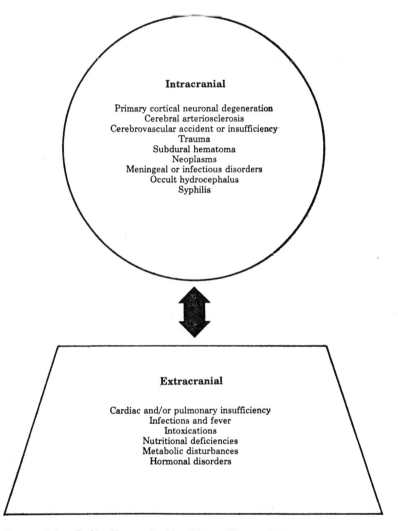

Intracranial

Primary cortical neuronal degeneration
Cerebral arteriosclerosis
Cerebrovascular accident or insufficiency
Trauma
Subdural hematoma
Neoplasms
Meningeal or infectious disorders
Occult hydrocephalus
Syphilis

Extracranial

Cardiac and/or pulmonary insufficiency
Infections and fever
Intoxications
Nutritional deficiencies
Metabolic disturbances
Hormonal disorders

Source: Gaitz, C. M., Varner, R. V., Calvert, W., and Linden, M. E.: Realistic Expectations and Treatment Goals in Caring for the Impaired Elderly. Scientific Exhibit, American Medical Association, San Francisco, California, June 18-22, 1977.

brain syndrome exhibit personality changes which seem to be related to their premorbid states. The person who tended to be suspicious is more likely to become paranoid, while the passive, submissive individual slips into a state of apathy and withdrawal.

Understanding personality dynamics helps the therapist choose interventions that will diminish the patient's distress and lead to a more satisfactory adjustment. One of our patients with dementia, for example, began to identify photographs as living persons. Removing the photographs only turned the patient's attention to magazines and then she talked to portraits in the magazines. Such a patient might do better if she were offered more opportunities for socializing with living persons.

A cursory review of the extra- and intracranial conditions associated with organic brain syndrome shown in Table 4 will remind the physician that many of the causes or associated conditions can be treated. A patient with acute organic brain syndrome associated with cardiac or pulmonary insufficiency or an infection will likely improve or recover when the underlying condition is treated. It is critical that patients have an adequate evaluation to uncover the remediable conditions; regardless of etiology, one cannot conclude that organic brain syndrome is chronic and irreversible. Furthermore, reducing external pressures on the patient to perform will significantly alter the clinical picture. The patient referred to above might not be able to recall addresses of her siblings or children. She might not be able to make a list of persons to whom she would want to give Christmas presents. But, with assistance, such a person might enjoy the experience of going to a store and deciding whether to give her daughter a green or a yellow blouse, although still not remembering the name of the store or how to get there.

Sexual Behavior in Old Age

Myths and stereotypes are hardier and more plentiful than facts. There is little empirical data upon which to base conclusions. The taboo against sex in old age persists in the "dirty old man" label, let alone comparable terms for women. Behavior with sexual connotations presents problems to caregivers in hospitals and nursing homes. Exhibitionism and pedophilia, the prevalence of which is by no means known, tend to tarnish the white-haired image of the aged, an image which itself is a stereotype.

Seidenberg (13) has written an interesting paper on older man-younger woman marriages, concluding that such marriages are neither to be recommended nor condemned. Our society has accepted the coupling of older men with younger women but still tends to look askance at the union of older women and younger men. Possibly this will change as the status of women in this society changes. Seidenberg cautions against "wild analysis" as a means of hurling insults at friends and relatives and states that even though economic factors may be important considerations, pairings of young and old may have mutual psychological rewards.

Pfeiffer (14) has given us a good review of data available from several research studies. Sampling problems are easily recognized and generalizations have been drawn from small samples. As Pfeiffer points out, not only are subjects reluctant to give information, but investigators also find it difficult to inquire into the sexual lives of aged persons.

Reporting on a longitudinal interdisciplinary study of older persons done at Duke University since 1954, Pfeiffer concludes that "Sexual interest and coital activity are by no means rare in persons beyond age 60, and patterns of sexual interest and coital activity differ substantially for men and women of the same age." About 80 percent of the men who were not significantly impaired reported continuing sexual interest at the start of the study. Ten years later, sexual interest had not declined but the percent of those still regularly sexually active dropped from 70 percent to 25 percent. Far fewer women than men were still sexually interested or coitally active. It is also of interest to note that some 20 to 25 percent of the men showed patterns of rising sexual interest and activity with advancing age. The Duke studies showed that the likelihood of continued sexual expressions in the later years is substantially greater for persons who have been highly interested and highly sexually active in their younger years. Married men did not differ markedly from unmarried men in the degree of reported sexual interest and activity, whereas married women differed substantially from unmarried women; only a few of the latter reported any sexual activity and only

20 percent reported any sexual interest. Pfeiffer recognizes that much additional information is needed to answer many of the questions raised about sexual behavior in old age.

One can agree readily with some of Pfeiffer's implications. Being aware of and accepting the fact that many elders continue to have or to desire an active sex life, practitioners must be willing to offer counseling and education. Provision of living arrangements that permit sexual expression is important to the aged. Intercurrent illnesses may temporarily lead to a change in sexual expression, but these are only temporary interruptions. Sexual expression is a rewarding human activity which should be encouraged as long as possible. Remarriage, especially for persons who have had reasonably satisfactory marriages in their younger years, has an excellent chance of succeeding. Sexual expression is one reason for getting married, but it is only one of many.

Sexual behavior represents an important area for understanding human beings. Silence on the subject has caused much suffering, anguish and guilt. It goes without saying that more research data would be helpful but, meanwhile, aged persons, their families and caregivers need to discuss the subject openly and to solve conflicts based on what we already know. Physicians have a particular responsibility to impart information about the psychological aspects, and then be well informed about the effects of various medications and physical conditions that affect sexual performance.

ON PREVENTION OF ILLNESS

Prevention of illness and disability is a goal that is laudable but difficult to attain. Several suggestions are in order.

Individuals can help themselves by planning for the future conjointly with significant family members. Denying the inevitable leaves one unprepared to cope with the stresses of old age, while open discussions and planning give one an opportunity to overcome fear and apprehension, anger and frustration, and the other negative emotions one may experience when one approaches the terminal stages of life. A reappraisal of values and goals, and some compromises, can be helpful.

Attention to physical health is essential. Periodic examinations and, more important, an ongoing relationship with a trusted and conscientious physician are important components in the network of services and supports from which older persons benefit.

Individuals participate in a network of community and family support systems. Even minimal contacts can turn out to be significant. As one ages and one's need for more support becomes apparent, more active participation with a reliance on others can be quite helpful. This is most obvious in the relationship to a physician or to an agency providing health service, but social contacts with volunteer groups, church-related activities, clubs and similar organizations nurture self-esteem and provide interaction. Familial ties with spouse, children and other relatives provide much emotional support. The option to continue working and the abolition of mandatory retirement will enable some persons to retain the gratification and income afforded them by the work done. Unfortunately, some will persist in working past the time when they are physically and mentally qualified.

The network of services and supports must be maintained or replaced when the need arises. New contacts must be made when, for example, a spouse dies, children move away, or one does retire. If one's physician dies or retires, it is important to establish quickly a connection with another physician rather than wait for an emergency. These and similar steps provide emotional security and contribute to a sense of self-confidence.

All of these practical suggestions for self-help sound so reasonable and self-evident that it may seem trivial to note them. They are part of the total planning for the future we are constantly reminded to do—making a will, planning for retirement income, and so on. But it is the kind of planning one is always going to "do tomorrow," when the duties of today are less pressing. We, as well as our patients of all ages, must provide ourselves with as much self-help as possible for events that might occur at different life stages.

Creative use of leisure is an aspect of self-help. In our research, we conceptualized a definition of leisure as discretionary personal activity in which expressive meanings have primacy over instrumental themes, in the sense that fulfillment of current needs, desires, or objectives is given precedence over practical preparation for later gratification (15). Development of personally satisfying leisure is frequently neglected until one has the "time" sometime in the future. Compared with work-oriented concerns, leisure is devalued by our society. Our survey strengthened our belief that leisure should be viewed as more than a dimension of time in this work-oriented culture. Viewing leisure merely as time not spent working leads retired individuals to the sudden dismaying discovery that they have time for leisure pursuits but few or no interests.

Successful adaptation to old age has sometimes been evaluated in terms of disengagement and activity. Continuing research on predictors of good adaptation is making it clearer that good adaptation is not related to any single life-style and only to some extent to a past life-style of participation and activity, that is, whether hobbies or interests were social or individual, active or passive, or a combination. Habits endure, however, and a recent report of different patterns of retirement among educators suggests that both choice and level of activity after age 65 depend somewhat on childhood experiences and attitudes toward retirement (16).

A persistent myth has it that retirement per se will cause a decline in physical or mental health. Research has shown that this is incorrect. Many factors enter into state of health and adjustment after retirement, not the least important being state of health and adjustment before retirement. Other variables are preretirement attitudes and expectations, voluntary or involuntary retirement, retirement income, and type of work done before retirement (17, 18).

At least for the present generation of elderly persons, these issues apply primarily to men. As more and more working women retire, the implications of retirement will probably be less related to gender. It is certainly desirable for couples to consider retirement and the impact it will have on their life-style. Many couples look forward to having more time together and to doing things that were not possible because of the demands of jobs.

Obviously, preparation for a "good old age" is not unlike preparation for a good middle age or adolescence. The ingredients are supportive family relationships and sensible health care practices, satisfying leisure activities, and attainment of the goals established earlier in life. Planning for economic security and fulfillment of other needs is reasonable. Realistically, persons with numerous problems of long standing have a different prognosis than those who present with relatively acute problems. For some elderly persons, however, social pressures that created disturbances in the past can be turned around and used effectively to resolve some of the current problems. It may be easier to provide dependency gratification and to lower expectations for a person at age 70 than for the same person at age 40. When an old person is helped to reduce tension and frustration, "mental health" improves. This should not be interpreted as an argument for considering any elderly person as a candidate for an institutional arrangement, which is certainly not the only method of achieving such goals.

Retirement means different things to different people. It is not a devastating experience for most people, and its depressing aspects have been overadvertised.

COMPREHENSIVE TREATMENT

It follows from this discussion that, when problems arise, all personal resources and help available from the network of community and family supports must be recruited. The importance of early recognition of problems and treatment is self-evident. As I have said, elderly people are likely to have a combination of psychological, social and health problems which must be recognized by the patient and the caregiver. Since an unidisciplinary approach frequently leaves some needs unmet, a comprehensive care approach should follow. A physician may believe his prescription is complete when he has determined a proper balance between diet and dosage of insulin. The treatment will fail if he has not also made certain that the patient or someone else can prepare meals and inject the correct dosage of insulin, that the patient is psychologically prepared and willing to follow the diet and take the insulin as prescribed, and that there is money and transportation available. In this relatively simple but common situation, the physician may well have to call in a dietician and social worker and possibly a psychiatrist. Similarly, patients with psychiatric disorders may have concurrent problems that require collaboration with a nurse, physician, social worker, home service agencies, and social welfare programs. A multidisciplinary treatment plan provides the mechanism and goals for delivering comprehensive service, but someone must coordinate treatment to assure attention to the many details. This is essential in long-term care, be it in an outpatient clinic, a hospital or residential setting. In a formal structure in which a team of specialists collaborates, the multidisciplinary approach is more clearly defined, but even when the services are provided informally, someone among the caregivers must continually monitor the patient's condition and the appropriateness of the treatment plan.

Diagnostic Evaluation

In appraising a patient's assets and liabilities, it is not enough to examine social or psychological or health factors independently of each other. As pointed out, medical evaluation and recommendations for treatment will fail unless other factors are considered. Even when a patient's income is adequate and family supports are available, both patient and family need some direction to help them find and make connections with services that may be available but are unknown to them. Emotional support to enable the elderly patient cope with changes in living arrangements, move to a new neighborhood, or adapt to restrictions imposed by an impairment in physical health is equally important.

In helping a particular individual to maintain or regain maximum functional capacity, abstract measurements of functional capacity are of little value. A more meaningful approach incorporates a study of the person's capacity to function in the environment in which he or she is living. Alterations in the physical environment may be necessary. An apartment, for example, might be quite adequate except that it is inaccessible to the tenant with arthritis or congestive heart failure who cannot climb stairs. Similarly, a person may be able to prepare meals but live too far from public transportation and a grocery store. To avoid social isolation and fear, issues related to safety from street crime must also be considered.

Physical Health Care

Persons concerned with the mental health of elderly persons are alert to the possibility that mental illness has a physical-illness substrate. In elderly persons, organic brain syndrome is often associated with a remediable condition and can be reversed if the underlying physical condition is recognized and treated adequately. Here, again, early diagnosis and treatment are especially important. Pathology in the cardiovascular, renal, pulmonary, and endocrine systems may produce psychiatric symptoms of an organic brain syndrome or other types of illness. "Depression" is often associated with chronic illness, and the behavior associated with acute and chronic illnesses can resemble that of psychiatrically ill persons. Psychological symptoms obviously cannot be ignored, but the possible association with a physical disorder deserves careful evaluation. If there is an association, prompt treatment of the physical condition may also relieve the psychological manifestations. The coin has two sides; emphasis on psychological manifestations may lead to neglect of underlying physical disorders just as a treatment regimen emphasizing the physical components may ignore important psychological aspects.

Rationale for Treatment Approaches

Understanding human development as a series of changes across the life span helps one to understand what happens to individuals as they age and generates information about specific age groups. The developmental approach is especially relevant for psychiatrists because it reminds them that changes occur throughout life. At each age the human being encounters unique stresses and central problems, to which he or she usually responds with a variety of adjustments that may lead to successful and satisfying experiences.

Common sense tells us that adjustment in one period of life is related to past experience, but good adjustment in one period does not guarantee uninterrupted happiness in the next one. Issues and conflicts change, so, for example, a successful adjustment in middle life is not guaranteed by a smoothly negotiated adolescence. Usually, however, persons in middle and late life have had more opportunities and more practice in making successful and satisfying adjustments.

Old age is a time when the future is shorter, but the past is longer, and old persons have had time to polish their coping mechanisms. Although old age is probably not a time for major personality changes or for dramatic alterations in life-style, it has potential for beneficial changes and modifications, achievement of happiness and ability to deal effectively with crises. One need not be naive and assume that changes do not occur as an individual ages. To be reassured, the patient and his or her therapist need only remember that ample resources remain to deal with most of the physical disorders, social problems, and other forces that impinge on older persons.

The rationale for treatment should be based on a theoretical formulation of all factors contributing to an individual's condition at the time of appraisal. A psychiatrist making such a formulation should consider theories related to aging and its processes, to brain function, to psychosomatic disorders, and to the nature of psychiatric illness. Sensitivity to what may transpire as individuals age is critical; myths and stereotypes about aging and the aged should be recognized as such and discarded.

Practical Considerations

Goals of treatment which are compatible with the physical health status of an individual should also take into account the patient's and the family's expectations. A patient deserves the opportunity to explore all problems and all possible solutions. Age per se does not determine what issues are important. A patient and his therapist should not be inhibited by the notion that an elderly person is inevitably occupied with certain issues and that others are irrelevant and inapplicable. Autonomy, dependency, sexuality, life satisfaction, and many other concerns are not entirely age-related.

Therapeutic intervention should be based on a judgment of what is wrong or maladaptive. A comprehensive diagnostic approach will often uncover multiple factors. A psychiatrist who limits his or her understanding of the patient's mental status to neurophysiological, neurochemical, or psychodynamic formulations—or any other single theoretical frame of reference—will probably deny a patient the full benefit of treatment currently available. A sophisticated, but limited, approach is usually inadequate. For example, if one treats impaired cerebral blood flow only with conventional drugs, one ignores the possibility that diminished blood flow is a phenomenon associated with scarring of brain tissues which results in diminished requirement. When this is so, improving circulation is a futile effort. Dealing only with circulation fails to take into account the patient's responses to the impairment, let alone the implications for, say, family members who are affected when their relative no longer functions effectively.

The intervention a physician chooses is often influenced by the attitude he or she holds about a particular diagnosis or condition. If one believes that manifestations of organic brain syndrome reflect an irreversible condition, therapeutic nihilism follows. The converse is true, of course.

For illness attributed to psychological mechanisms, a whole range of interventions are appropriate, but, here again, the patient's and therapist's attitudes are critical in determining what steps will be taken. Therapeutic outcome will depend on a careful appraisal of assets and liabilities, and the application of modalities already in the therapeutic armamentarium. Even though we recognize that the state of the art is such that we cannot cure, much can be done to alleviate pain and distress and even to delay progression of disability.

One should not minimize the potential of patients to help themselves and to serve as their own therapists. Given a chance, elderly persons are quite likely to respond to their own insights. They may need help in exploring what can be done when they are lonely, perhaps widowed. Remarriage and group living arrangements are sometimes possible. If children have moved away, the parent may decide to give up the security of an old familiar environment in exchange for closer contact with children. He or she may be helped to acknowledge impairments and dependence and to accept help and care. The essence of therapy is encouraging a patient to express feelings, to sort out issues, and then to help the person recognize available options and to select the best ones.

Psychiatric Treatment

Psychiatric treatment is an important component in a comprehensive treatment plan. Psychiatrists have a host of modalities to alleviate emotional distress and its manifestations. These include individual, group and family psychotherapy, psychological and social counseling, crisis intervention and psychopharmacotherapy. Environmental manipulation, social case work, behavioral modification, and electroconvulsive therapy may be effective. All of these treatment approaches are applicable to older and younger patients, based on the usual indications and contraindications.

Working with family members and other significant persons is an essential part of treating the elderly. This must be done with a consideration of the patient's feelings and attitudes. Many elderly patients will respond to individual therapy and interpret involving other persons as condescension or a reflection of their own weakness or inability to care for themselves.

Psychotherapy has been used quite effectively in helping patients confront and deal with a variety of emotional problems. This may be done as individual, group or family therapy. Marital counseling may prove useful, regardless of how long a couple has been married. Short-term therapy may be more effective for older than for younger patients, which perhaps reflects the strengths of the old and their ability to benefit from relatively little intervention. As with younger patients, the type of therapy and duration should be related not to age, but to an understanding of the patient's problems and the therapist's own potential.

Psychotropic medications—tranquilizers, antidepressants, and stimulants—have been demonstrated to be effective in elderly persons. Special precautions are necessary, however, because elderly patients respond differently to drugs from younger patients. The explanation for differences is by no means clear. One day we may be able to understand changes in drug metabolism as they relate to neurochemical or neurophysiological changes in the central nervous system or other systems. Elderly persons have often been conditioned to believe that treatment with pills is better than "talking" or counseling. This may explain why placebo effects are especially likely in older persons. When drugs are administered, it is relevant to remember that elderly persons are not a homogeneous group, either physiologically or psychologically, and that physiological changes associated with aging may affect absorption, drug distribution and excretion of a drug. The responses to drugs cannot be predicted simply on the basis of the age of patients. Therefore, we usually begin with small doses of medications and these may prove to be adequate. In some instances, patients probably do not obtain full benefit because of a physician's reluctance to increase dosages to a level that will be therapeutic for the individual patient. The indications for medications should be based on appropriate target signs and symptoms, not on the age of the patient.

Since elderly patients are likely to be taking other medications, "polypharmacy" may present some serious problems as a consequence of drug interactions. Patients may withhold information, or need prodding to remember other drugs they are taking, those prescribed by other physicians or self-administered. A detailed history of drug intake is a necessity and may often reveal an etiologic relationship between the medications and what appears to be a psychiatric disorder. One is very likely to find that patients with organic brain disease and associated psychiatric impairment also are in poor physical health status. When prescribing medications, a physician must obviously take into account not only the mental but the physical status of his patients.

Electroconvulsive therapy is still an effective treatment for patients with profound depressive disorders. Age per se is not a contraindication to this form of treatment. When elderly patients with affective disorders have failed to respond to other modalities, electroconvulsive therapy may prove to be quite effective.

Evaluation of Treatment

Evaluation of treatment, however, is more difficult with elderly patients. The aged are not a homogeneous group, and thus age alone rarely accounts for outcome. The explanation for treatment outcome probably rests in many factors, some of them understood. For example, though much interest and research have been centered on the kinetics of drug metabolism, few studies have paid attention to chronological age as a factor. Methodological problems arise not only because comparable samples are difficult to obtain, but also because so many variables affect results. Norms for health and social status are often lacking; tests validated with younger age groups may not be appropriate for aged persons. Much remains to be done in establishing baselines and profiles so that the impact of interventions, be they medical, pharmacological, social, or psychological, can be compared. Measures of life satisfaction, for example, need to be concerned with the quality of the experiences as well as the quantity of pleasant or unpleasant events. Persons in an institution may have lower levels of anxiety than those outside, but the effectiveness of a hospital treatment plan may be open to challenge because it has resulted in the patient's isolation from family and friends. A treatment plan that benefits a patient might carry considerable emotional and financial costs to family members. As I have said so many times, these and other questions are not unique to the care of elderly persons. Ultimately it is value judgments that determine what is to be done, by whom, and when.

Many problems arise in evaluating the effectiveness of a drug purported to be effective in alleviating symptoms or complaints of elderly patients. To begin with, the mechanism that produces the symptom often is not known. Neither is the action of the drug always clear, so that outcome can be attributed to a placebo effect or to the increased attention patients are receiving as a result of being involved in research. The possibility of intercurrent illness is always present, making prolonged studies difficult. Patients are likely to lose interest in the study. If treatment for intercurrent problems is needed, it might put data from the study in question.

Research on social problems is no easier. For example, there has been much concern about the influence on mental health of age-segregated vs. age-integrated housing. Even a superficial approach to the question uncovers many variables that influence results and are extremely difficult to control.

These remarks should not be interpreted as hopeless or apologetic. Those of us who have been concerned with the elderly can point out to our critics that persons of all ages suffer chronic disorders that are not treated very effectively with the methods we now have available. Our colleagues do not know why aspirin or digitalis are effective, but this has not eliminated these excellent drugs from the tool kits of physicians. In the case of the elderly, however, bias and prejudice are sometimes reinforced by an attitude that we cannot help because we do not know enough, or we do not understand, or no matter what we do our patients are likely to get worse. Ultimately, we must decide to give our energies and efforts to patients regardless of age. If we waited for absolute results to prove effectiveness of a treatment, I suspect many of our patients, young and old, would go untreated. We must work toward a better definition of problems and a better clarification of techniques that will satisfy the needs of our patients.

AGED PERSONS AND THEIR FAMILIES

The following discussion points out some of the attributes of families and familial relationships that affect outcome of treatment and sheds some light on the genesis of conflicts.

Intrafamily Relationships

Patterns of relating within a family may remain relatively constant as members of the family age. Some persons are able to maintain a parental role well past middle age, especially if they are healthy, active, and satisfy our society's concepts of success. Their children become independent and self-reliant. They complete their education, marry and have their own families, or not, as they may choose. The grandparents, and even great-grandparents, continue as active members of the family. They have the respect of the young members and, together, they reach compromises that enable all the members to balance autonomy, independence, and control.

Healthy families are not rare. When elderly persons can accept the physical and financial help they need, comfortable arrangements follow as the child assumes more and more of the parental role. Often, however, we encounter families whose conflicts flare up when their elderly members become dependent. In a family troubled by a long history of child-parent conflicts or intrapersonal problems, neither child nor parent may be able to make these accommodations. A parent with strong dependency needs, for example, may have had these satisfied through middle life. Death of a spouse, retirement or ill health will bring battles as the parent makes excessive demands. If the child's dependency needs were not gratified in early life, he or she may then refuse to do this for the aged parent. It is easy to understand how these conflicts come about.

Marital relationships are particularly important to emotional stability and gratification. Partners who have had a good, supportive marriage will help each other to cope with problems arising late in life. The possibility of a delayed response to frustration and resentment exists, however, and these reactions may surface after decades of marriage. When, for these and other reasons, the equilibrium in a marriage is disturbed, manifestations of illness may follow in one or both partners. As the partners in a marriage age, the needs of one may increase more rapidly or be more intense. If the other spouse remains healthy and psychologically able to provide attention, no difficulties may be encountered, but if the spouse becomes less competent physically, emotionally and intellectually, the loss of support may be felt intensely by the more dependent partner.

Stress in old age may disrupt a relatively fragile but continuous relationship. Illnesses, changes in social roles, retirement, losses, and other stresses are especially difficult to manage for such couples. Other members of the family may become involved when previously repressed hostility is expressed by wife or husband. Such situations require the same kinds of psychiatric attention as when they arise in younger persons. Psychotherapy, marital counseling, and environmental manipulation may help.

Attitudes of Family Members

The attitudes of patient and family members strongly influence outcome when interaction becomes an important part of a treatment plan (19). The capability of a family member or members to provide a service may or may not match performance, depending on many of the factors mentioned above. Therapists must be alert always to the interaction of family members when preparing a treatment plan. One cannot assume that family resources will inevitably be used. An adult child may have a room for a parent and a car, but that is no guarantee that the child will provide an elderly parent with housing and transportation. A wife or husband who intellectually understands a diet prescription or medical regimen for the spouse may refuse to participate in or actually sabotage a treatment plan. A willing, compassionate family member can be extremely helpful to an elderly person. Those of us who work with older persons have been heartened by numerous instances of devotion and love from spouses and other relatives. But we must be careful not to place unreasonable expectations on families. When help is not forthcoming, it is usually easy to understand why not.

Other pressures on a family may limit care. Often children of old patients are somewhat handicapped themselves; they may have a spouse who requires attention, and have neither energy nor time to spend on a parent. Conflicts may arise in middle-aged couples because of demands made upon one or both to care for their parents, and, of course, some individuals grow up incapable or unwilling to give of themselves to anyone—parent, spouse, or child. One must examine early relationships to understand the dynamics of interaction between a family member and an elderly person.

Conflicts that have been intense in childhood and adolescence may subside in adulthood, only to rise again when the parent is old. In such instances, therapist and patient must counsel together to determine whether or not the family members should be included in the treatment plan. Moral precepts and biblical commands to honor one's parents do not seem to be enough.

PHYSICIANS CARING FOR AGED PATIENTS

Attitudes

Physicians caring for elderly persons must examine their own attitudes and life experiences and make certain that they have dealt with the prejudices and biases that might interfere with delivery of service (20). Physicians, culturally bound to notions that disability, failure and death are associated with aging and the aged, are not immune to developing cynical attitudes about therapeutic intervention. From the few studies done (21, 22), it is clear that psychiatrists and other physicians harbor stereotyped views of the aged, and it is reasonable to assume that these attitudes affect their selection of patients and probably lead them to exclude elderly persons. Physicians generally have negative attitudes toward patients with chronic disease, dependence and disability, common features of elderly patients. Countertransference phenomena are likely to affect relationships with such patients and, in turn, influence the therapeutic relationship.

All doctors have patients, young, middle-aged, or old, who suffer from illnesses that do not respond quickly to treatment, and they also have patients who evoke negative reactions. Age rarely is the single differentiating factor. If prejudices associated with age are set aside, it is possible to establish satisfying and gratifying relationships with older patients. Mature physicians are able to accept responsibility for doing what is possible and to recognize the limitations of therapy. Obviously, a therapist who has resolved conflicts about aging, losses and death, is more likely to help persons who are attempting to deal with such conflicts.

A physician with a healthy degree of optimism and openmindedness is likely to find working with older people rewarding. If he or she also enjoys collaborating with other professionals and respects the contributions of practitioners from other disciplines, such a practitioner is likely to be successful. Although there are notable exceptions among young physicians, there is reason to believe that practitioners work more effectively with older persons after they themselves have had an opportunity to experience the joys and sorrows of life. This may only come about after the physician has reached chronological maturity. Elderly persons, in turn, may find it easier to relate to older physicians, but personality characteristics are more important than the therapist's age. Personal experiences with aging patients, parents and family tend to endow physicians with sensitivity and awareness of changes occurring with age.

Physicians must be sympathetic to the needs and values of their patients, arriving at agreement about treatment objectives and critical issues by mutual consent. Provision of adequate housing and income may, for example, be more important and relevant to a patient than an interpretation of dreams or an understanding of mental mechanisms. On the other hand, an aged person who is concerned about sexual performance will welcome an opportunity to discuss this with his or her therapist. Urging such a patient to follow a diet or to participate in activities at the neighborhood senior citizens center, while denying him or her an opportunity to discuss more personal problems, is a therapeutic error. No checklist of problems is unique to the elderly; each patient must be approached as an individual with special problems and attributes.

Physicians must guard against condescension. This attitude can be expressed in many ways and may begin when a history is taken from an informant rather than the patient. Although they may need a little extra time and patience, elderly persons are usually quite capable of giving a history and discussing treatment objectives.

Multidisciplinary Approach

Since elderly people are likely to have a multiplicity of problems and complaints, a multidisciplinary approach to providing comprehensive service is usually best. First, of course, the patient and his family must agree that this is desirable. For members of a treatment team, each of whom contributes his or her special skills to comprehensive care, coordination of service requires some concessions of autonomy. Physicians particularly, and for good reasons, have trouble sharing authority. This is related, in part, to issues of legal responsibility, but physicians have moral responsibility as well to give personal attention to their patients' social, psychological, and physical needs, or to be willing to collaborate with other professionals who work in areas other than health care. If a physician is willing to become a family counselor or a social worker or a welfare worker, there are no problems, but most physicians prefer working in a relatively restricted and traditional role. Their patients will benefit dramatically from the team approach.

All remarks directed to physicians apply equally, of course, to all specialists, including psychiatrists. The type of practice makes some difference; solo practitioners find it more difficult to participate in a team effort. These doctors have additional responsibilities to offer a broad spectrum of services. Psychiatrists in solo practice often provide services which, in an institutional setting, are given by social workers. Physicians practicing alone may find themselves performing functions that a physician's assistant, a nurse-practitioner or a dietician might provide. When the patient's welfare is the primary concern, and when the patient has varied needs, persons in one professional discipline will recognize their limitations. They will find ways of working with other professionals while arguments about professional roles, responsibility, and territory fade into the background.

Aging of Physicians

Until recently, physicians rarely encountered mandatory retirement and many of the other pressures faced by large segments of the aged population (23). As a group, they value work, achievement, independence, and self-reliance, and are strong proponents of the work ethic. It is understandable, then, that conflicts may arise between caregivers who cherish this value system and patients whose condition is characterized by passivity and dependence. The physicians' lack of empathy for persons with these qualities may be a serious barrier to treatment. The life experiences of most physicians leave them ill-prepared for old age and the changes it might bring. Their personal attitudes will affect relationships with, as well as selection of, patients. Many physicians do not like reminders that there are patients and diseases which they are relatively incapable of treating. Moreover, as physicians age, their patients age also, evidencing changes which remind the doctors that similar changes are occurring in themselves. Doctors are by no measure spared existential questions, questions of professional competence, and adjustments in marital and familial roles. The way a physician resolves these issues not only determines his adjustment but also influences his relationship to patients.

The physician is subject to all the pressures to which other persons are exposed as they age. The often used defense mechanism of hyper-achievement may not operate forever. Like other human beings, physicians must be aware that preparation for their own old age is not only personally beneficial, but also helpful to their families and patients.

In summary, a professional identification as physician does not protect against the prejudices about aging, nor does it rule out an irrational acceptance of stereotypes assigned to elderly persons in our culture. Therapy involves helping older people acknowledge some aspects of aging and related problems, and to accept treatment. A physician must also overcome the temptation to deny personal realities. He or she is less likely to reject and will be more effective with elderly patients when he or she is informed about treatment potentialities and discovers that elderly persons respond quite favorably to the application of basic and sound principles of medicine.

SUMMARY

By focusing attention on assets and liabilities of aged persons, one gains an understanding of how these characteristics sometimes lead to manifestations of psychiatric disorders. Social, psychological and physical health factors interact in a complex manner across the life span and, ultimately, in old age, result in varying degrees of mental health or illness. The manifestations and treatment of psychiatric disorders are not age determined. Special attention, however, must be given to the social pressures exerted on elderly persons and their physical health status. A very careful diagnostic assessment is mandatory to determine the importance of various factors and the most effective ways to intervene.

Diagnosis and treatment of aged individuals should also be based on an understanding of intrafamilial relationships. Across the life span, changes in the individual and in family members occur and influence adjustment and the outcome of therapy. Ignoring these interactions will result in inadequate treatment and possibly devastating effects on those concerned.

Finally, the care of aged patients is affected by the attitudes of physicians. They are not immune to culturally determined negative images of aging and the aged. A physician also ages, and associated changes in personality, attitudes and competence may also affect treatment.

These and other issues have been discussed with the ultimate purpose of demonstrating that aged patients have unusual opportunities to utilize their own resources. In addition, there are also many ways in which family members and physicians may help them achieve a high level of mental and physical health and life satisfaction.

REFERENCES

1. NOWLIN, J. B.: Physical changes in later life and their relationship to mental functioning. In: E. W. Busse and E. Pfeiffer

(Eds.), *Mental Illness in Later Life.* Washington, D.C.: American Psychiatric Association, 1973, pp. 145-152.

2. VERWOERDT, A.: *Clinical Geropsychiatry.* Baltimore, Md.: Waverly Press, Inc., 1976, p. 4.

3. SHANAS, E.: Health status of older people: Cross national implications. *American Journal of Public Health,* 64:261-264, March, 1974.

4. PALMORE, E. (Ed.): *Normal Aging II.* Durham, N.C.: Duke University Press, 1974.

5. BUSSE, E. W. and PFEIFFER, E. (Eds.): *Behavior and Adaptation in Late Life* (Second edition). Boston: Little, Brown and Co., 1977.

6. BUSSE, E. W. and PFEIFFER, E. (Eds.): *Mental Illness in Later Life.* Washington, D.C.: American Psychiatric Association, 1973.

7. MILLER, E.: *Abnormal Aging: The Psychology of Senile and Presenile Dementia.* New York: John Wiley & Sons, 1977.

8. BAER, P. E.: Cognitive changes in aging: Competence and incompetence. In: C. M. Gaitz (Ed.), *Aging and the Brain.* New York: Plenum Press, 1971, pp. 5-13.

9. GAITZ, C. M.: Depression in the elderly. In: W. E. Fann, et al. (Eds.), *Phenomenology and Treatment of Depression.* Jamaica, N.Y.: Spectrum Publications, 1977, pp. 153-166.

10. SCOTT, J. and GAITZ, C. M.: Ethnic and age differences in mental health measures. *Diseases of the Nervous System,* 36:389-393, July, 1975.

11. GOLDFARB, A. I.: Clinical perspectives. In: A. Simon and L. J. Epstein (Eds.), *Aging in Modern Society.* Washington, D.C.: American Psychiatric Association, 1968, pp. 170-178.

12. BROCKLEHURST J. C. and HANLEY, T.: *Geriatric Medicine for Students.* Edinburgh: Churchill Livingstone, 1976, p. 59.

13. SEIDENBERG, R.: Older man—younger woman marriages. *Human Sexuality,* 7-25, Nov., 1975.

14. PFEIFFER, E.: Sexual behavior in old age. In: E. W. Busse and E. Pfeiffer (Eds.), *Behavior and Adaptation in Late Life* (Second Edition). Boston: Little, Brown, and Co., 1977, pp. 130-141.

15. GORDON, C. and GAITZ, C. M.: Leisure and lives: Personal expressivity across the life span. In: R. H. Binstock and E. Shanas (Eds.), *Handbook of Aging and the Social Sciences.* New York: Van Nostrand Reinhold Co., 1976, pp. 310-341.

16. SNOW, R. B. and HAVIGHURST, R. J.: Life style types and patterns of retirement of educators. *The Gerontologist,* 17:545-552, Dec. 1977.

17. SHEPPARD, H.: Work and retirement. In: R. H. Binstock and E. Shanas (Eds.), *Handbook of Aging and the Social Sciences.* New York: Van Nostrand Reinhold Co., 1976, pp. 286-309.

18. SHELDON, A., McEWAN, P. J. M., and RYNER, C. P.: *Retirement: Patterns and Predictions.* Rockville, Md.: NIMH, Section on

Mental Health of the Aging. DHEW Publication No. (ADM)
74-49, 1975.
18. SHELDON, A., McEWAN, P. J. M., and RYNER, C. P.: *Retirement*:
elderly psychiatric patients. *Archives of General Psychiatry*,
22:348-350, April, 1970.
20. GAITZ, C. M.: Role of the physician in the comprehensive care of
elderly persons. *Lex et Scientia*, 11:204-211, Oct.-Dec., April,
1975.
21. CYRUS-LUTZ, C., and GAITZ, C. M.: Psychiatrists' attitudes toward the aged and aging. *The Gerontologist*, 12:163-167. Sum-
mer, No. 2, Pt. 1, 1972.
22. GARETZ, F. K.: The psychiatrist's involvement with aged patients.
American Journal of Psychiatry, 132:63-65, January, 1975.
23. GAITZ, C. M.: Planning for retirement: Advice to physicians.
Journal of American Medical Association, 237:149-151, July,
1977.

BIBLIOGRAPHY

BEREZIN, M. A. and CATH, S. H. (Eds.): *Geriatric Psychiatry: Grief,
Loss, and Emotional Disorders in the Aging Process*. New York:
International Universities Press, Inc., 1965.
BINSTOCK, R. H. and SHANAS, E.: *Handbook of Aging and the Social
Sciences*. New York: Van Nostrand Reinhold Co., 1976.
CARP, F.: *Retirement*. New York: Behavioral Publications, Inc., 1972.
DATAN, N. and GINSBERG, L. H. (Eds.): *Life Span Developmental
Psychology: Normative Life Crises*. New York: Academic Press,
1975.
GRANICK, S. and PATTERSON, R. D. (Eds.): *Human Aging II: An
Eleven-Year Follow-up Biomedical and Behavioral Study*. Rock-
ville, Md.: NIMH Section on Mental Health of the Aging,
D.H.E.W. publication No. (HSM) 71-9037, 1971.
LEVIN, S. and KAHANA, R. J. (Eds.): *Psychodynamic Studies on
Aging: Creativity, Reminiscing and Dying*. New York: Interna-
tional Universities Press, Inc., 1967.
NEUGARTEN, B. L. (Ed.): *Middle Age and Aging: A Reader in Social
Psychology*. Chicago: University of Chicago Press, 1970.
PALMORE, E. and JEFFERS, F. C. (Eds.): *Prediction of Life Span*.
Lexington, Mass.: D.C. Heath and Co., 1971.
STREIB, G. F. and SCHNEIDER, C. H.: *Retirement in American Society:
Impact and Process*. Ithaca, N.Y.: Cornell University Press, 1971.

Index

Acetylcholine, (ACH), 55, 70
ACHE, 68, 69, 71
ACTH, 51, 58, 73, 76-78
Activity Theory, 140
Acute Organic Brain Syndrome, 118, 119
Adaptation Study, 146.
  See Schaie, K.
AER, 101
Affective assistance, 192
Age gauge, 2
Aging, 1-17
  AER potential, 152-154
    fig. 3, 153
  age composition and impairment, 22-24
    table 1, 23
  cognitive, 109-120
    clinical issues, 118-120
    clinical studies, 116-118
    intellectual, 109-114
    memory, 114
    neuropsychology, 114-116
  death and dying, 116-181
  definitions, 130-132
  demographic change, 21, 22
  depression and suicide, 8, 9
  education, 26
  EEG changes, 148-152
    fig. 1, 149
    fig. 2, 151

electroencephalographic, 99-103
emotional and mental problems, 4, 5
galvanic skin responses, 103, 104
heart rate, 105
income maintenance, 24, 25
longitudinal studies, 144-146
making history, 40, 41
neuropathology, 146-148
nursing homes, 12, 13
organic brain syndromes, 5-8
patients, families and physicians, 206-237
personal adaptation, 37-40
professional neglect, 14-16
psychophysiologic and cognitive, 96-120
research, 129-162
role in depression, 47-83
  aging, of, 61-73
  biochemical studies, 64-73
    tables 1-5, 65-67
  differing views, 48-50
    fig. 1, 49
  endocrine studies, 73-79
    table 6, 74
    table 7, 75
  morphological studies, 61-64
    fig. 2, 62
  neurobiology of stress, 51-63
  neuroendocrine studies, 58-61

241

neurotransmitters, 53-61
scientific problem, 30, 31
services, 184-202
sex differences, 108, 109
sexual behavior and attitudes, 157-162
sleep, 154
social integration, 31-36, 39
  table 2, 34, 35
social issues—financial, 9, 10
social problems, 27-29
surviving spouse, 155, 156
theories of aging, 132-144
  biologic, 132-138
  problems in research, 140-142
  psychologic, 138, 139
  serendipity, 142-144
  social theories, 139, 140
transportation, 25, 26
values, 27
Akistal, H., 48
Alpha activity, 148
  rhythm, 100
Alzheimer, 61, 147
Alzheimer's type dementia, 5, 13, 61, 101, 119, 120, 147, 148
Amitriptyline, 57
Amyloidosis, 137
Anderson, B., 37
Antidepressants, 56, 57
Aristotle, 17
Arrhythmias, 175, 176
Arsenian, J., 27
Arsenian, J. M., 27
Autoimmunity, 136
Autonomic nervous system (ANS), 96-109
Average evoked potential (AEP), 101, 152-154
  fig. 3, 153

Bal, T., 117
Baltes, P., 109, 138
Baltimore Study, 3, 4
  Gerontological Research Center, 145
Bayley, N., 111
Beauvoir, S., 29, 36
Beck, E., 152
"Being Younger Is Better," 39

Benton, A., 115
Berger, H., 99
Berkley Growth Study, 110
Berkowitz, B., 113
Berle index, 180
Beta adrenergic blocking agent, 107
Birren, J., 107, 138
Blichert-Toft, M., 74, 75, 77
"Blind alley behavior," 168
Bondareff, W., 63
Botwinick, J., 110, 113
Bowers, M., 71
Bowman, R., 74, 76
Brain damage, 116
Breznock, E., 74, 76
Brody, H., 61
Brown, G., 58
Bruce, R., 169, 175
Burnet, F., 136
Busse, E., 99, 103, 104, 108, 129-165
Butler, R., viii, 1-19, 157

Cannon, W., 167
Cantor, M., 184-205
Caplan, G., 185, 186
Carlsson, A., 65, 69, 70
Carrell, A., 133
Cathecholamine biosynthesis, 54-56, 68
Cattell, R., 112
Central nervous system, 47-83, 96-109, 119, 120
  aging of, 61-73
  biochemical studies, 64-73
    table 1, 65
    table 2, 66
    table 3, 66
    table 4, 67
    table 5, 67
  endocrine studies, 73-79
    table 6, 74
    table 7, 75
  morphological studies, 61-64
    fig. 2, 62
  neuroendocrine studies, 58-61
  neurotransmitters, 53-61
  neurobiology of stress, 51-53
  physiological studies, 79, 80
Cerebrospinal fluid (CSF), 70, 71

Chan, S., 75, 78
Changes intrinsic to aging, 3, 4
  immune capacity, 4
Church, F., Senator, 13
Clark, M., 37
Classic symptoms of brain disorders, 7
Clemens, J., 75, 78
Cognitive studies, 109-120
  clinical issues, 118-120
  clinical studies, 116-118
  intellectual, 109-114
  memory, 114
  neuropsychology, 114-116
Cohen, D., 113, 137
Cohort approach, 140
Cohort disease, 170
Cole, J., 77, 78
Comfort, A., 22, 28
Commitment theory, 133, 134
Community mental health services, 12, 15, 184-202
  Community Mental Health Act, 185
  Massachusetts Mental Health Center, 197, 198
  need for, 193, 194
Computerized axial tomogram, 13
Concept of attachment, 139
Concept of disengagement, 139, 140
Corticosterone, 51
Corticotropin-releasing hormone (CRF), 76
Cortisol, 59, 60
Cotzias, G., 83
Cowgill, D., 32
Craik, F., 114
Crook, T., 116
Cross-linkage or eversion theory, 135
Crystallized intelligence (GC), 111-113
Cumming, E., 39

DA, 55, 58-60, 68, 69, 81, 82
Death and dying, 166-181
  aging, 171, 172
  arrhythmias, 175, 176
  coronary occlusion myocardial infarction, 174, 175
  crisis, 167, 168
  cultural expectations, 167-173
  disease, 169, 170
  fainting, 174
  infectious disease, 176, 177
  kidney function, water, electrolyte balance, 176
  living dangerously, 170
  psychophysiologic mechanism, 173-180
  respiratory system function, 177-180
  sin, 172, 173
  suicide, 173, 174
Delirium, 216
Demographic changes, 21, 22
  age composition, 22-24
  table 1, 23
Denckla, W., 75, 78, 79, 82
Depression, 4, 6, 7, 118, 120, 210, 211, 225
  aging and its role, 47-83
  aging of, 61-73
  biochemical studies, 64-73
    table 1, 65
    table 2, 66
    table 3, 66
    table 4, 67
    table 5, 67
  differing views, 48-50
    fig. 1, 49
  endocrine studies, 73-79
    table 6, 74
    table 7, 75
  morphological studies, 61-64
    fig. 2, 62
  neurobiology of stress, 51-53
  neuroendocrine studies, 58-61
  neurotransmitters, 53-61
  physiological studies, 79, 80
  suicide, 8, 9, 48, 53, 155, 168, 173, 174
Developmental theory, 38
DeWied, D., 77
Differential gerontology, 41
Differential mortality, 166
"Dirty old man," 218
Division of adult development of aging, 31

DNA, 54, 55, 64, 68, 133-135, 141
Doerr, H., 104, 106
Donahue, W., 16
Down's syndrome, 147
Duke Center for Study of Aging and Human Development, 40, 136, 145, 146
Duke Longitudinal Study, 110, 111, 160, 219, 220
Dustman, R., 152
Dyspnea, 178

Ebling, A., 133
Eichorn, D., 110
Eisdorfer, C., 96-127, 137
Electroencephalographic studies, 99-103
    EEG changes, 148-152
        fig. 1, 149
        fig. 2, 151
        fig. 3, 153
Eleftherion, B., 102
Emphysema, 137
"End of the rope syndrome," 168
Engel, G., 168
Erikson, E., 38
Error theory, 134, 135
Ettigi, P., 58

Fainting, 174
Falek, A., 113
Families, 231, 232
    attitudes, 232, 233
    intrafamily relationships, 231, 232
Financial assistance, 190, 192
Finch, C., 65, 66, 68, 75
Fisher, D., 36
Fluid intelligence (GF), 111-113
Follette, W., 104, 106
Force of mortality, 171
Formal support system, 194-196
    barriers to utilization, 195, 196
    current solutions, 197, 198
    principles underlying, 194, 195
Frank, L., 30
Freud, S., x, 8, 14, 16, 17
Friedman, M., 74, 77, 174
Froehling, S., 107
Frolkis, V., 80, 106, 107

Gaitz, C., 206-239
Galvanic skin responses (GSR), 103-105
Geinisman, Y., 63
Genetic studies, 50, 156
Gerbode, R., 71
Geriatric alcoholism, 119
Geriatric medicine, 14, 15, 25
Gerontology Research Center, 16
    gerontological research, 42
Gold, P., 73
Goldfarb, A., 16, 212
Golgi investigations, 63
Gomori staining techniques, 80
Gonadotropin (LH, FSH), 59, 82, 83
Goodwin, F., 52
Gorham, D., 117
Gottfries, C., 65, 66, 71
Grad, B., 74, 76, 77
Graham, D., 174
Green, R., 113
Greulich, R., 3
Grief reactions, 210
Growth hormone (GH), 51, 52, 58, 60, 77
Gurian, B., 184-205

Hackett, T., 168
Hallenbeck, C., 116
Hallucinations, 7
Halstead-Reitan, 115, 117
Harkins, S., 102
Harris, L., 39, 40
Haven, C., 139
Hayflick, L., 22, 134
Heart rate, 105, 106
Henry, J., 39
Herr, J., 106
Hess, G., 74, 76
Hirano bodies, 62
Holliday, R., 134
Holmes, L., 32
Holmes, T., 166-183
Honzik, M., 111
Horn, J., 110-113
Hreschyshen, M., 75, 78
Huntington's chorea, 64, 119
Hyperarousal, 107, 108

Hyperthyroidism, 60
Hypothalamic pituitary adrenal
  (HPA), 59, 60

Imipramine, 56, 57
Immune system, 135-138
Immunoglobin serum, 136, 137
Immunologic theory, 135
Income maintenance, 24, 25
Indoleamines, 56
Informal support system, 187-200
  additive, 188, 189
  asymmetrical, 189
  choice of, 190-192
    table 1, 191
  hierarchical-compensatory, 189
  models of, 188-190
  relationship between formal and
    informal, 200
  task specific, 189
Intellectual functioning, 109-114
Irving, J., 175
IQ tests, 101, 102, 112, 113, 116,
  117

Japan, 32, 33
Jarvik, L., 109, 113
John, E., 101-103
Johnson, A., 156
Johnson, V., 158
Jonec, V., 65, 66, 68
Jones, H., 171
Journal of Gerontology, 30
Jung, C., x, 14

Kalish, R., 139, 140
Kaplan, B., 40
Kaplan, H. G., 75, 78
Kennedy, E., Senator, 129
Kent, S., 136
Kibbutz movement, 33, 36, 37
Kleemeier, R., 113
Klove, H., 115
Knudtson, F. W., 139
Kovacs, K., 75
Kuhn, M., 16

L-DOPA, 57, 71, 83
Lacey, B., 105, 108

Leisure, 221, 222
Lewis, P., 120
Lewy bodies, 62
LHRH, 60, 73, 76, 78, 83
Liberson, W., 100
Linden, M., table 1, 213
Lipofuchsin, 62, 63
Lipton, M., 47-94
Litwak, E., 187-189, 193, 194
Lopata, H., 40
Lowenthal, M., 40, 139, 187
Luteinizing hormone (LH), 60, 78

Macfarlane, J., 111
Maddox, G., 20-46
Mania, 55-57
Manton, K., 37
Marsh, G., 99-102
Massachusetts Mental Health Cen-
  ter Geriatric Team, 197, 198
Masters, W., 158
Matarazzo, J., 116
McBurney's point, 7
McCallum, W., 102
McGaugh, J., 73
McGeer, D., 65, 67, 69, 70
McKinney, W., 48
McNamara, M., 72
McQueen, R., 74, 76
Medicaid, 9-11, 13, 197-199
  recommendations, 201, 202
Medicare, 9-11, 13, 196, 198, 199
  recommendations, 200, 201
Meek, J., 65-67, 69, 70
Meier, M., 115
Meier-Ruge, W., 72
Meites, J., 75, 78, 79
Memory, 114
  primary, 114
  secondary, 114
Menninger, K., 8, 9
Mental health support systems,
  184-202
  barriers to utilization, 195-197
  choice of, 190-192
    table 1, 191
  concept of support, 185-186
  current solutions, 197, 198
  formal support system, 194-196

informal support system, 187, 188
  models of, 188-190
  need for formal community support, 193, 194
  other support systems, 198-200
  principles underlying, 194, 195
  recommendations, 200-202
  relationship between formal and informal, 200
  social support systems, 186
  systems view, 187
Metabolism in brain, 6
MHPG, 56, 57
Michalewski, H., 102
Miller, E., 120
Modernization, 32, 33, 37, 40, 41
Monoamine oxidase (MAO), 56, 70, 71, 82
Moorhead, P., 134
Mutation theory, 133-135

Narotzky, R., 63
National health insurance, 13, 199
National Institute on Aging, 15, 16, 202, 203
National Institute of Mental Health, 15, 197
Nemeroff, C., 47-94
Neugarten, B., 162
Neurobiology of stress, 51-80
  aging of, 61-73
  biochemical studies, 64-73
  endocrine studies, 73-79
  morphological studies, 61-64
  neuroendocrine studies, 58-61
  neurotransmitters, 53-61
  physiological studies, 79, 80
Neuropsychology, 114-116
Nies, A., 65, 66
Norepinephrine (NE), 51, 52, 55-60, 68-70, 80-82
Norris, A., 79
Nowlin, J., 105, 107, 207
Nursing homes, 12, 13

Obrist, W., 99, 100, 152
Ordy, J., 65, 67, 70
Organic brain disease, 53
  syndromes, 5-8, 210, 216, 229

Organicity, 115
  See Neuropsychology
Overall, J., 117
Owens, W., 110

Palmore, E., 33, 37, 46
Paranoid states, 4, 210, 218
Parkinson's disease, 8, 64, 69, 83, 147
Parson, 193
Patients, 206-231
  becoming a patient, 207
  changes in physical health, 207, 208
  changes in social roles, 208, 209
  comprehensive treatment, 223, 224
  diagnostic evaluation, 224, 225
  evaluation of, 229, 230
  physical health care, 225
  prevention of illness, 220-223
  psychiatric disorders, 209-218
    table 1, 213
    table 2, 214
    table 3, 215
    table 4, 217
  psychiatric treatment, 227-231
  rationale for treatment, 225, 226
  sexual behavior, 218-220
Peng, M., 79
Personality of individual, 8
Pfeiffer, E., 219, 220
Philadelphia Geriatric Center, 12.
  See Nursing Homes
Physical health care, 225
Physicians, 233-237
  aging of, 236, 237
  attitudes, 233-235
  multidisciplinary approach, 235
Pituitary hormones, 51
  pituitary adrenal axis, 51
Polycythemia, 160
"Polypharmacy," 229
Powell, A., 105
Prange, A., 57, 66
Predilection to death category, 168
President's Bio-Medical Research Panel, 129
Prevention of illness, 220-223

Primary aging, 96
Primary depression, 53
Primary memory (PM), 114
Professional neglect, 14-16
  reasons for neglect, 14, 15
Prolactin (PRL), 51, 52, 58, 59, 78
Propranolol, 107
Prostatic hypertrophy, 160
Psychiatric disorders, 209-218
  table 1, 213
  table 2, 214
  table 3, 215
  table 4, 217
Psychiatrists, 14, 16, 235
  psychiatric treatment, 227-231
  psychotherapy, 14, 228, 237
  psychotropic medications, 228, 229
  role with aging, 1, 2
  See Professional neglect
Psychopathology, 4, 5
Psychophysiologic studies, 96-109
  electroencephalographic, 99-103
  galvanic skin responses, 103, 104
  heart rate, 105
Purkinje cells, 61

Rahe, R., 168
Reichlmeier, K., 67, 71
Reitan, R., 115-117
Relief of loneliness, 192
REM activity, 102, 154
Renner, V., 138
Research, 129-162
  definitions, 130-132
  EEG changes, 148-152
    fig. 1, 149
    fig. 2, 151
    fig. 3, 153
  longitudinal studies, 144-146
  neuropathology, 146-148
  problems in research, 140-142
  serendipity, 142-144
  sleep, 154
  surviving spouse, 155, 156
  theories of aging, 132-144
Reserpine, 56, 57
Respiratory system function, 177-180

Resting electrodermal levels
  (EDR), 104, 105, 107
Retirement, 40, 41, 222, 223
Reversible brain syndromes, 6, 7
Riegle, G., 74, 76
Robinson, B., 40
Robinson, D., 65, 66, 70
Rogerian, 14
Romo, M., 168
Rosenman, R., 174
Rostow, I., 36

Samorajski, R., 64, 65, 67
Schaie, J., 116, 117
Schaie, K., 109, 116, 138, 146
Schedule of Recent Experiences, 167, 168
Scheibel, A., 63
Scheibel, M., 63
Schizophrenia, 5
Scientific problem, 30-37
  social integration, 31-37
    table 2, 34, 35
  study of, 30, 31
Secondary aging, 96
Secondary memory (SM), 114
Seidenberg, R., 219
Seneca, 9
Senility, 5, 118
  senile dementia, 13, 119, 120, 216, 218
Serendipity, 142-144
Serotonin (5HT), 51, 52, 55, 57-59, 68-72
Serum free fatty acid (FFA), 105-107
Sex differences, 108, 109
Sexual behavior and attitudes, 157-162
Shanas, E., 208
Shih, J., 66, 70
Shmavonian, B., 103, 104
Shock, N., 3
Siegler, I., 113
Simmons, L., 30, 32
Sleeg EEG studies, 102, 154
Smith, G., 73
Snyder, P., 75
Social problems, 27-29

Social Science Research Council, 30, 31
Social Security, 9, 10, 24, 25, 198, 199
  recommendations, 202
Stage theory of adult cognitive development, 138
Stereotypes, 41
Steroids, 51
  See Neurobiology of stress
Storrie, M., 97-99, 102
Suicide, 8, 9, 48, 53, 155, 168, 173, 174
Surnillo, W., 100
Survival, 22
Surviving spouse, 155, 156
Sussman, M., 33-36, 187
  table 2, 34-36

Talman, Y., 36
"Tea and toast" syndrome, 6
Terminal drop, 113
Terry, R., 119
Testosterone, 160
Theories of aging, 132-162
  biologic theories, 132-138
  EEG changes, 148-152
    fig. 1, 149
    fig. 2, 151
    fig. 3, 153
  longitudinal studies, 144-146
  neuropathology, 146-148
  problems in research, 140-142
  psychologic theories, 138, 139
  sexual behavior and attitudes, 157-162
  sleep, 154
  social theories, 139, 140
  surviving spouse, 155, 156
Theory of disengagement, 39
Thompson, L., 99, 100, 102
Thyrotropin (TSH), 59, 60, 73, 79

Timaras, P., 67, 68
Townes, B., 168
Transient cerebral ischemic attacks, 7
TRH, 59, 60, 79
Tryptophan, 57, 69-71
Tsai, 75, 94

U.S. Senate Health Subcommittee, 129
Utiger, R., 75

Varner, R., table 2, 214
Vernadakis, A., 65-67, 69
Verwoerdt, A., 207
Visser, S., 101

Waldron, I., 155, 156
Walford, R., 136
Walpole, H., 142
Walter, W., 102
Wang, H., 99, 100, 108
Wechsler, D., 110, 116
  Test, 116
Weinberg, J., 17
Weisman, A., 168
Weiss, L., 157
Weiss, R., 186
Wernicke-Korsakoff Syndrome, 119
Wilkie, F., 103-111, 113
Willis, S., 138
Wilson, S., 100
Wisdom, 142, 143
Wisniewski, H., 119
Wolf, R., 74, 76
Wolf, S., 168
Woodruff, D., 100, 101

Yale cross-cultural area files, 30
Yen, S., 75

Zumoff, B., 75, 78